THE PRIVATE, THE PUBLIC, AND THE PUBLISHED

THE PRIVATE, THE PUBLIC, AND THE PUBLISHED

Reconciling Private Lives and Public Rhetoric

edited by

BARBARA COUTURE
THOMAS KENT

UTAH STATE UNIVERSITY PRESS
Logan, Utah

Utah State University Press
Logan, Utah 84322-7800

Manufactured in the United States of America
Cover design by Barbara Yale-Read

Library of Congress Cataloging-in-Publication Data

The private, the public, and the published : reconciling private lives and public rhetoric / edited by Barbara Couture, Thomas Kent.
p. cm.
Includes bibliographical references and index.
ISBN 0-87421-577-3 (alk. paper)
1. Rhetoric. 2. Written communication. 3. Privacy, Right of. I. Couture, Barbara. II. Kent, Thomas, 1947-
P301.P716 2004
808—dc22

2003026807

CONTENTS

ACKNOWLEDGMENTS

For their support and assistance in preparing this manuscript and contacting contributors we wish to thank Rebecca Allen, research assistant, who completed her Ph.D. in Political Science at Washington State University while working on this project, and Ellen Arnold, Assistant to the Dean, Washington State University, College of Liberal Arts. We also wish to thank the staff of Utah State University Press, in particular, Robin DuBlanc, copyeditor; Kyle Sessions, typesetter/indexer; and Michael Spooner, director, who championed this project and guided it to completion. Finally, we wish to thank those helpmates in all of our endeavors, our spouses, Paul Couture and Charie Thralls.

PREFACE

We live in an era where communication is virtually ubiquitous. The joys and hazards of living in a small town where everybody knows you are quickly becoming a reality for everyone. Television, the internet, cell phones, and a host of new communications technologies assure that anyone who does not already know you can quickly find out all about you. Indeed, as television exposés and Internet Web sites with streaming voice and video have revealed, if we wish, we can make everything we say and do available to nearly everyone. This ubiquity of access to personal communication has begun to blur the boundary of the private and the public. What meanings and consequences do our words have in a world in which there appears to be little that is private? Can and should our personal lives be separate from our public rhetoric? Indeed, what connection is there between what we privately think and how we publicly communicate with others? And what implications do our answers to these questions have for how we interact with others as speakers and writers?

This anthology contains sixteen essays by scholars in the fields of rhetoric, communication, and critical theory who examine the ways in which concepts of the private relate to public communication. The first essay, Barbara Couture's "Reconciling Private Lives and Public Rhetoric: What's at Stake?," serves as an introduction to this volume and addresses one of the central questions inherent in our attempts to reconcile private lives with public rhetoric: Does the blending of the private and the public in speech and writing contribute to the public good? The fifteen essays that follow Couture's introduction employ a wide variety of disciplinary and philosophical perspectives concerning the nature of private lives and public rhetorics, but each essay in its own way asks us to consider, as Couture phrases it, the ramifications of "saying that private lives, identities, and values remain out of the sphere of public rhetoric and, in contrast, in making a private value the standard for public rhetoric."

To address the central topic of this book—the intersections and the interactions of private lives and public rhetorics—we have organized the chapters of this volume thematically into four segments. The first segment,

"Public Expression Meets Private Experience," contains four chapters that address the complex interplay between our private lives and our public expressions in divergent social realms such as politics, jazz, and medicine. In the first chapter, "Ain't Nobody's Business? A Public Personal History of Privacy After *Baird v. Eisenstadt*," Nancy Welch examines milestone legal decisions concerning the protections of privacy, decisions that liberalized access to birth control information and devices and created a shift from what Welch calls the "politics of the personal" to the "politics of *privacy*." In "Virtuosos and Ensembles: Rhetorical Lessons from Jazz," Gregory Clark argues that the private jazz performance, although improvisational, may be understood nonetheless as a rhetorical model that teaches us "something about how private intention can be rendered publicly useful." In chapter three, "Keeping the World Safe for Class Struggle: Revolutionary Memory in a Postmarxist Time," John Trimbur describes what he terms "revolutionary memory" and explains how revolutionary memory might enable us to think beyond national borders and "articulate a program to extend literacy and the higher learning" to anyone who seeks a college education. In the final chapter of this segment, "Mary Putnam Jacobi and the Speaking Picture," Susan Wells examines Mary Putnam's personal fascination concerning the relation between word and image and how Putnam's experiments in visual representation reveal a medical "truth about the tempo and structure of complex bodily processes, particularly as they were actively constructed by human beings in displays and experiments."

Part two of this book, "Confronting the Public and the Private in Written Language," concentrates directly on the problematic intersection of private experience and public expression within the academy and within the academic disciplines that constitute our colleges and universities. In "The Collective Privacy of Academic Language," David Bleich points out that "in the history of the academy, only one sense of privacy has existed, the collective privacy of the male group," a group "bound together by a language few others in society knew." Bleich concludes his chapter by arguing that this limited sense of privacy and the privileged academic language that is allowed by this limited sense of privacy can no longer be assumed to be necessary, in that no justification now exists "for not letting the language speak of all the constituencies now entering the university." Addressing issues concerning the essay as a genre—issues central to the discipline of English studies—the second chapter in this segment, Lynn Bloom's "The Essayist In—and Behind—the Essay: Vested Writers, Invested Readers," argues that the work of canonical essayists is qualitatively different from the work of other essayists, and "[i]f more teachers wrote essays, or academic articles with presence that acknowledged their authorial investment, they would be better able to teach students not only the craft but the art" of the essay genre. In the third chapter of this segment, "Upon the Public Stage: How Professionalism Shapes Accounts of Composing in the Academies," Cheryl Geisler explores the ways in which writers construct professional identities, and she argues that professionalization shapes "the very language with which we account for our work, the daily stories we and our students tell of our progress in the academy, the stories through which we shape our identities." The final chapter of this segment investigates the role of the individual within groups of collaborative writers, an issue centrally important to a variety of academic disciplines. In his chapter "Ethical Deliberation and Trust in Diverse-Group Collaboration," Geoffrey Cross argues that common trust drives successful collaboration and that we frequently need to go beyond the logos of collaboration into the ethos or "spirit" of collaboration.

Part three, "Public and Private Identities in Popular and Mass Communication," brings together three chapters that investigate the role that personal identity and private experience play in a world dominated by popular media, especially the Internet. The first chapter of this segment, Douglas Hesse's "Identity and the Internet: The Telling Case of Amazon.com's Top 50 Reviewers," provides a provocative analysis of the process employed by Amazon.com to review the products sold through its Web site. In "The Influence of Expanded Access to Mass Communication on Public Expression: The Rise of Representatives of the Personal," David Kaufer investigates another aspect of mass communication. Kaufer poses the intriguing question, "What is public expression and what properties does it confer to ordinary expression?," and he concludes that "our increased access through technology has weakened the ties between ourselves as individuals and has further weakened our attention to one another's messages." In the concluding chapter of this segment, Marguerite Helmers, in "Private Witness and Popular Imagination," describes the "personal narrative of trauma," and she provides a remarkable analysis of several mass-media accounts of the 1996 "disaster season," when several professional and amateur climbers died while attempting to scale Mt. Everest.

The final section of this book, "The Public and the Private in the Discipline of Composition Studies," concentrates on the important debate regarding what has come to be called the "personal turn" now occurring in the areas of rhetoric and composition studies. In his investigation of this topic, Bruce Horner in "Mixing It Up: The Personal in Public Discourse" argues that the "confusion over what constitutes the *personal*... prevents us from more productive engagement with the personal in public discourse, in both our writing and our teaching." In "Cultural Autobiographics: Complicating the 'Personal Turns' in Rhetoric and Composition Studies," Krista Ratcliffe reviews the two "personal turns" that have occurred within the discipline of composition studies. She argues that "these two personal turns, though related, generate debates with different histories, definitions, and stakes," and she concludes her chapter "by imagining how autobiography theory, particularly a concept of cultural autobiographics, may productively complicate our field's thinking about 'personal turns.'" Addressing what he takes to be the false distinction between public and private discourse held by many scholars in the field of rhetoric and composition studies, Sidney Dobrin in "Locating Public/Private Discourse" argues that the reductive distinctions between public and private discourses often limit our understanding of communication, and he concludes that "[a]ny discourse, no matter what we chose to label it for the sake of convenience . . . is, then, always already public." In the final chapter, "Public Writing and Rhetoric: A New Place for Composition," Christian R. Weisser investigates some of the pedagogical ramifications of the personal turn, and he concludes with the observation that "[if] we wish to create assignments, courses, and pedagogies that enable students to interact more effectively with other groups and individuals in public arenas, we could begin by considering where and to whom meaningful and productive public writing might be delivered."

Taken as a whole, the chapters in this volume define, dissolve, and bridge the gaps that distinguish the private and the public as epiphenomena that have implications for theorizing and practicing rhetoric and composition studies. These chapters also serve as an important first step toward a better and more nuanced understanding of the intersections and interactions between private experience and public expression, and perhaps more important, these chapters stand as excellent examples of the informed, lively, and often controversial conversations that currently animate the disciplines of rhetoric and composition studies.

Thomas Kent
Utah State University

1

RECONCILING PRIVATE LIVES AND PUBLIC RHETORIC

What's at Stake?

Barbara Couture

"I tried it, but I didn't inhale." It is hard not to smile at the irony of former president Bill Clinton's wan attempt to place himself on the right side of the law in public when disclosing his private use of marijuana. And the irony is doubly inflected for us, knowing—as we do now—about his duplicitous public admission that he never "had sex" with Monica Lewinsky. Perhaps there is no figure in American life for whom private life and public rhetoric are more intertwined than for our nation's president. This consequence of public life in America's most visible office is well known and well accepted.

Lately, the conflation of private life with public rhetoric has become the norm for many of us in far less visible positions, with interesting and perhaps problematic consequences. Some intrusions of public discourse into private life are legislated and involuntary: none of us who travel by air nowadays escape the public questions of a stranger about the contents of our baggage, questions often accompanied by a search of our most intimate personal belongings—including our persons!—amid a crowd of onlookers. Other such intrusions are voluntary: some of us cheerfully encourage the ubiquitous distribution of our private dalliances in public chat rooms on the Internet, for instance.

Whether by wish or by force, there is no question that private lives are increasingly becoming the subject of public expression. Consider the following (far from exhaustive) list of examples:

1. The rock star Ozzie Osbourne's family life, displayed on television twenty-four hours a day, became one of the most popular American shows.
2. A new illness, now treated by psychiatrists, is "Internet addiction"; it involves the obsessive desire of individuals to talk about themselves in public chat rooms to strangers online.

3. TV, radio, and Internet talk-show hosts invite individuals to review intimate details of their private lives in forums for public discussion.
4. Increased electronic access to personal data allows news services, consumer outlets, and government agencies to "learn" more about private citizens, with thousands of nameless employees tailoring services to private individuals, often without their direct knowledge, and contacting them by phone, mail, or e-mail.
5. Academics who teach online courses report exhaustive involvement in public e-mail discussions of individual students' responses—often personal—to classroom materials, discussions viewed by entire classes.

The increased forced and voluntary opportunities to make the private doings of many or most of us the subject of public rhetoric have consequences for its function, content, and form—consequences that not only provide topics of interest for scholars and challenges for teachers of writing and speech, but that also affect the potential utility of public rhetoric in the service of the common good.

One could argue, of course, that rhetoric, by definition, is not necessarily an art in service of the common good; by far, its most common interpreted function is "persuasion"—with no assumption made as to whether the goal is to persuade for good or ill. Yet in the grand tradition of classical humanistic education, the aim of teaching the rhetorical arts has always been and today remains to prepare students to contribute to the public good. James Zappen, for one, made the point convincingly over a decade ago, arguing for a "pluralistic rhetoric" in the teaching and writing of technical and managerial discourse that encourages writers to serve organizational goals while relating decision making to the greater good (Zappen 39).

The question for our contributors, responding in this volume to the growing tendency to confuse and conflate private lives with public rhetoric, is this: Does this blending of the private and the public in speech and writing contribute to the public good? Or is increased confusion over the boundaries of the public and the private in communication a bad thing? In the discussion that follows, I suggest that this increased fusing of the private and public does not bode well for public rhetoric; it does not lead to expression that contributes to the public good. In making this argument, I will define the consequences of conflating private life with public expression, giving contemporary examples of how public expression that is confused with private life obliterates the possibility of public rhetoric—that is, communication for the public good. Referring to the scholarship of philosophers and rhetoricians, I will argue further that public expression that functions effectively as public rhetoric requires a reconciliation of private concerns with the ethical demand of relating to others, concluding with some examples of approaches to the study and teaching of rhetoric that meet this aim.

CONFLATING PRIVATE LIVES AND PUBLIC EXPRESSION

We have many amusing and some pathetic examples of the tendency of some individuals to make their private lives the subject of ubiquitous public expression. Cited earlier was the "glass house" example of Ozzie Osbourne and his family, whose public exposure of their private lives has led many to conclude that the rich and famous—at least those who appear to have grown up on the same side of the tracks as we—are not all that different. They argue, curse their spouses and children, do goofy things, have disgusting personal habits, and harbor questionable prejudices—just like us. As Internet users, we have daily access to the twenty-four-hour "Webcams" of persons who have invited us into their rooms, the personal Web pages and diaries of yet others, and the dominators of public chat rooms who reveal their personal likes and dislikes to hundreds.

Such voluntary exposés of private life on the public scene are not new: we are all familiar with the appeals of the lovelorn and love-happy in newspaper want ads and with the occasional ebullient suitor who sky-writes a declaration of love or proposal of marriage. All of these public expressions of private business appear quite harmless, though perhaps annoying. Yet even voluntary "harmless" exposure of private life in the public forum can have deleterious consequences. Many find worrisome, for instance, the talk-show exposés of Jerry Springer and Jenny Jones, where individuals choose to reveal personal secrets before millions of onlookers whose prurient interest is piqued by the emotional trauma that enfolds before their eyes when the speaker's relatives and friends learn as we do about the speaker's faults and transgressions.

What is common to these examples of private life revealed in public expression is the effort to use identity as a way to reach and influence someone else. The aim is either to erase the distinction between the communicator and the audience—there being nothing private about me that is not shared with you—or to confront an audience with one's identity, as does the talk-show guest, revealing secrets that effectively reduce the significance of someone else in public.

In short, this conflation of private life with public expression demands that the audience absorb, deny, refuse, or obliterate difference, specifically what is different from the identity of the speaker. Ozzie Osbourne's family and the twenty-four-hour Webcam hosts have imposed their lives on the public, giving us the options of finding ourselves to be the same as Ozzie or the Webcam host, denying or refusing affiliation with the likes of them, or obliterating them by simply "turning them off." Such communication of one's private life as an expression to the public does not contribute to a development of some shared understanding of what it is to be human because there is no shared effort on the part of either the exposer or the voyeur to reach a mutual understanding of this communication.

Private life that functions as public expression in the modes just described poses no unavoidable threat: we can always choose not to participate in the imposed assimilation of or conflict with the private identity being thrust upon us. But what happens when private lives conveyed through public expression become representative—exclusively—of the interests and welfare of others? In short, when a public expression of private life becomes the standard for public participation? This phenomenon has been treated by a number of prominent scholars lately, notably by Jacques Derrida in his philosophical treatise on the ancient concept of friendship as a form of identity politics that was opposed to democracy. In composition studies, Dianne Rothleder similarly has explored private identity as a substitute for public expression as this substitution figures in rhetorical theory and writing pedagogy.

In *Politics of Friendship*, Derrida tells us that the classical valorization of personal friendship as a virtuous activity—one that assumes accepting a person as a friend, unconditionally, despite his or her faults and regardless of reciprocal devotion—had a dark side that intruded upon public political life. He explores what he claims to have been Nietzsche's nagging question about the nature of friendship, that is, how does one maintain a friend without having enemies, without identifying those who are excluded from the circle of friendship? Derrida extends this concern to the framework of public policy: to define the bonds between compatriots as friendship is to assume that those outside this bond are enemies of the state. The classical concept of friendship held these consequential political overtones.

Nietzsche, claims Derrida, was also troubled by the classical conception of friendship, seeing there a contradiction that calls into question not only the antithesis of friendship and enmity, but also by extension all antitheses, including good and evil, truth and error. Nietzsche was obsessed with a comment on friendship often repeated by Aristotle, and later noted by Montaigne, that Aristotle had attributed to a sage who lay dying: the old wise man whispers to a young friend, "O my friend, there is no friend." Derrida claims that Nietzsche found this comment so intriguing because it disguises a truth about friendship as classically conceived.

The sage says to his friend that there is no friend because friendship cannot exist without the possibility of enemies. To believe in enemies is to hold the possibility of friendship. But a deeper truth concealed in this phrase, suggests Nietzsche, is one far more maddening: friendship, unconditional friendship, hides from truth. True friends ignore the faults of one another, keeping a silence that is required to keep friends, to close a circle against a presumed enemy. The closed classical conception of friendship involves, as Derrida tells us, "making each other laugh about evil. Among friends" (56). We do not need to look far for contemporary examples of this kind of friendship, a friendship closed to truth. Abuse of others handily persists in the name of friendship, by those who count one another as friends against others: be they a nation such as Nazi Germany, a faction such as the ultraconservative Right, or a family that disowns a son or daughter for living a life to which its other members cannot subscribe.

What defines this kind of friendship is a closed and singular identity, a private circle of like minds, exclusive of others. This is what friendship means when self and others are linked through an exclusive bond of identity. Because it is based in loving, this kind of friendship has the moral force of virtue—yet it is a love that categorically excludes difference. It is a love that, when practiced by many, obliterates the possibility of democracy and a public forum that acknowledges and respects difference.

The forced or voluntary display of private life as public expression can have the same exclusionary effect as "classical friendship" when practiced by those who claim to represent others through this display. A striking example is the now famous spectre of Osama Bin Laden, who has addressed the public on tape while among friends and devotees from his home or other protected site. The chilling power of these messages lies in their presentation of his private identity as the emblematic representation of a virtuous friendship of the faithful that excludes nonbelievers as the enemy. It is not insignificant that these presentations, meant to be broadcast publicly, were made in his home or barracks, exclusive of any site where a public other may reside or be acknowledged. Through this private communication in public he has imposed an identity on the public that speaks to and acknowledges no one but himself and those who have become as himself. For Bin Laden—who remains hidden or dead as I write—this private life or identity expressed in public but not interacting with the public is the standard for public interaction in the closed society he advocates; on his terms, private life as public expression is the model for public rhetoric.

For public expression to function as public rhetoric requires a reconciliation of private identity with the ethical demand of relating to others. This movement cannot occur if we merely substitute private identity for public expression. And it cannot occur if we hold that our identity is defined and preserved through excluding rather than acknowledging others. In short, to transform private life as public expression into a public rhetoric is to transform private identity.

FROM PUBLIC EXPRESSION TO PUBLIC RHETORIC

It is important to elaborate at this point what is at stake in distinguishing public expression from public rhetoric, that is, in distinguishing a "private life made public" from the reconciliation of private life with the ethical demand of relating to others. I have already noted that the imposition of private life through public expression can only be accepted, rejected, or obliterated by the audience responding to such display. Such public expression of private life allows no opportunity for a shared understanding of identity developed through acknowledging or listening to others, a conversation that may result in the speaker reconsidering his or her identity in light of what is learned about others and vice versa.

One could argue that a reconsideration of identity is not needed—or desired—in a community of speakers who are already satisfied with their shared identity and interactions among their members. One can imagine, for instance, a small town, an industry, or an academic department where like minds have created tight friendships based on shared identity—places where presumably no one feels excluded. Public expression in these domains easily can be relegated to a mayor, executive, or department head whose private desires, beliefs, and affiliations expressed in public are assumed to be—and, in fact, are—representative of the group. We can imagine, for instance, a mayor who speaks for everyone when he talks of the dangers of building a public housing unit that will attract jobless immigrants "not like us," an executive who strikes in her board of directors a single chord when she calls a family-leave plan "bad for business," or a department chair receiving nods of approval when he rejects a job candidate's scholarship as lacking the test of rigor as applied to himself and, of course, others already in the department. We can draw a picture here of an ideal social group in which conflict does not exist about the identity the group shares.

The problem with limiting public expression to such displays of singular identity, as these examples suggest, is not so much that the speech reflects the homogeneous identity of the speaker with the group as that it does not leave an opening for debate about that identity. And why is this important? It is important because private identity accepted as public without debate poses a threat to an open society and this in turn threatens pursuit of an ancient value that stands above identity, affiliation, and social politics—truth itself.

To forestall sidelining this argument by introducing a debate here as to whether "truth" is obtainable, let me say that I am referring to "truth" as it is most popularly conceived—as a commodity that a society values as a common pursuit, that is, knowledge that reveals individual or societal motives, desires, and needs publicly without deception. Karl Popper has elucidated most clearly the threat to public truth that exists by posing private identity or affiliation as public rhetoric in *The Spell of Plato,* volume one of *The Open Society and Its Enemies.* To keep society open, capable of revealing public truth, he advocates competition among individual viewpoints and warns against identity politics, that is, the tendency for individuals to "accrue privileges by virtue of membership in a specific group, whether that be defined by race, creed, politics, or profession" (153). He further warns against the uncompromising viewpoints of radicals, who promote an aesthetic ideal at the expense of social systems and individual freedom through fanatical identification with an idea—such as fascism, communism, or white supremacy, for instance (see Popper 146–47).

Derrida, in his own fashion, has come to similar conclusions about identity and public expression. In *Politics of Friendship,* he argues that the conditions for a democratic, open society could not be met in ancient society until the conception of friendship as a closed circle of persons who share an identity outside of which lies the enemy changed to include others not previously defined by that shared identity.

A democracy thrives by allowing an ever-widening public circle of possible friends to develop and prosper. A democracy requires the participation of persons who are not defined by the enemy that exists without, but rather by the anticipation of human connection of persons known and yet unknown, across societies, space, and time. A democracy ideally supports the reciprocal, equal participation of all in dialogue toward public truth, a circle of possible friends—as Derrida has put it—friends connected across the divide of space and time. We can think of all who form a democracy as connected to that possibility of a future friend who will answer the questions we cannot answer, uncover the public truths we seek but cannot yet find.

Modern political democracies, like ancient democracies composed of those who share a political bond, thrive in part on the virtue of friendship as classically defined, a shared identity, but they are also linked "to loving, to friendship as well as to love—more precisely, to the Greek, Jewish, and Christian history of this link, of the binding and unbinding of this link" (Derrida 79). Unlike classical friendship, which was based on a desire to maintain exclusivity, modern democratic friendship is based on a constant "binding and unbinding" of a link to others through love. The fraternization that typifies modern democracies is dependent both on the loving that overlooks—the ancient ideal of virtuous friendship that accepts affiliation with another, regardless of what that other does—and on the loving that looks for truth: in short, a love that hopes to find in another a better understanding of our own lives and purpose, one that leads to a better society. It is this latter act that requires a reconciliation of private identity with the possibility of having that identity challenged, changed, and expanded by virtue of contact with others in a public forum.

For the mayor, business executive, and department chair of my earlier examples, a reconciliation of private life or identity with the aim of democratic participation in an ever-expanding fraternity of possible friends could inspire a move from public expression to public rhetoric. Consider, for example, that our mayor could view the immigrants' presence in public housing as an opportunity to expand his own and his community's customs, languages, and beliefs; or the business executive might interpret a family-leave policy as an opportunity to expand the talent pool of a workforce by bringing in more single parents and change—for the better—the relationships of employees to the company; or the department chair might regard a candidate's research as groundbreaking and innovative when it differs from the norm, as presented by the measure of his own work and that of his colleagues.

All of these rhetorical moves require the speaker to reconcile a previous conception of a private, closed identity—albeit shared—with the needs of an outside individual or group with whom they will build a relationship, a future, that will change them both in the common pursuit of a public good. This is the aim of public rhetoric, as I see it.

RECONCILING PRIVATE LIVES AND PUBLIC RHETORIC

In many ways, linking rhetoric with participation in an open, democratic society in pursuit of the public good underlies much of modern rhetorical theory. Note, for instance, Habermas's theory of communicative action, which links discourse interaction to moral sensitivity to the needs and perceptions of others; Burke's advocacy of the conversational parlor, an environment for continually renewed, healthy, and reciprocal exchange within an environment of safety; and, Rorty's model of building knowledge by "recontextualizing belief," that is, exposing oneself to as many new contexts and beliefs as possible and then contributing one's own view in reciprocal exchange (80). My coeditor and I also have linked rhetorical practice and reciprocal, democratic participation in our scholarship. Thomas Kent's theory of paralogic rhetoric defines textual meaning as the function of a dynamic interaction that involves charitable linguistic exchange (*Paralogic Rhetoric*). Taking this notion yet further, I have characterized meaningful rhetoric in public contexts as a phenomenological outcome of altruistic attention to others (Couture, *Phenomenological Rhetoric*).

In short, contemporary rhetorical theorists have fairly widely acknowledged that if rhetoric is to serve the public good, it must involve the reciprocal exchange of views in a charitable context. What is perhaps less widely acknowledged is the threat to such open exchange that is embedded in the increased opportunity to offer private life—whether individual or community—as a substitute for public rhetoric. Also rarely acknowledged is the threat to public rhetoric that lies in distinctly Western notions of how knowledge is created.

Although intrusions of private life in the public forum afforded by television and the Internet are relatively new developments, the justification for making public exposé of private life a substitute for public rhetoric is embedded deep in Western culture and continues to be strongly advocated in rhetorical theory today. I speak here of the literary and rhetorical tradition of the "strong poet." Those individuals who emulate this tradition are valued for the ways in which they distinguish themselves, separate themselves from others, in their private quest for truth, a quest that they can choose to make—or not to make—public. Furthermore, if the quest is made public, the strong poet who reveals his or her beliefs ideally remains resistant to critique, valuing original, individual expression over collaborative dialogue. Such is the generally admired behavior of the independent critic, for instance—the one who is better than, smarter than, richer than—and, perhaps, more holy than—others.

The rhetorical stance of the strong poet provides a significant challenge to modern theories of rhetoric that advocate democratic participation. To illustrate, Dianne Rothleder, in *The Work of Friendship,* tests Rorty's rhetorical ideal of "solidarity," for instance, against the demands of participatory democracy as practiced in the classrooms where we teach children how to play, work, learn, and communicate together. In these settings, she finds that Rorty's rhetorical project falls short. She concludes that participatory democracy requires a transformation of private life in the public forum, one that is in direct conflict with Rorty's rhetorical ideal of the strong poet. Because Rorty preserves the strong poet ideal by defining "solidarity as a public phenomenon that is kept far from private concerns," as Rothleder explains (xiv), he develops a negative vision of how private belief contributes to knowledge in a public rhetoric. For Rorty, individual genius—or the ability to create radically new knowledge—is not debated in the public forum; genius is always "other," outside of the familiar space that the public shares. Idiosyncratic difference and individual suffering also are circumscribed as private phenomena by Rorty and not discussed as public issues. As Rothleder tells us: "Solidarity, for Rorty, is based solely on each person's desire not to have his or her idiosyncracies judged in the court of reason" (44).

Instead of interpreting communal solidarity as the outcome of individuals communicating openly with one another, Rorty appears to define it as the result of a common desire not to be in pain or to cause others pain. Consequently, he limits discussion about personal experiences that may illuminate difference to the private sphere. He advocates reading as a good way to experience private life as others do, lacking or even avoiding direct conversational acquaintance with them. For Rorty, Rothleder concludes, "Others and otherness are instrumental, experimental curiosities to be experienced and then used privately. Rortian self-creation is a negation of others, is anti-social, is friendless, and is indeed cruel" (52).

The desire to experience difference only in private shifts public responsibility for dealing with difference to the private sphere. Furthermore, because difference and suffering are dealt with in the private sphere where they are personally reflected upon and interpreted by the sole voice—that is, the strong poet—we relegate to the public sphere only those matters about which there can be no disagreement. According to Rothleder, Rorty assumes there is consensus about basic values in the public sphere and "makes what might be controversial seem entirely noncontroversial." "Who," Rothleder exclaims, "could comfortably argue against freedom?" (95). In American contexts, it is simply not a subject for debate.

Rothleder offers a new vision of public rhetoric, a rhetoric based in friendship that fosters reciprocal engagement in knowledge creation for the public good—the kind of rhetoric that Rorty presumably advocates, but that is hampered by the image and presence of the strong poet. Instead of asking students to emulate the ideal of the strong poet who retreats from society, Rothleder encourages them to develop "friendships of play," taking as her model the pedagogical practice and theory of educator Vivian Paley.

Friendships of play are safe havens where individuals can share their life stories without fear of retribution. However, the sharing of one's life story here does not result in conveying an obsessively pure, unchallenged, exclusive identity. Storytelling, she says in reference to Paley's classroom methods, must bridge the gap between private self-creation and public justice: "My self-creation needs to be just, and justice needs to give a turn to tell stories; I direct no cruelty to others and no one directs cruelty toward me" (138). Yet others are free to redescribe me and themselves in an experience that is shared, unlike Rorty's vision of self-narrative, which valorizes only the strong poet who is not the victim of others' redescriptions of themselves. (The irony, for Rothleder, is that those who are doing the redescribing are the very strong poets whom Rorty admires.) By relegating these critics to the private sphere, they remain protected from others and are never forced to engage with them. Having to participate in the public sphere occasionally would keep them from becoming too self-centered, but in Rorty's vision, the public sphere is not destined to be the place where meaningful ideas are exchanged. Rothleder concludes: "The strong poet . . . is Rorty's regulative ideal for the private sphere. We cannot, any of us, realize this strength, but we are obligated to set up the world so that we can keep trying. And we preserve the public sphere insofar as it guarantees that we cannot withdraw completely into solipsism" (106).

In contrast to life as the strong poet, engagement in friendships of play, as Rothleder describes them, makes it possible for us to be changed by others through our interactions with them. She envisions rhetorical interactions within friendships of play as scenes where we can address private life in the public sphere without relapsing into solipsism on the one hand or destroying our individual integrity through vulnerable overexposure on the other. At the same time, within friendships of play mere public expression of private life is deemed an unacceptable imposition on others; what is expected is a speaker's transformed presentation of private life that anticipates and respects the stories of others already told and yet to come. Moreover, the creative mission of the strong poet is not abandoned within friendships of play. In contrast to emulating the artist who values only his or her own depiction of the world, within friendships of play our goal should be to become "a poet whose creations have room for parents, for the tradition, and for change" (Rothleder 141). Finally, Rothleder advises, we must both tell and listen within the friendships of play: "If we only read, we are limited by what has been written, and thus we must write and tell stories as well" (120).

Rothleder's appeal to transform the ancient and powerful value of friendship into a scene for public rhetoric that will lead to good rings true for me. The obligation to create the conditions for this kind of interchange lies within those who "play" in forums where public rhetoric dominates: in our classrooms, in community and corporate meeting rooms, in our Congress, and in the White House—all places where private lives need be reconciled with the ethical demand of public rhetoric to let everyone play.

I have outlined here just a few of the implications of relaxing and strengthening the contrasts and distinctions between private life and public rhetoric. This discussion began with some amusing examples of the imposition of private life on the public scene, but it must end with a reminder that horrific consequences of not reconciling private life with public rhetoric are daily present. In a recent *New York Times* editorial, Beena Sarwar speaks of the decision of a tribal council in a Pakistani village to have a young woman raped as revenge for a crime that her brother committed—a decree of Jirga law, which is "rooted in tribal customs and the power of elders," a power that the state chooses to ignore by calling these "private" matters. As Sarwar explains: "This often means, in practice, giving this small portion of the population private power over others, particularly women." The state's excuse for calling this a private matter is that this ceding of power leads to social stability—for all those who hold private power. Within very recent memory we have repeatedly heard our American president declare the private value of American freedom to be the justification for invading Iraq and uprooting Saddam Hussein. This private value, repeated as public rhetoric, is in effect assumed to be the voice of the people—a community of like minds and identity—and assumed to be a position unchallenged, not only by nations other than America, but also by those living in America. Yet, freedom demonstrably has not always had one value for all who live here. As W.E.B. DuBois poignantly remarked: "few men ever worshiped Freedom with half such unquestioning faith as the American Negro for two centuries" (7), two centuries when freedom was granted only to white Americans.

Much is at stake in saying that private lives, identities, and values remain out of the sphere of public rhetoric and, in contrast, in making a private value the standard for public rhetoric. It is a topic worth our study and a problem that should continue to hold our attention as teachers, scholars, and practitioners of public rhetoric.

PART ONE

Public Expression Meets Private Experience

2

AIN'T NOBODY'S BUSINESS?

A Public Personal History of Privacy after Baird v. Eisenstadt

Nancy Welch

For women the measure of intimacy has been the measure of oppression.

Catherine A. MacKinnon
Toward a Feminist Theory of the State

One can agree that privacy is not enough without concluding that the choice of privacy arguments in the Roe context was a setback for women.

Ruth Garrison
"Feminism and the Public/Private Distinction"

What is needed . . . is not the abandonment of rights language for all purposes, but an attempt to become multilingual in the semantics of evaluating rights.

Patricia J. Williams
The Alchemy of Race and Rights

TAKE ONE: THE PRIVACY GENERATION

Some years ago my mother told me the story of how, when she was twenty years old and the mother of two, she drummed up the courage to ask the family doctor about something called "birth control." "Oh, no," the doctor replied, "Not until you have six children at least."

"So you were born ten months later, and your brother, fourteen months after that."

"And then?" I asked.

"And then your father learned the word *vasectomy.*"

At the time my mother told this tale, I was twenty years old, working in Boston, and had just gotten myself down to the Bill Baird Clinic on Boylston Street to be fitted for a diaphragm. I didn't tell her about my visit to Bill Baird; there seemed little to tell. Between her story of a humiliating exchange and my entirely unremarkable after-work appointment lay the Supreme Court decisions of *Griswold v. Connecticut* (1965) and *Baird v. Eisenstadt* (1972). Like *Roe v. Wade,* soon to follow, these landmark decisions, which liberalized access to birth control information and devices, extended the protections of privacy to (some) sexual practices and decisions. The 125-year-old Massachusetts law that would have shut down the Boylston Street clinic just ten years before in the name of protecting future generations' "virility" and "virtue" had been overturned. When I made my appointment, words like *purity* and *chastity* were as far from my mind as my ninth-grade, Cliff Notes–assisted reading of *The Scarlet Letter.* (On my mind instead: would I have the money for the $35 appointment, the diaphragm, and a tube of spermicidal jelly, given that my secretary's paycheck was $230 a week *before* taxes?) I didn't have to tell my mother about my appointment or why I needed a diaphragm because I understood such matters to be *private.*

Out of this story—or out of this assertion that, thanks to Bill Baird and the Supreme Court, I, unlike my mother, have no story to tell—I might conclude that I was born into the first generation of women to experience the lucky boon of privacy. I might celebrate the good fortune of being granted the "right to be let alone" (Warren and Brandeis) without even having to have argued for it. There would be obvious weaknesses in such a conclusion: the Supreme Court's refusal to extend privacy protection to lesbians and gays (*Bowers v. Hardwick,* 1986); the use of the privacy argument to rule against state funding for medically required abortions (*Harris v. McRae,* 1980); the erosion of geographic and economic, as well as legal, access to birth control and safe abortions through thirty years of legislative and extralegislative activity including presidential gag orders, parental notification and consent statutes, waiting periods, and the shutting down of clinics. I could note these weaknesses—and the ways in which privacy rights have not been uniformly extended to poor women, people of color, immigrants with and without green cards, anyone receiving public assistance—and maybe, noting these limits, I might argue that women of my generation and beyond need to come together for renewed arguments, renewed activism.

There's a catch here, though, a problem with the idea that "women like me"—white, heterosexual, and, back when I was twenty, urban and a part of the pink-collar workforce—can agitate to extend privacy rights to others. How does one argue—publicly—for that which has been defined as private, outside rhetoric's realm? The Supreme Court rulings on reproduction between 1965 and 1979 did not, after all, expand women's *spheres of liberty* but instead marked new *zones of privacy*. These rulings weren't aimed at granting women *freedom to* do as they wished but instead (some amount of) *freedom from* public interference and also, by implication, from public debate. Of course, I've felt pressed many, many times to join phone banks, stuff envelopes, lift banners, raise my voice. But that's just it: I've felt pressed to defend that which I've been raised to believe should need no defense. As a member of the privacy generation, I've been raised to regard sex, birth control, and abortion rights (for starters) as self-regarding, not other-regarding (to adopt John Stuart Mill's classic distinction from *On Liberty*)—nobody's business but my own.

Indeed, I had no idea, until my mother told me her story, that the right to birth control—no, the right to privacy regarding birth control decisions—had such a recent history, more recent than, say, the nineteenth century.

Do We Have (Too Much) Privacy?

The common wisdom is that in this hypercommunicative age, the boundaries between private and public are giving way, our sense of privacy and rights to privacy eroding. "There is less privacy than there used to be," write Ellen Alderman and Caroline Kennedy at the start of their critique of contemporary publicity (xiv). If I bracket the question of who has less privacy than before—who, historically, has been granted and who denied privacy and according to what racial, gendered, and classed markers—I can see plenty of evidence for this claim. At this moment, I look up from typing to see the U.S. attorney general argue on TV for increased wiretapping powers. I check my neighborhood Listserv and find a posting, subject heading "Homeland Security," that offers tips for exercising surveillance on our street. I check the rest of my e-mail and find half a dozen action alerts: an antiwar activist interrogated by the FBI for her involvement in the (Nobel Peace Prize–nominated) Women in Black, a library worker suspended for using her university e-mail account to compose a message critical of U.S. foreign policy, a Green

Party member prevented from flying from Bangor to Chicago because she showed up on a computerized list as a security risk. Confronting these encroachments upon the individual freedoms of private citizens in the name of public interest, I can agree: there's not as much privacy as there used to be.

Yet even though I can see stark examples of privacy under siege, I want to disturb the common wisdom long enough to reveal an opposite and at least equally pressing problem that we—particularly as teachers of writing and rhetoric within a would-be democratic society—need to address: we don't live in a world of too little privacy but, increasingly, too much.

Consider:

1. At the same time people lament a loss of privacy, millions of Americans live in 5,000-plus square-foot homes in gated communities and incorporated cities (such as Disney's Celebration, Florida) where not only public spaces are privatized (and policed) but the social responsibilities of citizenship and government are turned over to private enterprise (see Blakely and Snyder).
2. This privatizing trend affects virtually all areas of public life—schools, prisons, hospitals, policing, trash collection, transportation services, and, in the news most recently, airport security—as local, state, and national governments "outsource" public services to private companies, transforming citizens into consumers (see Bunker and Davis; Giroux).
3. Since the 1980s companies have increasingly asserted a "corporate right to privacy" (Gilbert, Hare, and Ollanik) to justify a growing use of confidentiality agreements in the settlements of sexual harassment, workplace discrimination, and products liability lawsuits (Ramsey, Durrell, and Ahearn; Hans 70–111). Well known, for instance, is the 1985 California court settlement that sealed all evidence of the dangers of silicon breast implants and thus protected manufacturer Dow Corning from publicity while thousands more women were implanted with the potentially toxic device (see Gilbert, Hare, and Ollanik.).
4. The agents of neoliberalism such as the International Monetary Fund have made privatization a key condition for any country seeking economic aid. As third world countries have privatized airlines, telecommunications, and energy to meet IMF mandates, U.S. and European multinationals have stepped in to scoop up these prizes—converting a country's public resources and services into another nation's private property (see Green 51).

With these examples, it may appear that I'm conflating *privacy* and *privatization*. *Privacy* is a word we typically associate with *personal* and *domestic* realms, realms in which we may feel entitled to freedom from observation and interference. Though the entitlements of private life are certainly subject to periodic debate and dramatic revision—as birth control is renamed from moral menace to private choice and as domestic abuse made the opposite shift from personal prerogative to public crime—we most often think of private life as "self-regarding," that is, outside the public interest. *Privatization*, in contrast, we associate with political economy and particularly as one piece of the larger trend of neoliberalism. It would seem to be distinct from our ideas of personal privacy first because neoliberal economic tenets are always presented as impersonal (that invisible hand of the market) and second because, feminism's critique of Victorian "separate spheres" notwithstanding, we're still so schooled to distinguish between the (self-regarding) realm of home and the (other-regarding) realms of market and government. Given these usual distinctions, it might seem, then, that I'm confusing the problem of growing economic privatization with the separate issue of personal privacy.

Yet that's precisely my point: the distinctions are confused, as anyone must surely feel driving by a gated community or, maybe more to the point, living in one. The rights of privacy, as I've found growing up after *Baird v. Eisenstadt*, do have some liberalizing potential. It's because of privacy rights that I could choose, as my mother could not, when to bear children or, in fact, whether to bear children. Yet these privacy rights, specifically, the right to *exclude* a woman's decisions about reproduction from public regulation and debate, have proved shaky, to the say the least. It has turned out that the right to privacy is not really the same thing as having full, publicly articulated and publicly defended reproductive rights and full, publicly assisted access to exercising these rights, since our rights and access currently are very much tied to our economic standing.

Moreover, privacy rights have also shown potential to collude with the aims of neoliberal privatization, which, after all, likewise seeks to exclude some or most (business/market) matters from public regulation and debate. In fact, when it comes to writing out definitions, as Nancy Fraser points out, domestic and economic privacies wind up sounding much the same. "The rhetoric of domestic privacy," Fraser writes, "seeks to exclude some issues and interests from public debate by personalizing and/or familializing them." Similarly, the "rhetoric of economic privacy . . . seeks to exclude some issues and interests from public debate by economizing them" (*Justice Interruptus* 88). The means—familializing, economizing—may be different, but the ends—excluding a set of interests and issues from public debate—are the same.

Hence, as Fraser has argued elsewhere, if we want to get a critical purchase on this idea of privacy, we might need a shift in terms from "private" experience to "privatized" experience (*Unruly Practices* 135). That shift can remind us that experiences marked as "self-regarding" are not naturally and inevitably outside social jurisdiction but have been placed there, raising the questions of by whom, for whom, and with what interests and aims. By thinking in terms of active, historic privatization, not immutable privacy, we can examine how issues become privatized and thus removed from public debate.

We can also, I think, extend Fraser's critique of domestic and economic privacies, with their shared aims of exclusion, by considering those uncanny moments when constructions of domestic privacy don't just collude with economic privatization but become indistinguishable from it. These are moments in which our existence suddenly appears so thoroughly economized that what we find under siege isn't privacy but publicity: our rights and access to a public self. Maybe I can dramatize this sort of threat through a recent example.

The public radio program *Marketplace Morning Report* aired a story on the minifinancial boom experienced by hearth-and-home stores in the aftermath of the Twin Towers and Pentagon attacks. Amid grim reports of falling stocks and rising joblessness, stores such as Williams-Sonoma reported robust sales. People want to "cocoon" at a time like this (the first day of the bombing of Afghanistan), one interviewee explained. They feel a psychological need to "nest." The story's reporter, Aaron Schacter, also went on to speculate that there may be more at work than individual psychology. Perhaps people (people, that is, with spending power) were shopping as an expression of their patriotism, answering the president's call to boost the economy. (Perhaps, I would add, such shoppers had seen the October 15 cover of *Us* magazine—Laura Bush accompanied by the bold heading "Comforter in Chief"—and understood their own feminized roles to provide domestic comfort rather than direct or protest public policy.) Viewed from this angle, such shopping expresses people's strong desires to *do something*—protecting the "homeland" symbolically with duvet covers and cookie sheets. (After all, ordinary citizens hadn't been invited to join politicians, policy makers, and the corporate media in shaping or debating the military attacks. We were sent off instead to silent candlelight vigils, then to malls.) So maybe such shopping isn't about nesting, cocooning, or retreats into privacy at all. Maybe it signals the very opposite: an attempt (one that ought to give any rhetorician pause) at *something like* public voice, *something like* public action—an attempt not only channeled into consumerism but defined from the very start *as* consumerism.

A few minutes later, a news story aired on the latest threats to our privacy. I didn't listen. I was too busy thinking about a different sort of threat: the threat to our publicity rights, to our sense of being public selves. When I tried to explain this issue to my husband, who is not a U.S. citizen, he shrugged. "There's nothing new about Americans going shopping."

On the one hand, I want to say there *is* something new about this blunt, unapologetic championing of consumerism as the only sanctioned form of civic participation, the only way to *do something* other than display a flag or give blood. (As I write, teach-in, rally, and debate are decidedly not among the currently sanctioned forums in which to *do something.*) I want to say there's something breathtaking and terrifying about the dropping of all pretense: the measure of America isn't democracy but capitalism, the measure of one's citizenship isn't one's participation in public decision-making forums but one's spending in the private retail sector. Breathtaking, terrifying, what's dropped to dust in the aftermath of September 11.

On the other hand, if I can resist the current national chorus—the one declaring "Everything's changed!"—long enough to reread my own history, I have to say my husband's right: there is nothing new about privatization.

TAKE TWO: THE PRIVATIZED GENERATION

Looking back, I see that my family associated privacy not only with matters of sexuality and reproduction but with just about every realm of daily experience: religion, politics, family economics, employment and joblessness. This reign of privacy probably had little to do with the Supreme Court and much more to do with my parents' upbringing in lower-middle-class Yankee families where morality was measured by the ability to mind one's tongue.

"Who did you vote for?" I asked my parents in 1972.

"Shush," Mom replied. "That isn't polite."

"Are we at war?" I asked.

"No," Mom said. "That has nothing to do with us." Even Vietnam was none of our business.

To be fair, I have to recognize that my parents were also products of the McCarthy era—enough to make entire English departments stop talking about anything but beauty and form—as well as the cold-war dread of privacy rights violations that had produced *1984* and *The Naked Society* (see Hasian, especially 97–100). They were the first in each of their families to move away from the tiny corner of southeastern Massachusetts where Welches, Winslows, Gauntlets, and Shoveltons had subjected one another to daily scrutiny for more than two hundred years. Now my mother frets that giant grocery store chains like Kroger's and Big Bear are tracking her purchases through her use of a membership card.

Even my father's choice to be an on-the-road salesman—no shop floor or office cubicle for him—appears bound up in an idealization of individual privacy that's so American: it's a shock to realize that nowhere is the right to privacy constitutionally guaranteed. (Supreme Court decisions like *Roe v. Wade* were argued through the constitutional guarantee of due process, with privacy understood to be an implied or a priori right enabling that guarantee.) When twice in six months, by two different companies in two different states, my father was laid off, we experienced the other side of privacy, the side not associated with freedom and mobility but (as my mother had experienced in the doctor's office years before) humiliation and shame. *Laid off* is how the companies put it. *Canned,* my father always said, though whether to emphasize his sense of personal disgrace or to expose what lay beneath corporate euphemism, I don't know, because really this event wasn't a matter for family discussion. Twice in one year my father came home, handed my mother a letter, and announced, "I've been canned." Twice we children were sent outside to play, then called back in, nothing more said about the matter until the day came to pack and move. We'd have brought up sex at our dinner table, I think, sooner than the word *unemployment.*

In later years—having witnessed the journey of my sister's family from Lincoln to Rochester to Lafayette to Columbus in a search for full-time, not contract, employment; having listened to my university president announce a faculty downsizing program, then counsel us to learn to live with "anxiety"; having witnessed with my in-laws in France what Pierre Bourdieu later called a "social miracle"—legions of unemployed French workers organizing to protest for increased benefits, the vast majority of the country, feeling the insecurity of their own jobs, supporting their aims—I would understand, finally, that these are not private, self-regarding matters. *Neoliberalism. Globalization. Underemployment.* If the extension of privacy rights to (some) women appears to mark a radical break between my mother's experience and mine, the trend of *privatization* binds us all back together.

Privatization. It's a word I think of not only in relation to the dominant economic paradigm since Reagan but also in relation to my own increasingly constricted and privatized world between 1978, when my vocational high school began sending me to work in lieu of classes, and 1986, when an unusual and lucky combination of public funding and prominent, public-space advertising brought me to the University of Massachusetts at Boston. By saying that I lived in an increasingly constricted and privatized world until I started college, I'm not invoking the usual tale of liberal education. According to the usual tale, the university transforms the asocial or self-centered individual into a public, civic-minded citizen. What I experienced was very different. My education didn't take me from private to public but instead offered glimpses into—a critical purchase on—the ways in which I was already socialized and, especially, socialized to regard virtually everything in my world as strictly personal (and so not discussible) or strictly impersonal (and so not discussible either). For example, in 1982 when I left my $230-a-week secretarial job for one that paid $265, I handed my boss a neatly typed letter of resignation. (Write a letter, the employment agency I'd visited on my lunch hour had counseled. Keep it vague. Say you're resigning for "personal reasons" and refuse, on the grounds of privacy, to reveal any more.)

"You can't do this," my boss protested. "We paid a lot of money for you." She was referring to the $230 fee they'd paid to the same employment agency for bringing me to them three months before.

"You have to give a reason," she said. "Otherwise . . ." She looked me up and down, her eyes coming to rest on my midsection. "Otherwise, we have to assume the worst about you."

When still I refused to explain, she concluded, "You can't give notice. Clearly we can no longer trust you. You're fired."

"Whatever you think is best," I said, and then—this is how I would remember that moment in years to come, a denouement created more from my reading of Carson McCuller's "Wunderkind" than from actual fact—I took the elevator down forty-seven floors, spun out into the noontime world of fresh air and light.

I've told this story many times over the past twenty years, adding that this boss used to follow me into the ladies' room and dictate telexes through the closed stall door—so much for privacy. It's one of a dozen or so back-when-I-was-a-secretary tales I cart about like battle honors. In each telling, I stress how this woman regarded me as she might a cow she'd purchased and now had doubts about, how I'd smiled right back and then broke away—*free! independent! a wily deal maker able to get herself $35 more a week!* I hope the paucity of that pay increase and the ridiculousness, or pathos, of that wily deal-maker image of myself is apparent. Consider that Tom Wolfe at this very moment must have been gathering material among Wall Street's billionaire bond barons for his *Bonfire of the Vanities*. Now picture me on the sidewalk outside Boston's Hancock Tower, rifling through my empty briefcase—leather, Aigner, a Katharine Gibbs graduation gift from my Aunt Joan—and panicking because I couldn't find my monthly T pass. That subway pass cost $22, the first two weeks of my raise, after taxes, already eaten up.

What I always leave out when I tell this tale is the perplexing question of just why I heeded in the first place the employment agency's advice: Be vague, don't mention the new job, let her think you're knocked up if she wants to. (Of course, I understand why the employment agency gave me this counsel: they wanted to continue business with this company, wanted me to invoke personal privacy as a cover for them.) Why not say, "I've found a new job that pays more, and you ought to be paying more, too"? Why not go back out into the secretarial pool and—instead of silently picking up my briefcase and sneakers—shout, "Everyone! Listen! There's more money out there! Not much, but it's a start, and if we just band together . . ."?

The answers to these "Why not?" questions are pretty obvious: my family history joined to New Right Reaganism where employment is a personal matter of self-created success or self-inflicted failure. (For an examination of the Reagan-era semantics transforming social issues into "lifestyle" choices, see Howell and Ingham.) As for shouting out loud, calling on others to rally around: the very thought of this possibility would have overwhelmed me with embarrassment (a feeling I finally had to confront and fight head-on when I took a public role last year in my university's faculty union drive). Though I'd found the final scenes of *Norma Rae* thrilling, the movie *9 to 5* deeply satisfying, the idea of actually joining NOW or the Boston chapter of *9 to 5* ran entirely counter to my Mary Tyler Moore idea of making it through by being plucky, pert, and indispensable. Feminism? I had my diaphragm, needed nothing else.

My new boss was the treasurer for what would turn out to be a successful U.S. Senate campaign. He enjoyed hitching his thigh up on my desk, lighting a cigar (since I smoked at my desk, I didn't regard this as rude, just characteristic), then telling me how politics really work: "You pay them; they do what you want."

"So what about me?" I asked. It was an honest question, not cynical or sarcastic. I really wanted to know, really hoped he'd tell me. Somewhere out there was the public world, and despite my keen discomfort at the thought of joining anything (what if I accidentally joined the wrong group, like the Hari Krishnas I saw every weekend in front of the Harvard Co-op?), I wanted desperately to find that world, "a world just a little inaccessible," as Susan Wells writes, "like live theater or downtown department stores" ("Rogue Cops" 326). It's the usual story: I wanted to *do something, be someone, belong somewhere.* I felt this desire especially when the handsome man who would become Massachusetts' next senator came in—sailed in, really, never pausing at my desk, never knocking at my boss's closed door, entirely free from the usual business-office rules of entry. Sometimes while I typed my boss's fund-raising letters, I tried to imagine myself as a political candidate and then, failing that, I entertained fantasies that I would become someone by becoming a writer.

"So what about me?" I asked my boss. "What can I do?"

"Ha," he said. "That's funny."

It was about this time that I bought myself a journal. I still have it, one of those cardboard-cover composition books, and it contains a single entry: "I know I want to write but what?"

Rhetorical Questions

For as long as I've been in the fields of composition and women's studies, the questions of what we and our students should write and how we should write have been framed in terms of "personal vs. public." Recently, for instance, Deborah Brandt and Anne Herrington have argued for composition researchers to distinguish between personal lives and public interest. It's not the person writing or being written about who matters, Brandt argues: "What matters are the ideas or knowledge that research yields for public use" (42) and is in the "public interest" (44). To this argument for research that serves the public interest, Herrington adds: "We should make the choice as to what of our personal lives we feel should be made public on the basis of our own sense of professional and political purposes" (48).

It's tough to argue against the good of writing in the public interest. But in my teaching and writing that's exactly what I've tried to do. Or, more accurately, what I've tried to do is make the classifications of public, private, personal, and social *arguable.* The terms public and private, as Fraser underscores, aren't "straight-forward designations of societal spheres" but are "rhetorical labels and cultural classifications," labels and classifications that function "to delegitimate some interests, views, and topics, and to valorize others" (*Justice Interruptus* 88). What counts as public interest? Whose interests are protected under the banner of privacy? What has gone into creating our guiding sense of what to include, what to exclude? These are crucial rhetorical questions for any class to take up.

In recent years, as I've sought to place these questions at the center of my teaching, I've also shifted from talking with students about the "politics of the personal" to the "politics of privacy." That word *privacy* carries with it a history that the term *personal* simply does not. Bound up with *privacy* are stories of benefit and protection and simultaneously stories of exclusion and denial, including countless examples of how privacy rights have been used to justify the power of a husband over a wife, a master over a slave, a boss over a worker, and North American interests over Latin American. Though in the end, I can't join with Catherine MacKinnon in arguing that we should abolish the very idea of privacy, for I've benefited too much from the strategic if incomplete privacy arguments advanced through *Baird v. Eisenstadt* and *Roe v. Wade,* However, analyses such as MacKinnon's, my own uneasy history, and the many stories my students bring to class keep me mindful of what the measure of privacy has too often been. I want that tension between privacy as boon and privacy as bane in my classroom and in my scholarship.

For my classes, then, I look for texts offering prime examples of how voices and views get "worked up" as strictly private. (This idea of looking at how things get "worked up" into institutional categories comes from feminist sociologist Dorothy Smith. Her book *The Everyday World as Problematic: A Feminist Sociology* provided me with the inspiration to approach this chapter as I did: using my history as what Smith calls a "*point d'apui*" for grasping the cultural construction and social regulation of privacy.) I look, too, for examples of what Fraser calls "discursive contestation" (*Justice Interruptus* 86) over the highly political questions of who gets to draw the public/private boundary. Other texts that not only show the persistent problems of public/private boundaries as experienced in specific contexts but also how individuals and groups labor in language to contest these categories include Patricia Williams's critique of the privatization of racial segregation (in *The Alchemy of Race and Rights*), Fraser's examination of challenges to the liberal model of the public sphere in the Clarence Thomas confirmation hearing (in *Justice Interruptus*), and Jacqueline Jones Royster's detailed historical account of African American women's work to create democratic counterpublics in which they could be heard (in *Traces of a Stream*).

With and through published examples, I also want my students to have the means to examine and contest what's been worked up as merely self-regarding or entirely other-regarding in their own histories. These are, after all, writing classes I teach, and I know from that single journal entry I wrote in the 1980s—"I want to write but what?"—that a precondition of writing is the belief that one's experiences, perceptions, and spheres of participation are discussible. Fulfilling that condition takes an act of double consciousness that I've tried to dramatize in my approach to this chapter and that I try to foreground in my teaching, particularly through revision exercises aimed at filling up margins and backs of pages with both contextual detail and analytic speculation. One exercise, "Reseeing the Argument," for instance, asks a writer to look again at a draft, no matter what the genre and no matter how seemingly "personal" the approach, and to draw out in the margins the arguments this early draft may be advancing or implying. The point of such an exercise is not to move students from "private" to "public" or from "narrative" to "argument" but to dramatize, visibly in the margins, how experiences and genres we've been taught to regard as personal and private are very much bound up in what is social, public, and arguable. The exercise might lead a student to a revision that does indeed highlight the teased-out argument. It might also lead a student to delve all the more into the complexities of context.

Regardless of the final product that results, what I want my students to experience through such an exercise is a growing, heady, and also very possibly disorienting sense of how much social history and public debate is packed into a single rough-draft paragraph—even and especially a paragraph about a matter typically marked as merely personal. I want them to have a sense of how hard it is to write about such a subject, how necessary, too, to exercise real choices between the *freedom from* intrusion and the *freedom to* articulate. The exercise of such choices in writing isn't enough, obviously, to unseat the dominating logic of neoliberalism and halt the privatization of public services, public spaces, and public issues. Much more than classroom work is needed here. But it does mark one point of resistance, one way that teachers of writing can refuse to participate.

TAKE THREE: BE VERY AFRAID. BUT STAND UP ANYWAY

When I started this essay, I had it in mind to argue that the much publicized threats to individual privacy in an Internet age distract us from the real and growing threats to our democratic publicity rights. That's an argument I've backed away from, though, because the more I unpack my rhetorical terms, the more I recognize that privacy and publicity exist as two sides of the same coin. For example, today among my e-mails is an ACLU action alert detailing the latest legislative proposal to defend national security through electronic surveillance, detainment without due process, and secret searches. (The U.S. Patriot Act has, of course, with overwhelming and dismaying congressional support, gone on to become law. One of Vermont's senators even snapped a photo of George Bush signing the act into law—a Kodak moment for his personal photo album, I suppose.) The U.S. Patriot Act has profound and damaging consequences for our rights of privacy. In a crucial twist, however, what this e-mail alert emphasizes are the devastating effects these invasions of personal privacy will have on democratic publicity: on people's ability and willingness to assemble, dissent, be noticed in any way. The alert ends with this ambivalent call to public action: "Be very afraid. But stand up anyway."

I read those lines, remember my mother saying, "Shush. That has nothing to do with us," and I realize that the lesson she imparted wasn't specific to her own post-McCarthy era but still operates, and must be resisted, in ours.

3

VIRTUOSOS AND ENSEMBLES

Rhetorical Lessons from Jazz

Gregory Clark

Reconciling our desire for individual freedom to act with our practical need to establish and maintain with others a working consensus might well be the foundational project of human sociality, and it is certainly the reason for rhetoric. Particularly in a democratic society, this binary structures the experience of social interaction and, consequently, rhetorical practice. It structures conventional rhetorical practice in the form of a conflict that is resolvable only when one element of the binary concedes to the other, or, at its most democratic, when each relinquishes enough to the other to effect a momentary compromise. Conventionally, then, we use rhetoric to manage the ongoing confrontation of two conflicting aspirations. The familiar conflicts between individual and collective, private and public, autonomy and consensus, so pervades our experience that the very suggestion of fully reconciling the two seems at least to be naive. By almost every definition we have, rhetoric is a method for engaging, not reconciling, that conflict.

However, one definition does seem to admit that possibility, offered some time ago by John Poulakos as a "Sophistic" definition of rhetoric: "Rhetoric is the art which seeks to capture in opportune moments that which is appropriate and attempts to suggest that which is possible" (26). Absent from the terms of this definition is any reference to that persistent conflict between our desire for individual freedom and our need to build and maintain consensus that traditionally gives rhetoric its form and function. Instead, these terms suggest the general shape of a discursive practice that joins people together in activities of collectively beneficial innovation. Rather than reconciling competing interests, the purpose of the discourse defined here is to move its participants more or less together from what Poulakos calls "the sphere of actuality" to an altogether new sphere, "a place in that of potentiality" (26). Functionally, this notion of rhetorical practice seems to structure an alternative relationship between individual and collectivity. What, exactly, might this relationship be? Beyond conflict, what sort of relationship between the two is possible?

Poulakos envisions a rhetoric that would be "ultimately more persuasive" than the familiar rhetoric of conflict (29). Functionally, what he seems to describe is an aesthetic act within which those engaged in discourse together leave the realm of the actual to imagine a new realm comprising their common potential. But such a process remains difficult to envision using the language of the rhetorical tradition. Perhaps Kenneth Burke came the closest when he reconceived rhetoric in terms that rely heavily on aesthetic experience. But the problem that remains is that the concept of *persuasion* is itself constituted of this conflict of autonomy and affiliation. Using rhetorical terms, we can hardly conceptualize any other sort of discursive exchange.

But there is another set of terms, these derived from another sort of communicative practice in which the contending opposites of autonomy and affiliation seem, indeed, to be reconciled. That practice is the ensemble performance of jazz music. Its reconciliation of this conflict is observed, though not analyzed and explained, by the dean of twentieth-century jazz critics, Martin Williams, in his history of jazz performance, *The Jazz Tradition.* The book concludes with this description of what that music can teach:

> The high degree of individuality, together with the mutual respect and cooperation required in a jazz ensemble carry with them philosophical implications that are so exciting and far-reaching that one almost hesitates to contemplate them. It is as if jazz were saying to us that not only is greater individuality possible . . . but that such individuality, far from being a threat to a cooperative social structure, can actually enhance society. (253)

And Williams himself hesitates to contemplate that possibility, offering this observation only at the end of his book. But his chronicle of great jazz performances documents this reconciliation of autonomy and affiliation in action. In jazz performances, neither the virtuosity of the soloist nor the unified authority of the ensemble is subordinated to the other. Rather, the two are inextricably interwoven and absolutely interdependent. In Williams's descriptions, the more individually unique and expressive the solo, the more powerful the performance of the ensemble. And, at once, the more cohesive and intense the music of the ensemble, the more each soloist is enabled to perform as a virtuoso. In jazz, the virtuoso performance is the moment when the private is made public. The individual performer brings the resources of skill and feeling to a moment of public expression, and in jazz that moment is most powerful when the individual performance is deeply embedded in the performance of a group.

In the best jazz performances, the individual and the collective interact in relationships of collaboration. But *collaborate* is a very weak term for describing what happens in an ensemble performance of jazz. What I hope to explore here is the possibility of finding in jazz performance some better terms to describe the possibilities for a positive relationship between individuals and collectives, a relationship in which private individuals can join in a powerful public expression, together, of their individuality. Some terms that describe this aesthetic practice that, at its best, enacts a seamless joining of individual and collective, might help us envision ways that the contentious competition of autonomy and affiliation might be transcended in rhetorical interaction. Specifically, this "new language" for collaboration in communication may help us envision a rhetorical practice in which collectives are created by a project that enables the individuals who share interest in that project to thrive. It renders rhetorical practice a pragmatic social context in conflicts between the private aspirations of individuals and the public performance of the group where these conflicts can be rendered productive.

DEFINITION

Poulakos's definition suggests that considerable rhetorical power is wielded by collective aesthetic effort in which people work together using resources available in "opportune moments" to construct images of "that which is possible." And that, to most jazz critics, commentators, and performers, is precisely the power of jazz music, a music they treat as wielding considerable rhetorical power. At the end of his book, Williams hesitates to contemplate the "philosophical implications" of the stunning reconciliation of individual and collective that he witnesses in a good performance of jazz, but he does contemplate in detail its rhetorical effect. Art, he writes, "does not reflect society and environment and consciousness so much as it tells us what environment and society and conscious do not know." In other words, art "reveals to us that there are other, perhaps opposite, but still tenable ways of looking at things, of feeling about things. Art tells us what we do not know or do not realize," presenting us with "resolutions to the problems of paradox" (253). In particular, the art of jazz

> not only exalts the individual finding his own way, it also places him in a fundamental, dynamic, and necessary cooperation with his fellows. It handles paradox—the paradox of emotion but also the paradox of thinking and doing—in ways that perhaps no other music has. It does not deal with absolutes, and it does not deny the relative function of time. (256)

The individual finding his or her own way within a "fundamental, dynamic, and necessary cooperation" with others and individuals working together through shared paradoxes, using the resources made available by a particular place and time, together constitute jazz performance. However, they also constitute rhetorical practice, at least by its more dialogical definitions. And in that sense, rhetoric functions aesthetically in the same way that, according to Williams, jazz does. Although rhetorical interactions merely reflect "society and environment and consciousness," they can also produce innovations that, as he puts it, tell "us what environment and society and conscious do not know" as, like jazz, they reveal "other . . . ways of looking at things, of feeling about things" (253).

Like rhetoric, jazz is perhaps best defined in terms of its functions rather than its forms. By *function*, I mean both how the practice itself—whether rhetoric or jazz—prompts people to interact as well as the effects of those interactions on their participants. This focus on function is readily apparent in many definitions of jazz—those, for example, from one of the most articulate of contemporary jazz musicians, Wynton Marsalis. When asked by an interviewer to define the *essence* of jazz, Marsalis first listed three central elements that, he noted, "have nothing to do with music." The first is "play"—that primarily aesthetic experience of making something new from something else. The second, which immediately follows from the first, is a "desire to play with other people." The third is what success in the second requires—"learning to respect individuality" (Scherman 30). And that is learned in the practice of improvisation, which, along with the rhythm of swing and the harmonics of the blues, is conventionally one of the three formal characteristics of jazz music. "Classical music doesn't prize improvisation," Marsalis notes. "It doesn't place a premium on individuality. In jazz the point is to achieve your identity on your instrument, no matter what role you play" (31). However, that individuality is most fully expressed when jazz improvisation occurs within the common project of an ensemble where individuality must be made accessible to and usable by cooperating others. At its best, then, jazz improvisation "mediates" individualities but does not diminish them. Marsalis describes swing—that rolling rhythmic jazz feeling that resists any musical notation—as the "great mediator" of the individuality in a jazz performance as each participant both internalizes and expresses this common feeling (interview 2000). The crucial fact is that the ensemble swings best only when all of the participating individuals swing together.

Another definitional discussion of jazz—this one from Martin Williams—resonates more immediately with the terms of rhetorical theory. Also emphasizing its function over its form, Williams observes: "Jazz knows of no absolutes: there is no one 'best' way of performing a piece. Each day, each moment has its way, and hence its own meaning" (251). So a jazz performance is always contingent, always an expression of the situation within which it occurs. But within that situation, successful performers *function* as fully and integrally human: "To a jazz musician, thought and feeling, reflection and emotion, come together uniquely, and resolve in the act of doing." That is because what jazz demands from each performer is a "spontaneous individual invention of new melody, individual articulation of emotion, and individual interpretation of musical sound." Yet the success of the performance itself depends entirely "on group cooperation"—on the capacity of these performers to devote their individuality to "collective ensemble improvisation" (252). For Williams, as for Marsalis, jazz is more than music—it is an occasion in which individuals are at their best as they enact community by directing their private goals toward the public purposes enacted in an ensemble performance. For Williams, "jazz not only exalts the individual finding his own way, it also places him in a fundamental, dynamic, and necessary cooperation with his fellows" (256). For Marsalis, who tends to define jazz in rhetorical terms, jazz is participation in a conversation (Scherman 35); specifically, it creates "harmony through conflict, like a good, hot discussion"—one in which individuals are both transformed and unified by each other's influence (Marsalis and Stewart 146).

Jazz, like rhetoric, does the aesthetic work of inventing new ideas through collective interaction. Like participants in a rhetorical exchange, performers in a jazz ensemble are cooperative and competitive at once in ways that render the two complementary. But unlike rhetoric, in the best jazz, the separate work of those individuals is almost perfectly coherent, suggesting that the conflicts of autonomy and affiliation that are inherent in most social encounters might be rendered productive for the individuals *and* the collectives that comprise them. That is what seems to happen when a great jazz ensemble performs. As Martin Williams explains, "It is as if jazz were saying to us that not only is far greater individuality possible to man than he has so far allowed himself, but that such individuality, far from being a threat to a cooperative social structure, can actually enhance society" (252–53). Ralph Ellison was more specific about what that process would entail:

> True jazz is an art of individual assertion within and against the group. Each true jazz moment . . . springs from a contest in which each artist challenges all the rest, each solo flight, or improvisation, represents . . . a definition of his identity as individual, as member of the collectivity, and as a link in the chain of tradition. Thus, because jazz finds its very life in an endless improvisation upon traditional materials, the jazzman must lose his identity even as he finds it. (36)

The language of Christian transformation is deliberate here. Ellison explains that after learning the fundamentals of the instrument and the music, the performer "must then 'find himself,' must be reborn, must find, as it were, his soul. All this through achieving that subtle identification between his instrument and his deepest desires which will allow him to express his own unique ideas and his own unique voice" (60–61). That language seems to exalt the private individual—but it is a private individual already rendered public. The unique self expressed by a fully formed jazz musician is not the autonomous self that first entered the ensemble. That self has been transformed by the experience of the ensemble's performance. Writer Albert Murray describes how this transformation happened to the members of Duke Ellington's orchestra, an ensemble where "each solo participant fulfills a role that is as immediately distinguishable as a character in a story." That could only occur, however, after each was transformed by what Murray calls "the Ellington process." Playing in that ensemble "did not reduce musicians to robots."

Instead, as he says: "[It] brought the very best they had in them. Indeed, in almost every instance, the musician found himself being featured before he himself realized that he had something special to offer" (111).

Students of rhetorical theory will detect elements of Kenneth Burke's very important redefinition of rhetoric in this description of what happened to the individuals who joined Ellington's ensemble. As a cultural critic and social theorist, Burke—a contemporary and compatriot of jazz music—lived through all but the last seven years of the American twentieth century. It was a century that saw countless wars, more acts of genocide than anyone would care to count, and the creation and use of weapons capable of ending human existence altogether. Burke witnessed all that. By the third decade of the century he had already defined his lifelong project of articulating a communicative method that would enable people to move themselves toward "the purification of war," as he put it at midcentury in the epigraph to *A Grammar of Motives.* Simply put, he worked to describe a mode of interaction that would render human conflicts constructive rather than destructive. Summarizing the method at midcentury as "dialectic," a concept and term borrowed from classical philosophy and rhetoric, he described interactions that would encompass both "the competition of cooperation, or the cooperation of competition" (*Grammar* 402–03). The outcome that would follow from that sort of exchange is, in his preferred term, "transcendence." In one of his more precise descriptions, transcendence is "the building of a *terministic bridge* whereby one realm is *transcended* by being viewed *in terms of* a realm beyond it" ("I, Eye, Aye" 151). For Burke, that aspiration to build a bridge from *what is* directly to *what might be* is universally human. We all have a need to "stretch forth our hands through love of a farther shore"—a place where we might consider things "in terms of a broader scope" than our own (163). That entails a transformation of individual identity and private ambition, as people leave interactions with others understanding themselves and their place in a shared world differently than they had before.

Rhetoric redefined in this sense extends well beyond a discursive genre to encompass a kind of interpersonal relationship. In this sense, rhetoric describes relationships in which selves are mutually transformed by the influence of each other. This is what Burke meant by *rhetoric*—a mode of relationship that enables the transformation of self that follows from a dialectical encounter with others. Here is Burke's redefinition:

> If I had to sum up in one word the difference between the 'old' rhetoric and a 'new' . . . I would reduce it to this: The key term for the old rhetoric was "persuasion," and its stress was upon deliberate design. The key term for the new rhetoric would be "identification," which can include a partially "unconscious" factor in appeal. "Identification" at its simplest is also a deliberate device, as when the politician seeks to identify himself with his audience. In this respect, its equivalents are plentiful in Aristotle's *Rhetoric.* But "identification" can also be an end, as when people earnestly yearn to identify themselves with some group or other. Here they are not necessarily being acted upon by a conscious external agent, but may be acting upon themselves to this end. ("Rhetoric" 203)

The term *persuasion* suggests one individual dominating another, the sort of relationship assumed by traditional rhetoric. But the term *identification* suggests a genuine sort of intimacy shared among interacting individuals—even, it seems, a momentary experience of communion. That is the place at which Burke's revisionist rhetoric is distinctly different from the traditional. "In such identification," he continues, "there is a partially dreamlike, idealistic motive, somewhat compensatory to real differences and real divisions, which the rhetoric of identification would transcend" ("Rhetoric" 203). Living through the twentieth century, Kenneth Burke saw unthinkable destruction caused by difference and division, as well as by the most insidious of communions. So he focused his attention on the project of explaining how individuals are transformed by a community. This, he hoped, would enable them to seek the right sort of communions. That is the "idealistic motive" that directed his work.

Burke's definition of rhetoric significantly expands the category. In his *A Rhetoric of Motives* (1950), he described as rhetorical any encounter that prompts a "persuasion 'to attitude'"—a description that extends the term beyond the traditional concept of "persuasion to out-and-out action" by treating attitude itself as "an incipient act." It also extended formal notions of what counts as rhetoric, noting that defining rhetoric as "persuasion to *attitude* would permit the application of rhetorical terms to purely *poetic* structures" (50). Indeed, for Burke, the "simplest case of persuasion" is more precisely a kind of human relationship than it is a rational argument: "you persuade a man only insofar as you can talk his language by speech, gesture, tonality, order, image, attitude, idea, *identifying* your ways with his" (55). So rhetoric remains a matter of persuasion, but the experiences it includes are so diverse and pervasive that the term is hardly useful. Essentially, rhetoric is what happens when individuals interact and, through the influences of that interaction, come to understand themselves and their connections to others differently. The consequence of rhetoric is a new identity, individual and collective. This outcome constitutes the experience of playing in a jazz ensemble that Ellison described, and of the "Ellington process" that transformed individuals into virtuosos by integrating them into the ensemble. This process seems to be what Marsalis was getting at when he said that "the ultimate achievement in jazz music is the interplay of distinctive personalities through . . . a musical form [within which] the group establishes its identity" (Marsalis and Stewart 148).

For Burke, then, rhetorical power resides in the full range of relational experiences that comprise a life in society, life constituted of "rhetorical situations" that shape the identities of those who share them. The shaping forces there are those others who are "participants in a common situation" as well as "the words one is using *and* the nonverbal circumstances in which one is using them" ("Rhetorical Situation" 263; my emphasis) that together provide a common set of "resources of identification" (267). Simply put, individual identity is constituted from the resources of social experience as the private self is continually re-created in response to engagement with the public other. In Burke's words, it "may involve identification not just with mankind or the world in general, but with some kind of congregation that also implies some related norms of differentiation and segregation" (268). And the experience of jazz performance suggests that it is in the context of this congregation that individual identity becomes most rhetorically powerful and socially productive.

IMPROVISING IDENTITIES

Kenneth Burke's redefinition of rhetoric as identification rather than merely persuasion entails a particular definition of identity: "Personal identity comes to a focus in the complex of attitudes . . . that constitute the *individual's* orientation (sense of 'reality' with corresponding sense of relationships)" (*Permanence* 309–10). For Burke, identity both encompasses and expresses an individual's role in the social world. And rhetoric is always about transforming that identity—for better or for worse. For Burke, the study of rhetoric is the study of "the rhetorical constitution of the subject" within human relationships (Wess 136). That is the project of inquiry into the origin of human motives that he developed as "dramatism." Dramatism focuses on the actions and social roles of individuals, a study Burke extended when he began to explore "constitutional relations" as a way of understanding the mutual influences of individuals and groups. The aging Burke once briefly explained this aspect of his project in these terms:

> . . . I having gone from my first book of critical theory (*Counter-Statement*), built around the subject of literary form in such texts as the plays of Shakespeare to my realization that our Constitution is a literary form. And quite as Shakespeare's literary forms were "enacted" in historical situations largely non-literary, so the Constitutional principles, or ideals, or wishes involve enactments in the largely and ever-changingly extra-Constitutional situation. (letter)

Indeed, near the end of his life (for example, his 1989 talk at the Conference on College Composition and Communication, titled "Speaking on Language and Power"), Burke was locating this study of constitutional relations at the center of his lifelong project of envisioning a more constructive engagement of individual and collective.

Burke defined a constitution as "an enactment of human wills" (*Grammar* 323) that addresses a collective for the purpose of establishing the common ground upon which the individuals who comprise it will interact. Consequently, constitutions are intensely rhetorical, functioning primarily as "hortatory" (332) assertions of a collective identity that demands something of the individuals addressed. In effect, they constitute identity, individual as well as collective. As Burke put it, "in actual point of fact, a Constitution is addressed by the first person to the second person" (360), and when people adopt a constitution—when they acknowledge individually its address and in that process accept the identity it imputes (Charland 138)—they "in their present person . . . address commands to their future person" (*Grammar* 361). Burke uses the U.S. Constitution as his primary example of that fundamental sort of rhetorical act.

The first words of its preamble, "'We, the People,'' demonstrate that the primary rhetorical function of the Constitution is to articulate to a collective of individuals their identity as a community. That is the task of a constitution, to unite diverse people in a common identity that is at once philosophical and practical. A constitution addresses the people whose individual and private identities it makes public by attributing to them all the collective identity of "the people." As one rhetorical theorist puts it, "the people" is a rhetorical reality that remains in existence only so long as the rhetoric that describes it has force (McGee 345). Burke's work suggests that this constitutional function can follow from many communicative forms—from policy documents, shared narratives, even nondiscursive social practices. Whatever the form, each reconstitutes individuals by addressing them as a part of a "people," an address that asserts a "new version of collective life" with which they should aspire to identify (*Grammar* 347). So this sort of rhetoric addresses individuals in ways that reconstitute them as members of a community that shares perspectives, values, commitments, and projects. And that constitutional process is necessarily ongoing.

In the case of the U.S. Constitution, that ongoing process proceeds, as Kenneth Burke and contemporary jazz critic Stanley Crouch both observe, through the process of amendment. Crouch notes that by mandating a mechanism for its own revision, "the Constitution recognizes that there may be times in the future when what we now think of as hard fact might be no more than nationally accepted prejudice" that needs to be eliminated from national policy (*All-American Skin Game* 10–11). That rhetorical process of amendment, central to the survival of that Constitution and the nation it constitutes, mirrors the practice of improvisation in which the conflicting identities of individual and group are rendered complementary in the performance of jazz music. As Crouch puts it, "perhaps no society so significant has emerged over the last five centuries that has made improvisation so basic to its sensibility" (15). And it is probably not coincidental that the culture that has sustained itself into a third century by an amendable constitution is also the culture that created jazz music. When Crouch writes that "jazz is an art in which improvisation declares an aesthetic rejection of the preconceptions that stifle individual and collective invention" (16–17), that "jazzmen" provide a model for "how freedom and discipline could coexist within the demands of an ensemble improvisation" (17), and that what characterizes jazz virtuosity above all is "the ability to *make musical sense* during the act of playing" with a group, he describes a sort of civic interaction to which the structure of their constitution invites U.S. citizens to aspire.

Essentially, improvisation in a successful jazz ensemble enacts a practical ideal of democratic citizenship. It requires people to work constructively with paradoxes, uniting the dichotomies of tradition and innovation as well as of individual and collective. "The demands on and the respect for the individual in the jazz band puts democracy into aesthetic action," writes Crouch.

> Each performer must bring technical skill, imagination, and the ability to create coherent statements through improvised interplay with the rest of the musicians. That interplay takes its direction from the melodic, harmonic, rhythmic, and timbral elements of the piece being played, and each player must have a remarkably strong sense of what constitutes the *making* of music opposed to the *rendering* of music. (15)

In the process of jazz performance, then, individuals can confront and resolve conflicts that construct human experience in general and are perhaps intensified in an American experience. At least, they can resolve them "aesthetically." In jazz, writes one of its scholars, "expressions tending toward complete formal freedom have always been placed within well-respected structures," one demonstration of its "successful joining of invention and order" (Lichtenstein 229). An aesthetic resolution is not actual, practical resolution. But it can be instructive, suggesting what reality might become. Indeed, the aesthetic explores alternative futures that address present needs and aspirations. And in jazz, innovation is born out of the aesthetic resolution of problematical opposites—freedom and discipline, virtuoso and ensemble, invention and order, private and public.

TOWARD A JAZZ RHETORIC

But jazz is not rhetoric. Jazz, as Stanley Crouch recently put it, "is an art, not practical politics" (interview). And practical politics, as Aristotle and many others have observed, is precisely what much of rhetoric is about. Given that definitional disjunction, is there any value in this project of looking to jazz performance as a model for an alternative sort of rhetorical interaction? I think that depends on how we define *art.* When Albert Murray writes about jazz as an art, he draws upon Burke's definition and describes art as a particular kind of "equipment for living," one that provides "images, representative anecdotes, emblems that condition us to confront what we must confront, and it disposes us to do what we must do." For Murray, then, jazz fits that functional definition of art, and he concludes that the sort of interactions that produce jazz music in a "jam session" may be the best "representative anecdote" for life in the United States, a term he borrows directly from Burkean rhetoric (112). In that situation, "the musician is always engaged in the dialogue or a conversation, or even argument. . . . He achieves his individuality by saying 'yes and also' to that with which he agrees, and by saying 'no,' or in any case, 'on the other hand,' to that with which he disagrees" (113). This rhetorical vocabulary is being used to describe the art of jazz. Jazz is not politics, but it is an intensely collaborative art that models modes of individual interaction that have a potential to improve our social and political life. Consequently, it is worthwhile to examine jazz and to do so in terms of how it is made. As the pianist Bill Evans once put it: "Jazz is not a 'what,' it's a 'how,' and if you do things according to the 'how' of jazz, it's jazz" (Mehegan 150).

Jazz is made democratically. Its varied and infectious rhythms, its simple and memorable harmonies, its canon composed largely of the familiar melodies of American popular song rendered anew for each new situation—all draw upon resources of common experience. And jazz is democratic in its social functions. For Wynton Marsalis, that function is to reach people at a common root of rhythm and song and invite that part of them to a "gathering place" (interview 2001). There, those who have the skill and experience improvise an expression of themselves as a productive community using the resources they find available at the time and place of their gathering. And there, those without the skills gather to listen, transcending their inherent isolation and separation as they share together a very accessible and inviting aesthetic experience. They not only listen to the music but also move along with it, once filling dance floors and now, much more subtly, nodding heads and tapping feet and fingers all together.

Jazz enacts a mode of sociality that intensifies individuality and, at the same time, propels the process of creating community. But that, ideally, is precisely what rhetoric would do. A great jazz performance prefigures a rhetorical interaction that would enable people to encompass and transcend the conflicts of competing selves in order to create from the potential chaos that is inherent in any group of individuals something unified in beauty and order that is satisfying to all. And jazz does that in the moment that this creation is needed, and using the resources at hand. Jazz improvises order out of chaos, cooperation out of conflict, art out of the everyday. That improvisation is what every jazz musician must be prepared to enact. And it is also, increasingly it seems, what every citizen must be prepared to enact as well. Especially in a time when new situations continually surprise us. In an hour, the crime of hijacking became a mode of genocide and, for millions, the world changed. This new world required individuals actively to become a society, and it required that society immediately improvise ways to return order and meaning and direction to the common life that the individuals who compose it must share. Perhaps now more than ever before we need to learn the civic lessons that jazz can teach. Now, more than ever, we need to attend to, in Crouch's words, "what jazz has done, with its improvising attention to the details of memory, imagination, experience, passion, and design." What it has done "is make the velocity of creation equal to that of destruction" (*All-American Skin Game* 144). Now rhetoric and politics must do that as well.

This attempt to find in jazz a set of terms we might use to recast our concept of rhetorical interaction in ways that will enable us to do that has produced only one term, *improvisation.* And it is a very general term with much implicit within it. But it offers a starting point for thinking about resolving the conflict of individual and community in ways that conventional terms of rhetoric don't allow. But thinking that through will be difficult. It is difficult for the best of jazz musicians. Bill Evans was a piano virtuoso whose trio aspired to an improvisational ideal that would transcend the turn-taking exchange of most of his contemporaries. "I'm hoping the trio will grow in the direction of simultaneous improvisation," he wrote, "rather than just one guy blowing followed by another guy blowing. If the bass player, for example, hears an idea he wants to answer, why should he just keep playing a background?" (liner notes, "Portrait"). He envisioned "the very provocative revelation of two, three, four, or five minds responding simultaneously to each other in a unified coherent performance" (liner notes, "Conversations"). But this ideal was unstable in practice, perhaps because it is finally difficult for individuals to "respond simultaneously to each other in a unified coherent performance." In fact, this statement of Evans's vision is from the liner notes to a recording in which three pianos improvise together, each played by Bill Evans on overdubbed tracks.

Occasionally, Bill Evans's trio achieved the ideal of "simultaneous improvisation," but it may have been, finally, inadvertent, in the moments when these three custodians of their separate egos each lost themselves at once in their ensemble performance. But it clearly was *not* for those moments that Bill Evans preferred playing in trios. Late in his career, when asked about that preference, he replied:

> Well, for me it's a very pure group. But primarily, I'm more in control of the music. I can shape the music and I state the theme, I keep the flow going . . . and it becomes a totally musical experience for the group and also the audience. If I just added a horn—now, I enjoy playing with horns; I record with horns frequently—but that's the main reason. Even if I use one horn, it changes the whole concept, because then, the thematic statements and all are out of my hands. (interview)

Yet for me, one of Bill Evans's most powerful performances of jazz is given that power precisely at the moment when a horn takes all that out of his hands. The performance begins with his solo piano playing his poignant composition, "Waltz for Debbie," a song about a beloved little girl grown up and gone. I was alone when I first heard it, listening during a long day of driving, and lamenting the loss of my own little girls to adulthood—until Cannonball Adderly's saxophone, backed by a bass and drumset, picked up the song from Evans's piano and he joined their ensemble in an swinging testament of gratitude for the past and hope for the future that entirely transformed my mood. Evans was a virtuoso whose lovely opening solo prompted me to lonely reflection. But when the ensemble took the song out of his hands and he was no longer playing alone, I found myself moving to the music and thinking about how and when to get together with my daughters again.

The aesthetic experience of listening to this jazz performance was, for me, a powerful rhetorical experience as well. And Kenneth Burke's claim that rhetoric is primarily an experience of identification suggests that the aesthetic and rhetorical are not entirely different experiences. Indeed, Burke's first book, *Counter-Statement*, was written to counter conventional notions of the aesthetic by examining the rhetorical functions of the sort of "art" that "deals with life for a great many people" by "symbolizing" for the individuals it addresses "such patterns of experience as characterize a great many people" (191). Some twenty years later, his *Rhetoric of Motives* similarly countered conventional notions of rhetoric, described there as that vast "intermediate area of expression that is not wholly deliberate, yet not wholly unconscious"—an expansive realm of communicative symbols that occupy an intentional space "midway between aimless utterance and speech directly purposive" (viii). Clearly, jazz performance does not provide a usable model for argumentation or a practical method for conflict resolution. It does not teach us very much about the rhetorical formation of public policy. But it does teach us something about how private intention can be rendered publicly useful. And it does model interactions—and attitudes toward interaction—that acknowledge the extent to which individuals are necessarily interdependent, and the extent to which their success is dependent upon their cooperation as they make their separate ways together in the world.

4

KEEPING THE WORLD SAFE FOR CLASS STRUGGLE

Revolutionary Memory in a Post-Marxist Time

John Trimbur

In the last few months, I have gone to demonstrations against the "war on terrorism" and rallies on behalf of a living wage for Providence city workers. I attended a public hearing of the Workers Rights Board—a grassroots organization of trade unionists, clergy, and community activists—to investigate the conditions of undocumented workers in Rhode Island's fish-packing industry. I've made phone calls, written letters and e-mails, signed petitions, and raised money for a workers' housing project in South Africa. To be honest, I don't consider myself much of an activist these days. Instead, I see my participation more as acts of solidarity with the struggles of working people worldwide, to stay connected to the tradition of revolutionary Marxism that has shaped my way of understanding the world for nearly forty years now.

I am grateful to the editors of this volume for providing the occasion to think about how personal affiliations influence public rhetorics and published work. To do this, I want to shift away from the autobiographical questions of why I—as an individual—take part in the public rhetorical performances of the demonstration, the petition, and the letter of appeal or how I'd like my published work to push my field of study, rhetoric and writing, to the left. A more interesting question, as I see it, is why would anyone remain a Marxist in an apparently post-Marxist time. The answer, I hope to show, is that Marxism, in the first instance, is a tradition to keep revolutionary memory alive.

Now, I must say at the outset that the account I present of Marxism as an endangered tradition of revolutionary memory runs counter to what you read in the newspapers. After all, if you believe the syndicated columnists, op-editorialists, and cultural commentators ever since Richard Bernstein coined the term *political correctness* and set off a moral panic about leftist "thought police" putting free speech, white males, and the Western tradition under siege on college campuses, you might well think that American universities are dominated by Marxist ideologues. Through the culture wars of the 1980s and 1990s, writers at the *Weekly Standard* and *New Republic*, not to mention radio talk shows and fringe Web sites, refashioned the anticommunism of the cold war era to turn it on radical literary critics, feminists, and multiculturalists, finding an infiltration of alien and anti-American ideas in the academy at just the time the old Soviet threat seemed to be fading away.

I do not mean that this ideological struggle to discredit leftist ideas—and to deflate the pretensions of postmodern scholarship—is just a matter of the opinion makers needing an enemy, an other, a species of "un-American activities" to delineate a coherent, mainstream version of the American nation-state. There really was and continues to be something genuine at stake in the culture wars, as this country tries to understand itself as a pluricultural, polyglot, racially mixed, and complexly gendered society in the vortex of a globalized economy that is everywhere making and remaking the relations between working people and international capital. There is no question that a cultural Left did indeed form in American universities during the 1980s and 1990s, joining race, class, and gender to continental thought in its various poststructural manifestations. The resulting mix of cultural studies, feminism, critical race theory, queer theory, and postcolonial theory produced an invigorating effort to rethink teaching and learning and research and curriculum in the American academy, drawing generational and ideological lines in departments and fields of study that divided, often in painful and conflictual ways, traditional scholarship from the new thing and called into question the very meaning and nature of intellectual work. Writing and rhetoric were no exceptions, and I doubt that you will be surprised I consider all of this a good, even remarkable, development, an altogether fitting response to a national culture dominated by the free marketeering, deregulating ethos of the Reagan/Bush/Clinton administrations, the now burst bubble of the "new prosperity," and the social irresponsibility of "personal choice" (for the consuming classes) and "personal responsibility" (for the poor). Nonetheless, I must hasten to add that what the cultural Left did *not* do, despite all the charges of Marxist hegemony on campus, was to prepare a fertile ground for the revolutionary Marxism of the Old Left.

This is not to say that the academic cultural Left did not draw on Marxism for theoretical insights to maintain a properly cultural materialist attitude and approach. Rather, the cultural Left appropriated Marxism from a *post-Marxist* perspective, a sensibility that is not anticommunist in its allegiances but is not exactly devoted to class struggle or the historical mission of the proletariat, either. To my mind, two decisive events shaped the post-Marxist sensibility of the academic cultural Left: the emergence of postmodernism as a pervasive structure of feeling in the 1980s and 1990s and the fall of the Stalinized worker states in 1989. I want to look at each in turn to explain what I see as the present position of revolutionary Marxism in contemporary intellectual life.

As everyone knows by this point, the characteristic sensibility ascribed to postmodernism—its catchword slogan—can be found in Lyotard's "incredulity toward metanarratives." This incredulity, it is crucial to note, does not amount so much to an outright repudiation or disproof of modernist metanarratives, such as the Marxist tale of the emancipation of the working subject, though it is sometimes, mistakenly in my view, taken this way. Instead, Lyotard's postmodern incredulity is a distancing mechanism that props up modernism by making us "post" to it. This sensibility, for example, is not at all like *The God That Failed* days of the 1950s and McCarthyite anticommunist witch hunts, when writers and intellectuals who had been party members or fellow travelers denounced Marxism through public confessions and reintegrated into Eisenhower's America. As a rule, postmodernism does not produce renegades such as the notorious provocateur David Horowitz, who has turned infamously from his Old Left background and the New Left activism of *Ramparts* magazine, the antiwar movement, and support for the Black Panthers into a red-baiting gadfly. On the contrary, postmodernism offers an ironic detachment that puts the keywords of Marxism in quotes, unavoidable perhaps for the analysis of contemporary culture but never quite spoken with a straight face.

The second decisive event, the fall of the Soviet Union and the Eastern European workers' states in 1989, intertwines with the postmodern sensibility to discredit further the historical legacy of revolutionary Marxism. At face value, it seems hard to lament the fall of the Stalinized workers' states, with their secret police, gulags, psychiatric prisons, and totalitarian regimes. Still, it should be pointed out how the results of 1989 have affected working people and the oppressed not only in Russia and Eastern Europe but worldwide. What occurred was not simply the collapse of a parasitic bureaucracy but a victory for capital internationally. Russian and Eastern European workers are paying dearly for the sins of Stalin and his successors. Instead of ushering in a new era of democracy and freedom, the fall of the Iron Curtain has made available to the world market the socialized property that Stalin and his henchmen maintained at least in a degenerated form, thereby instituting a kind of anarcho-capitalism that is breathtaking in its corruption and venality. Moreover, the fall of Soviet Union and its sphere of influence removed a critical buffer between the third world and the capitalist metropolis, clearing the way for the imperialist expansion of NAFTA, GATT, the International Monetary Fund, and the World Trade Organization. The possibility of neutrality, national autonomy, and indigenous development once imagined in Nehru's India, Nasser's Arab socialism, Nyerere's Tanzania, or postapartheid South Africa has been profoundly constricted. To put it bluntly, the bosses are winning the class struggle worldwide.

Combined with the Reagan/Bush offensive against labor, the equation of the stock market's performance and national well-being during the Clinton years, the conservatism of the American trade union movement, and the absence of a workers' party in the United States, postmodernism and the fall of the Soviet Union can be seen as an actual and psychological Thermidor, a waning of revolutionary energies and the hope for social transformation. In this context, Marxism does not seem revolutionary or dangerous but corny and sentimental, left over from a prior time with little relevance to the present. Unlike the 1930s, when writers, intellectuals, and workers turned to Marxism as a guide to theory and practice—or even the early 1970s, when a fraction of antiwar New Leftists regrouped into Old Left tendencies, whether the Communist Party or Trotskyist and Maoist sects—Marxism appears not so much to have been overturned as to have withered away.

So why remain a Marxist in this post-Marxist world? As I mentioned earlier, the continuing pertinence of Marxism to our current situation can be described best in terms of revolutionary memory, the desire to keep alive the Marxist romance of history where socialism looms as not just the overthrow but the culmination of capitalist development, the design of a social future dedicated to the elimination of scarcity and the full participation of all in determining our common life. As I see it, revolutionary memory constitutes the psychological "interior" of revolutionary Marxism, where it figures as a personal and affective investment in the long-deferred dream of an international workers' commonwealth. For Marxists, theory amounts to the codification of past struggles, and revolutionary memory in turn embodies theory at the level of lived experience. There is a certain nostalgia, to be sure, that inflects revolutionary memory, not a wistful longing for a lost past but a personal affiliation with past struggles that seeks to realize their meanings and potentialities. To put it in rhetorical terms, revolutionary memory is a storehouse of knowledge—the lessons of the past that link memory, the fourth canon of rhetoric, to invention of a better future.

By convention, Marxism is often divided into its humanist and scientific wings, with the early Marx of the *Economic and Philosophical Manuscripts* and *The German Ideology* counterposed to the late Marx of *Capital.* In certain respects, of course, this is a useful distinction to map the terrain of Marxist thought, but it misses nonetheless the actual "interior" of revolutionary Marxism I am trying to describe. It may be easy enough to see how the humanist side of Marxism, in the work, say, of E. P. Thompson, Raymond Williams, or Richard Ohmann, extends Marx's vision of eliminating alienation, exploitation, and oppression and of replacing the individualist fragmentation and self-interest of bourgeois society with what Marx and Engels in the *Communist Manifesto* calls an "association, in which the free development of each is the condition for the free development of all" (53). But even the "scientific" designation must be seen as part of the pathos of Marxism, where the term *scientific* refers to neither the chilling power of a Stalinist bureaucrat nor the supposed disinterestedness of the bourgeois technocrat but instead to a process of immersing oneself, experimentally, in a history of struggle. The "science" of revolutionary memory begins, in my account, not with the desire to manage or observe but with the desire to make history, as Marx says, in conditions not of our own making. This kind of optimistic experimentalism is all the more valuable today when history appears, in fact, to be going in the wrong direction.

Let me put it a different way. Revolutionary memory is a Januslike, backward- and forward-looking maneuver that links lives to lives in the history of actual struggle. Revolutionary memory universalizes the particular moment when one does not cross a picket line, when one observes a boycott or goes to a demonstration by linking that moment to past picket lines, boycotts, and demonstrations. It makes one accountable to the struggles and sacrifices of the past—the Paris Commune in 1870, the Russian revolutions of 1905 and 1917, the Spanish Civil War, the Hungarian uprising in 1956, the Chilean Unidad Popular in the early 1970s, and the antiapartheid movement in South Africa. Revolutionary memory provides access to a tradition of heroes and martyrs, gains and betrayals, in an unfolding and now endangered narrative of emancipation.

This "interior" of Marxism, I should be quick to note, has its own historical circumstances. It has long been an axiom among liberal historians and social scientists that the appeal of Marxism in the United States is in large part due to the fact that it offers deracinated intellectuals, displaced immigrant workers, and others caught up in the turmoil of social change a way to deal with the demands and uncertainties of modernity. In this view, Marxism provided a means of acculturation for immigrants to the United States in the first half of the twentieth century to adjust to the new world of the capitalist metropolis, in the ethnic class cultures of industrial cities. Similarly, the "class treason" of Marxist intellectuals during, say, the Great Depression is often pictured as an alternative path of upward mobility, when other outlets were blocked for economic reasons. At one time, when I was studying American history as an undergraduate and graduate student, I thought this liberal view of Marxism's appeal was the worst kind of psychological reductionism, which made its revolutionary tradition of theory and practice into a compensatory gesture. But today, I must say, there is an important grain of truth here, though one that needs to be reformulated.

My sense is that, indeed, the "interior" of Marxism—the felt sense of revolutionary memory I'm trying to delineate here—*does* provide intellectuals, workers, and others with a means of dealing with the limits and pressures of modernity. But I want to highlight the positive side instead of the negative connotations. In other words, given the flux, fragmentation, and loss of traditional beliefs in the modern era (the shift from gemeinschaft to gesellschaft in the literature of the social sciences), I believe Marxism offers in the first instance not so much a compensatory gesture as a constructive reidentification. The uprootings of modernity, in which, as Marx says, "everything that is solid melts into air," brought with it the conditions to imagine a larger human community—no longer the family, neighborhood, village, or even nation-state but the bonds of working people worldwide.

Revolutionary memory is inseparable from revolutionary internationalism, the belief that workers have no fatherland and only their chains to lose. This is the profound (and poignant) side of "scientific" Marxism, that points out how unfettered capital creates simultaneously a world market and an international proletariat whose historical mission is to transcend national divisions and to remake the world. To my mind, revolutionary memory depends on this commitment to the international solidarity of working people. The precedents are clear enough: the revolutionary internationalism of Lenin and Trotsky, Rosa Luxemburg and Karl Liebknecht, and Eugene Debs during World War I, which held to the traditional Marxist view that war among the capitalist nation-states was no more than a matter of dividing the world market and political spheres of influence. The revolutionary internationalists, unlike their former comrades in the Second International who supported the war aims of their respective nations, urged intellectuals and workers to see they had no stake in the conflict among ruling classes.

At a time when the United States has embarked on a "war against terrorism" whose aims and boundaries are difficult to determine, it is helpful to recall this principled opposition. Don't get me wrong. It is hard to see the September 11 attacks on the World Trade Center as even a deformed response of the oppressed and exploited to American hegemony. Certainly, the conditions of the attack have been prepared by such U.S. policy as the Gulf War, the blockade and bombing of Iraq, and the tacit and explicit support of Israel's refusal to grant Palestinians self-determination. But, to me, the upshot is simply "commit a crime, do time." I'd even be willing to accept extraordinary police measures to bring the terrorists to trial—in an international court and not Bush's kangaroo military tribunals. But the bottom line, as I see it, is that working people have no interest in this war.

This volume of essays, of course, is not the place for my personal views of current events; it is about how personal affiliations and public rhetorics, in my case what I describe as revolutionary memory, influence published work. What remains to be seen—and what I take up in the next section—is how revolutionary memory influences the questions I think are important in my field of study, rhetoric and writing.

First of all, the revolutionary memory I describe suggests a particular orientation toward postmodernism in the realm of cultural and rhetorical theory. As anyone who reads the journals in rhetoric and writing knows, postmodernism has turned into an honorific term, a warrant to distance intellectual work from the supposed illusions of modernism, whether Enlightenment rationality, the autonomous subject, or the historical mission of the proletariat. If anything, the label "modernist" has become a convenient and now thoroughly conventionalized rhetorical gesture to critique, discredit, and dismiss. In my view, however, postmodernism does not offer the theoretical leverage it claims. Instead, postmodernism must be seen as an intellectual, artistic, and cultural trend *within* modernity, not the articulation of a new historical epoch but a sign of the persistence of late capitalism.

From this vantage point, there is less than meets the eye to postmodernism. Its postiality, when linked to such notions as globalization, postcapitalism, postindustrialism, post-Fordism, and postnationalism, amounts to a type of presentism that mistakes conjunctural developments (such as the unprecedented incorporation of information into the means of production, the shift from manufacturing to service economies in the metropolis by outsourcing production to the third world, niche marketing, and flexible specialization) for deeper, underlying changes in the relations between capital and labor. For Marxists, postmodernism's characterizations of the present moment are not only insufficient historical accounts but implicitly an accommodation to the current lull in the class struggle internationally. Revolutionary memory enables the view that it has not been changes in the "objective conditions" of capitalism that have blocked the path to socialism so much as it has been the defeats of the Left (in France in 1968, in Chile in 1974) and the consequences of Stalinism in 1989 that have bottled up revolutionary energies.

The now common claim that globalization has dramatically changed economic relations through the transnationalization of capital, rendering national markets and economies irrelevant and creating in their place an interconnected world economic system of immediate communication and exchange, ascribes to late capitalism a capacity it simply does not possess. As Paul Smith says, globalization embodies a kind of magical thinking: of a "fully global space replete with an ecstatic buzz of cyber communication," an "instantaneous mobility of people, goods, and services," and a "global market place hooked up by immaterial money that flashes around the globe many times a minute"—a world where time and space have been overcome and the "necessary navigational and communicational means so fully developed and supremely achieved that they can eclipse even reality itself" (13).

Behind such millennial dreams of a new postcapitalist, posthuman order, the very notion of globalization remains what Samir Amin calls a "reactionary utopia," a neoliberal fantasy that the world market can overcome the contradictions inherent in capitalist production. For all the breathlessness in theories of postiality, what appears to be a novel rupture with the past is, in fact, capitalism's familiar and relentless urge to maximize profits by revolutionizing the means of production. Despite the tendency toward universalization inherent in capitalist development, as Amin puts it:

> Capitalist globalization remains truncated, generating, reproducing and deepening global polarization step by step. The historical limit of capitalism is found exactly here: the polarized world that it creates is and will become more and more inhuman and explosive. (75)

Globalization does indeed seek to dismantle national borders for the free circulation of capital—but not of human beings or the products of their labor. The Marxist contradiction between use value and exchange value remains a key site of struggle, as is evident, for example, in the pharmaceutical industry's attempt to maintain patent rights and intellectual property claims against AIDS-stricken third world countries' demand for affordable generic drugs to alleviate human suffering. In this regard, the revolutionary memory of international solidarity—the imaginary community of working people worldwide—can remind us that the choice is still, as Trotsky put it in the shadow of fascism and World War II, "socialism or barbarism."

The fascination with postmodernism in rhetoric and writing studies, I must say, is both understandable and alarming. It is understandable because postmodernism, as an intellectual and artistic trend within modernism, is interesting in its own right. Postmodern notions of hybridity, border crossings, and nomadic subjectivities, for example, provide important correctives to orthodox Marxisms by showing how complicated racialized and gendered identities figure in the dynamics of class formation and reformation. Along similar lines, only the sternest Stalinist commissars of culture would deny the pleasures of such postmodern artists and architects as Cindy Sherman and Frank Gehry. In this regard, I agree with Trotsky in *Literature and Revolution* that the experimentalism of the artistic avant-garde, and not a narrow socialist realism, must be encouraged and appreciated.

Still, as you have probably detected, I want to hold such postmodernism at arm's length—and to subject it to the scan of revolutionary memory. There are two problems I find insurmountable. First, as I've already suggested, postmodernists posit a break with the past that makes revolutionary memory irrelevant. Its aggressive presentism wants to style history as rupture and discontinuity. Second, this desire to see the present as novel and unprecedented, instead of as the product of a knowable past, reveals the interests of a particular fraction of the professional managerial class—the consultants, artistic directors, information designers, editors and publishers, media specialists, human relations staff, public relations experts, and trend watchers, whose perspective is cosmopolitan, politically liberal, consumerist, gentrifying, and relentlessly hip. These are the sign and symbol managers in the culture industry and the information economy, professional semioticians whose cultural capital resides in their ability to interpret and explain. In certain respects, the predispositions of this postmodern fraction of the professional managerial class have insinuated themselves into curriculum design and textbooks for writing instruction, especially the cultural studies approach to composition, with its emphasis on the student as a knowing consumer, viewer, and spectator, and community service learning, with its emphasis on doing good work for the less fortunate.

Revolutionary memory calls for something different than informed and critical consumerism or community service learning. Both are important but inadequate alone. The critique of consumerism, for example, threatens to lead not to a reevaluation of production for profit instead of for human needs but to a hipper advertising message, what Robert Goldman and Stephen Papson call the production of sign values by addressing alienated and media-savvy spectators. Along similar lines, community service learning may well reinforce an old story of middle-class benefactors providing for the needy instead of leading to a critical and active understanding of class formation in contemporary America. I do not mean to suggest that either outcome will inevitably follow from these pedagogical and curricular practices. My point is that without the international solidarity of revolutionary memory, both cultural studies and community service learning remain at risk of accommodating critique and service to the postmodern middle classes' bid for cultural authority.

What is to be done? That is the question Lenin posed when the revolutionary forces in czarist Russia split into Bolshevik and Menshevik camps. I do not pretend I can answer this question in any kind of satisfactory way, given our present circumstances in contemporary America. But Lenin's insistence on intellectual elucidation and ideological clarification can be useful here. Within the confines of my field of study, I want to close by raising the issue of access to higher education and advanced literacy.

Rhetoric and writing studies have been shaped in many respects by the long-standing allegiance of writing instructors, theorists, and program administrators to democratic education, in particular to the aspirations of basic writers and to affirmative action and open admissions programs. Mina Shaughnessy's *Errors and Expectations*, the work of David Bartholomae and Patricia Bizzell, Mike Rose's *Lives on the Boundary*, and Tom Fox's *Defending Access* all affirm the educability of ordinary people and attack the class privilege of higher education. These works have played a central role in defining the identity and social affiliations of the field. Still, as the title of Fox's book indicates, we find ourselves currently fighting a defensive battle against a conservative backlash that has restricted access in the name of "standards." In my view, this is a necessary struggle, but it can also be one that keeps us in a holding pattern, trying to preserve the limited gains of the past, and it wears people down. For this reason, I believe there is an urgent need to articulate a program to extend literacy and the access to higher learning.

There are various ways to do this. At elite colleges and universities, the demands to institute need-blind policies and end legacy admissions can be raised to point out the class bias in the supposedly meritocratic premises of "selectivity." In a broader sense, given the unaffordability of private college for poor, working-class, and many middle-class families and the tracking system in higher education that distributes resources and life chances unequally to community colleges, state colleges, liberal arts colleges, and research universities, I think we should demand the right to a college education for all who wish it by democratizing higher education "through open admissions to *all* colleges and universities, free tuition, and a livable student stipend" (Trimbur, "Literacy" 294).

At least, as you can see from this citation, that is what I wrote over ten years ago, and I hold to its relevance today. The idea of overturning the prevailing class system of higher education, of course, is not a popular one, but to my mind, the issue is a matter of socializing education by removing it from the "free market," in which colleges and students compete with each other, and making it a thoroughly public and democratic institution. Such a demand, moreover, provides a way to point out how existing social arrangements in capitalist America cannot realize the most basic democratic task of educating all its inhabitants—native-born, documented, and undocumented—according to their talents and needs. Teaching in community colleges and adult literacy programs for recent immigrants, I have been struck forcefully over and over again by how class society wastes human potential and popular intelligence through its divisions of mental and manual labor, experts and laypeople, official and vernacular literacies. Class society not only erects barriers to the development of all its members, it also amounts to a system of subsidizing the children of the professional and upper classes. The issue, I am trying to persuade you, is not simply that this is unfair but that it also—and crucially—means we cannot solve the problems of poverty, exploitation, oppression, and environmental degradation that face us because we cannot activate the human ingenuity required. I have no doubt that the needed ingenuity is there and that it can be tapped. But to do so, I believe, would involve thinking beyond national borders, and that is why the revolutionary memory of international solidarity—the vision of how working people worldwide can remake society—gives me some measure of hope in an otherwise dark time.

5

MARY PUTNAM JACOBI AND THE SPEAKING PICTURE

Susan Wells

Mary Putnam Jacobi was a remarkable nineteenth-century physician and medical researcher. As a writer and speaker, she was always fascinated by the promise and difficulty of seeing the inside of the body, of representing dynamic bodily processes. Since medical illustration is a relatively well-documented field (Cazort, Kornell, and Roberts; L. Dixon; Herrlinger; Jordanova; Petherbridge and Jordanova; Roberts and Tomlinson; Rousselot; Stafford, *Body Criticism*), an analysis of Jacobi's practices of visual representation can help us trace the relation between her personal absorption in such images and the ways they are used to construct scientific facts.

We can conveniently begin by recalling two stories Jacobi told about failed encounters with the human heart. Jacobi dated the beginning of her medical career from a discovery she made in the family stables at the age of nine. The discovery is reported in a family memoir, written in 1902:

> I found a big dead rat and the thought occurred to me that if I had the courage I could cut that rat open and find his heart which I greatly longed to see. I had it in the corner of the stable but in the course of the day, thinking of this my courage failed me but with the sophistry of childhood I didn't propose to back out of this venture on my own initiative but put the responsibility on my little mother as often afterward. That evening I told my mother what I proposed to do hoping to elicit an expression of admiration at my daring. Instead I only aroused her fright and disgust and she promptly forbade me to touch the rat. I professed great disappointment but I was secretly [excessively?] relieved at the forcible delay of my anatomical studies. (autobiographical manuscript 5)

Not until Mary Putnam had persuaded her parents to let her leave home and attend medical school at the Women's Medical College of

Pennsylvania would she be sanctioned in her desire to see inside the body and learn what those images might say to her about health and sickness.

Jacobi wrote her second story of an inaccessible heart some seventeen years after her discovery of the rat, in 1868, while she was a medical student in Paris. Paris had provided Jacobi with a densely woven fabric of connections, linking her scientific and political interests with her personal life. So close were these connections that, for Jacobi, privacy and publicity were mutually determinative. Her politics, her friendships, her very presence in the medical amphitheater were all interdependent. In Paris, Jacobi was a very busy young woman, attending all of the lectures she could manage and writing extensive anonymous reports on Parisian medicine for the New York *Medical Record.* Of these reports, medical historian John Harley Warner observes: "It is quite possible that Putnam, during her time abroad, wrote more on Paris than any other nineteenth-century American physician—in private letters, in professional journals, in popular periodicals, and in newspapers" (328). Her interests were not limited to medicine: she participated in the politics of the Commune and supported herself with additional journalism, and, in her spare hours, wrote fiction and political essays. Within that context, Jacobi's short story "A Martyr for Science" returned to the theme of the hidden heart.

In this story, a physician mourning his wife and child becomes fascinated by his own death and undertakes a project of opening his own chest to display his beating heart. He trains a young medical student and pressures him to comply with the project: the physician will be paralyzed with woorara; his chest will be opened with acid cautery (a process expected to take several days); and his heart will be exposed, for at least a short period. The student will therefore become the first person to study the action of a beating heart. The heart itself is understood, and presented to the reader, as mysterious, tantalizingly close but irreducibly invisible. In its published form, the story ends with the student consigning his mentor to an insane asylum—the youth, like Mary Putnam's disgusted mother, stands between a potentially self-destructive desire to see and the desire's object. Seeing, for Jacobi, carried the thrill of the forbidden; in these stories, the heart, never seen in life, can be invoked verbally.

Jacobi was not the first person to puzzle about the relation between word and image. Since the Renaissance, an exceptionally vivid or provocative picture was seen as "speaking," while a very good poem could hope to work on the reader's imagination as if it were a picture, *ut pictura poesis.* And some of the more interesting forms of visual culture—emblem books that juxtaposed pictures with poems, allegorical paintings, book frontispieces, map cartouches—as well as a group of very interesting literary genres—place poems, shaped poetry, travel writing—investigate these boundaries between text and visual representation, between delight and instruction. While the concept of the speaking picture risks reducing words and images to a thematic lowest common denominator, it also draws our attention to the connections between words and images, to their specificity as forms of representation. Medicine has traditionally explored those boundaries: the sixteenth-century emblem books often included images of the heart or the skull that anatomists reworked for their own books, adding new mottoes and explanatory texts (Cazort, Kornell, and Roberts 30). Nor is the idea of a speaking picture completely archaic: in John Law and John Whittaker's account of how they designed a graphic representation of current research on acid rain, they speak of the need to make a picture that would, "so far as possible, make some qualitative sense . . . [; the image] should, as it were, 'tell a story'" (168).

Medical writing has drawn on what Simon Schaffer calls "literary technologies," which include "the design and use of instrumentation, the social organization of the scientific community and the assignment of credit and status," to give verbal representations the force of images: these mediating devices seemingly transform the text into a direct representation of the working of nature. Such technologies "help fashion the bearer of knowledge as authoritative and competent, and the item of knowledge as independent from the contingencies of human judgement." According to Schaffer, literary technologies "make authors and they make facts" (183). Mary Putnam Jacobi made facts and made herself as an author by using the technologies available to her, particularly by traversing boundaries between text and image. Jacobi was deeply interested in literature, and although she does not seem to have had any talent at visual art, she had a strong interest in visual representation. While Jacobi hated having her own picture taken—we have only three photographs of her—she was intrigued by the emerging technologies of visual display.

She wrote a great deal throughout her medical life—her bibliography includes nearly 140 items—and her medical writing was always marked by vivid and precise description. She was never one to leave the

Figure 1. Mary Putnam Jacobi, circa 1863. The Schlesinger Library, Radcliffe Institute, Harvard University.

resources of a genre in the relatively undeveloped state in which she found them, and so her writing was also marked by formal experimentation, by a search for new ways of presenting complex information. Very often, those experiments focused on ways of presenting visual information, of mediating between word and image. It would be wrong to celebrate Jacobi as particularly adept or artistic in her use of images: the illustrations in her books and essays are in themselves unremarkable. But her practices of representation, in both writing and in oral performance, tell us a great deal about how medical writing developed as a specific professional and disciplinary form in the late nineteenth century, and they complicate our understanding of how that form was gendered and how it was developed by particular writers. In that development, the writer's singular desire intersected with new medical practices of visual representation.

Steven Peitzman calls Mary Putnam Jacobi "probably the most brilliant of America's nineteenth-century women physicians" (27). After finishing high school, Jacobi cast about for her life's work—in the mid-nineteenth century, women did not exactly look for careers. She did some private teaching and tutoring; during the Civil War, she traveled to Union-occupied New Orleans to nurse her sick brother, and she preached to the "contraband" escaped slaves. Throughout her late teens and early twenties, she struggled with the evangelical beliefs her beloved grandmother had encouraged, finally declaring herself a "disbeliever" but resolving to abstain from the theater and the opera for ten years to prove that her disbelief was not motivated by a desire for amusement (*Life and Letters* 58). She studied chemistry and attended lectures at the New York Pharmacy School, eventually prevailing upon her father to allow her to attend the Woman's Medical College of Pennsylvania, reminding him of the "large liberty" that had always marked their family life (110).

The new Woman's Medical College and young Mary Putnam were not well matched; the school's atmosphere of Quaker piety and its openness to irregular medical practices tried her patience. Unlike more compliant early students, she applied to take her examinations after hearing the course of lectures for only one year: the faculty met several times on her case and wrote to New York for confirmation that she had attended lectures there. Mary Putnam, never very punctilious with institutional regulations, produced a scattered collection of lecture tickets, made some rude comments about the quality of lectures at the Pharmacy School, and turned in the second Latin medical thesis the Woman's Medical College faculty had seen. The faculty passed the thesis around—there is no evidence of it having been read through by anyone—and admitted Mary Putnam to examinations, which she passed. A few days later, Dean Edwin Fussell wrote a letter to the faculty protesting this action. He summed up his reasons: "And, lastly, firstly and all the time—because in my opinion we are not therein true to our own professions—we violate our long published standard of rules—degrade the College, injure the cause in which we labor—give reason to our enemies to rejoice at our dereliction, and to our friends to mourn over our weakness" (Woman's Medical College minutes, March 10, 1864).

In later life, although Jacobi participated in the Woman's Medical College Alumnae Association, she was sometimes critical in her accounts of the school, describing its early students, for example, as "really, and in the ordinary sense, illiterate," a charge that was simply not true ("Woman" 162). When she finally was permitted to register as a medical student in Paris after graduation from the Woman's Medical College, she was completely taken with her education, attending lectures and clinics at various hospitals, training herself in therapeutics and in the techniques of anatomical preparation. She also negotiated a visually rich environment: Paris was rich in wax models, celebrated for adept anatomical preparations, and also the center of publication for massive, detailed, anatomical atlases (Roberts and Tomlinson 538). Putnam became politically active through her friendship with the Réclus family of anarchists–after she overcame her shock at seeing Mme. Réclus clearing the table herself. Her friendship with the Réclus family brought her into the political life of the Paris Commune; she handily survived the siege of Paris on jam, wine, chocolate, and coffee, reassuring her mother that as long as these were provided, "one can not be very miserable" (*Life and Letters* 276). The Commune interrupted Mary Putnam's medical studies, but the bloody repression that followed—and perhaps the end of her engagement to a communard soldier—led her to finish her degree quickly and return to New York, where she taught at the Blackwells' school, the Woman's Medical College of the New York Infirmary.

The seventies and eighties were an enormously productive time for Mary Putnam. She published widely, entered a broad range of professional societies, and successfully joined the world of New York's academic and clinical elite medical institutions. Mary Putnam married Abraham Jacobi, a German socialist physician, one of the defendants in the Cologne Communist trial, who was practicing medicine in the German neighborhoods of the Lower East Side and also making his own way into the scientifically active professional associations of New York physicians. The two physicians shared commitments to the emancipation of women, scientific research, and radical politics. In New York as in Paris, Jacobi's professional life and her personal relationships were densely interconnected.

Recognition came quickly to Jacobi. She won the Boylston Prize for medical writing in an anonymous competition, became an honored member of the faculty of the New York Medical College, was inducted into a bristling handful of honorary professional societies, and published in the most prestigious journals. Her research broadened in scope: she followed her book *On the Use of the Cold Pack Followed by Massage in the Treatment of Anaemia*, an obvious, if tacit, critique of S. Weir Mitchell's work, which had been published in 1877, with a compelling collection, *Essays on Hysteria, Brain Tumor, and Some Other Causes of Nervous Disease* in 1888. She treated C. P. Gilman, the author of "The Yellow Wallpaper," with a regimen of structured intellectual work, regular doses of phosphates in wine, and periodic galvanic treatment; she encouraged Gilman's participation in a women's basketball team. All in all, Mary Putnam Jacobi's medical career was exemplary. Hers is an individual story worth telling, if only to direct our attention to the singularity of her engagement with science and medicine.

But, of course, this story did not take place in a vacuum. By the 1880s, a sturdy corps of women doctors had been educated in the United States, mostly in women's medical schools. Where these women were not integrated into the male profession, they organized themselves to share medical information, often through their alumnae associations. Women physicians were also integrated with a vast network of reform-minded lay women interested in questions of health and medicine—only a score of women practiced as regular physicians in mid-nineteenth-century Boston, for example, but over 250 women attended meetings of the Boston Ladies' Physiological Society, where they might look through the society's treasured collection of skeletons and anatomical preparations or consult its library. Lectures on health, including the display of anatomical images, were very popular, and popular anatomical texts were broadly distributed (Sappol). And many nineteenth-century women testify in letters and diaries that, at least in reform circles, curiosity about the interior of the body was common, accepted, understood as an edifying pleasure (Wells, *Out of the Dead House* 193–226).

Jacobi took her own writing seriously, and it was seriously read. She insisted on the highest scientific standards, and she pioneered a number of significant research strategies, including the use of survey information in medical writing. Her use of images, whether evoked by verbal description or graphically displayed, was not the least of her concerns as a writer. Throughout her medical life, Jacobi found ways of giving free rein to her desire to see; as time went by, she made fewer concessions to the convention that ruled a searching medical gaze inappropriate to women. As Jacobi's medical career developed, the medical technologies of the visible also advanced, and she took full advantage of them.

Taken together, Mary Putnam Jacobi's practices in deploying visual representations are an anthology of the ways in which late-nineteenth-century medical culture came to terms with the image. Looking at these practices quite specifically, we can begin to recognize the inadequacy of the two current lines of research in gender and visual scientific representation. One research program has understood the development of visual apparatus as a critical strategy in the construction of a modern gendered subject; to learn to see the objectified world through the developing armamentarium of scientific apparatus was to learn a practice of vision that entrained an immobile subject to an alienating apparatus. In this view, the early modern understanding of vision as a male penetration of female nature is mediated by new, industrialized, means of objectification (Jordanova; Crary). The other line of research on the scientific image, associated with Barbara Stafford, understands the image as a source of instruction and delight; in this view, the loss of visual literacy, the decline of visual education, and the valuation of text over image have been tragic losses.

Looking closely at the particularity of Jacobi's visual practices suggests that neither of these two lines of investigation does justice to the complexity with which medical images were displayed, understood, and appreciated in the nineteenth century, or to the very nuanced ways in which such images were gendered. Mary Putnam Jacobi associated medical images with transgression and with pleasure; her experiments with images met with resistance. But these pleasures, unlike those associated with other feminine practices of visual representation, like botanical drawing, were not oriented to producing an image that represented things that the eye could see: she was interested in abstractions, in relations, and above all in change. Her experiments do not map, in any easy way, onto the known gender markings of the territory of visual representation: she herself would have taken any suggestion that she saw "as a woman" as an incitement to satire. Nor was Jacobi alone among her sex; women whose visual practices diverged from a received feminine norm are continually lost and discovered. Consider, for example, the anatomical wax artist, Anna Morandi Manzolini, who shared Jacobi's interest in the movement (Messbarger), but who worked in a relentlessly realistic medium.

Let us consider an early *Medical Record* letter from Paris in which Mary Putnam gives an uncharacteristically enthusiastic account of a device "too good, or at least too striking, to pass over in silence," the somatoscope—essentially, a lightbulb that a physician would insert into a body cavity (48). The young Mary Putnam was fascinated by the somatoscope's ability to turn the walls of the body from curtains into screens, displaying what was inside. It is difficult to imagine a more convincing reversal of the usual logic of anatomy, which has been understood since Galen to turn on the process of dissection, an opening of the body "in order to see deeper or hidden parts" (2.3). The very skin that hides the interior organs becomes a means for visualizing them. Although the history of the somatoscope was brief and inglorious, this tool offered the young Dr. Putnam a model for medical representation: the object of representation would remain intact; the image would be directly produced by the object, but in an abstracted form (here, the shadow of the organ); the display would offer both instruction and pleasure.

When Jacobi began to teach at the Medical College of the New York Women's Infirmary, she experimented with visual display as a mode of medical education. In her lectures on Materia Medici, she would ask students to directly observe the effect of a drug on a patient and reason out its mode of operation. The demonstrating patient became, as it were, a picture of the drug; Jacobi, as lecturer, would tease out the medical information implicit in this picture from her class. One of these lectures, "On Atropine," was reprinted in the *Medical Record* and is included in Jacobi's collected works. Jacobi announced that she would not follow the conventional program of the Materia lectures, which "compelled" students to "listen to accounts of the remedial action of drugs, that their ignorance of pathology rendered completely unintelligible to them" (204). In her lectures, students would learn the "properties of drugs in their natural and commercial condition," beginning with that day's lecture on atropine:

> In the three cases where we tested the action of the atropine before your eyes, we observed a fall of the pulse within ten minutes. In the first case the patient was a delicate, lymphatic, but not nervous woman, to whom one-fiftieth gr[ain] of sulph. Atropine was given by the mouth, the pulse then being at 96, probably from some emotional excitement. In ten minutes the pulse had fallen to 80, and remained at 80 to the end of an hour, notwithstanding the occurrence of other symptoms of atropism, a slight flushing of the face, dryness of mouth and throat, and very slight dilations of the pupils. (205)

Jacobi went on to describe the effects of atropine on the other two patients, to draw conclusions from these demonstrations, and to extend them to a very comprehensive discussion of the whole clinical and chemical literature on atropine. All this is well and good to read as a finished text; it is painful to imagine this information, or the subsequent analysis, being elicited from a group of reluctant students. If, as the astronomer William Herschel claimed, "seeing is in some respect an art which must be learned"(qtd. in Schaffer 190), these students did not especially want to learn to see what Jacobi was showing them. They rebelled, demanding more accessible instruction. This lecture is a rare example of Jacobi attempting a direct display of the physical processes she wanted to explain: the effects of atropine and the changes in the patient that students were directed to observe were one and the same thing. There was no abstraction, no distribution of information, no redundancy: there was simply brutal, dense, information. However much Jacobi herself might have enjoyed such a display, she did not often attempt it again.

Sometimes, she textualized the image. While it is generally acknowledged in science studies that words and images are not translations of each other, Jacobi, at certain stages in her career, strove to make them equivalents by deploying the richly developed medical vocabulary for physical description. In an address originally given to the New York State Medical Society in 1874, "Remarks upon the Action of Nitrate of Silver on Epithelial and Gland Cells," Jacobi began by reviewing the literature on experimental use of silver nitrate and then outlined a series of experiments that she had performed herself. Jacobi was able to bring with her a number of tissue samples from the stomachs of dogs and rabbits that she had treated with silver nitrate. She describes these preparations as seen under a microscope—itself a fairly advanced piece of medical apparatus—noting especially any differences between her observations and those recorded in the literature, and her descriptions are vivid, precise, and comprehensive. For example:

> In the dog I have remarked one detail, not mentioned by Heidenhein or Rollet. The epithelial border seemed to consist of two layers of cells, of which the external was deeply spiculated. The lower part of the cell, deeply colored, was thus surrounded by a broad, clear, border. This appearance suggested an analogy with the spicules described by Frey on the pavement epithelium of the mouth and pharynx, and that as in this locality the epithelium is held

> more firmly in place, the clear space below the epithelium is much less distinct in the dog; the gland tubes larger, and the polygonal cells larger and more distinct. (251)

Besides bringing the experience of viewing the epithelial cells that she had prepared directly and vividly before her audience, Jacobi is here using verbal description to do specific intellectual work, work that we would today do with various enhancements of the visual image: Jacobi's verbal image demonstrated the relations between parts, including the attachment of the epithelium and the clear space below it (see also Baym 192–93). And Jacobi also inserts her verbal image into a conversation with other researchers: this sample shows something that Heidenhein had not seen, and it reminds her of something that Frey had seen in a different context. It is entirely possible, of course, to stage a visual conversation: contemporary advertisements are in many ways arguments among images, and the history of anatomical art includes many instances of illustrations that are specifically designed to argue with received opinion. However, citation of a previous researcher by name is quite difficult in visual conversations, and in this talk, a demonstration of Jacobi's membership in the New York Medical Society, direct citation by name would have been an important marker for intellectual affiliation.

Mary Putnam Jacobi's apprenticeship as a writer, her way of teaching herself to describe objects in their relations, argue about them, and compare them to each other, had been organized in unlikely locations, including fashion reporting. Her letters on French fashions, possibly written for the *New York Herald Tribune* or the *New Orleans Times* in the late 1860s, were precise in their designations of color, position, size, texture, material, and attachment, the traditional rhetorical topics for descriptions of objects. Consider this description of bonbon boxes:

> But the highest art of the master is not expended on the sugar plums. The boxes that hold them furnish a field for infinite ingenuity. The paper bag has been replaced by a box of enameled pasteboard, white, blue, rose or magenta colored, tied with a ribbon of the same shade. The Lancret basket is composed of a handkerchief of point d'Alencon, the four corners of which are raised by four bouquets of flowers, and are held by two handles covered with satin. The Trianon basket is coquettishly pretty, made of rice straw, garlanded with branches of roses, or of straw of gold, lined with white satin ornamented with grapes made of pearls. ("Our Paris Correspondent")

If Ludwig Fleck was right in arguing that facts are constructed in the spaces between the practices of the laboratory and the assumptions and beliefs of popular culture (111–24), the young Mary Putnam offers us a remarkable instance of a physician negotiating those spaces, moving from bonbon boxes to epithelial cells.

Further, for the young Mary Putnam, images of the body were politically significant and consequential—emblems, as it were, for the nineteenth century. In a short descriptive essay she wrote for *Scribner's Monthly*, "The Clubs of Paris," she joins fascination and unease in her description of the raucous and democratic political clubs of the Commune:

> Such an impression is made by a human fetus scarcely formed,—with its immense head,—its exaggerated nervous system,—its shapeless, powerless limbs,—its huge uncouthness,—in which, like pearls hidden in a mantle of rough skin, lie concealed unlimited possibilities of power, and beauty, and grace. (107)

It was very unusual for a writer in an American magazine to treat the Commune so sympathetically; for months, subscribers had been reading laments for the vanished gaiety of the Parisian boulevards. The embryo, an organism full of possibilities, however ungainly and disproportioned, would have offered such readers a new way of thinking about social movements and social change. What is of interest is not the "huge head," but the process that the embryo suggests, the changes it promises. Jacobi is fascinated here, not by structure or position, but by relationship, process, possibility. These complex ideas are concentrated in an analogy, a form which Barbara Stafford identifies as an "uncanny visual capacity to bring divided things into unison or span the gap between the contingent and the absolute" (*Analogy* 28). Putnam was able to link disparate registers, to resolve divisions, and to activate the visual capacities of her readers in an extended verbal analogy.

Jacobi also found nonverbal strategies for bringing processes and changes before her readers, for making them speak: her favorite strategy was that of abstraction, especially as mediated by the sphygmograph. The sphygmograph made pressure tracings on a spinning roll of paper, allowing physicians to trace changes in pressure as a result of treatment or experimental interventions. Like other graphic tracings, the sphygmograph mediates between the optical culture of early-nineteenth-century science and the digital culture we are now learning to navigate (Drorr 361). Jacobi included a number of sphygmographic tracings in her first book, *The Question of Rest for Women during Menstruation* (1876). In her second book, *On the Use of the Cold Pack Followed by Massage in the Treatment of Anaemia* (1880), the long strips showing the effects of cold packs on anemic patients' blood pressures were tipped into the book, so that they could be folded out and compared with one another. Jacobi found, in this relatively simple modification of the conventional form of the book, a way to bring one picture into conversation with another. Any medical reader, even one uninformed about technical innovations, could see the differences in tracings laid out in a row. Moreover, since the sphygmographic tracing presented an image of change over time and could be read and interpreted as a representation of a process, it was very closely adapted to Jacobi's scientific preoccupations. Like the early but ultimately unsatisfactory somatoscope, the sphygmograph did not lay open the structure of the body: brain, heart, and veins stayed where they were, intact. Sometimes, the sphygmograph was applied to wounds, as in a series of experiments performed on "Josie Nolan, aged ten, a very healthy Irish boy" with a convenient head fracture that exposed the membrane covering his brain. (Jacobi reassures her readers that Nolan has "so far, never experienced the least inconvenience from this partial exposure of the brain" ["Sphygmographic" 300].) Like the shadow of the somatoscope, the sphygmographic tracing was produced directly by the organ under investigation. Like the somatoscope, the sphygmograph was a technique that spoke to Jacobi's own preoccupations, to her desire to visualize what was hidden without destroying it.

Although the sphygmograph and similar instruments were sometimes valued for their ability to circumvent language, to get directly at physical processes, Jacobi often offered a very full discursive translation of her sphygmographic tracing. She would describe each tracing, interpret the description as evidence about what was going on in the system being studied, and draw some conclusion from the analysis. It is important to realize that Jacobi had to work out the linguistic means for writing these descriptions; there were no received forms for translating sphygmographic tracings (Drorr 374). Sometimes, Jacobi compares one tracing to another, giving verbal expression to the conversation between images. Always, she uses the single line of the sphygmograph tracing to support a verbal picture of the effects of the drug, as in this description

Figure 2. Sphygmographic tracings

of the effects of atropine on exposed brain tissue: "relaxation of cerebral blood-vessels; consequent diminished intra-cranial resistance to percussion stroke; more rapid collapse of arterial walls; diminution in mass of blood retained in brain" ("Sphygmographic" 307). The sphygmographic tracing works as a displaced and mediated picture, as a spatialized representation of the passage of time; Jacobi makes it speak to her reader about the invisible interior of the brain, heart, and veins. There was no optical reference, no model, for the processes that the sphygmograph traced; the pictures that it suggested were evoked by comparing one tracing with another (Rheinberger).

It took longer for Mary Putnam Jacobi to learn to use more direct, unmediated images, images that did correspond to optical experience—simple pictures of physical structures. Her "Studies in Endometritis," a relatively late work, is among her first illustrated articles. The work was published serially in the *American Journal of Obstetrics* through 1885 and 1886. (Illustrations appear in the "Studies in Endometritis" on 126, 262–63, 266–67, 269, 811–16, and 923. Other significant illustrations occur in "Case of Absent Uterus" and"Remarks upon Empyema.") Medical journals, of course, had long included small inset graphics: from midcentury, woodcuts and other engravings appeared in monthly journals such as the *Archives of Medicine*, although never in the weekly medical bulletins. But by 1879, images had appeared even in the weekly *Medical Record* and "illustrations" or "cuts" were common in the *American Journal of Obstetrics* throughout the 1880s. These pictures might show a surgical procedure, a design for bandages or other apparatus, a pathological specimen, or cellular structures. The "Studies in Endometritis" are profusely illustrated, including a score of woodcut engravings from microscopic slides. Some illustrations were copied from other texts, but others were apparently produced for this essay.

The figures extend Jacobi's prose argument: they are often arranged in series to facilitate comparison ("Studies" 814), and are labeled obsessively: the illustration's title identifies a sample of cells, the caption repeats that information, and the text will repeat it yet again. The redundant text, caption, and label imply that readers could not be expected to see what Jacobi wanted them to see: she had, perhaps, learned the lesson of her early Materia lectures all too well, compromising her usual brisk exposition. In contemporary scientific illustrations, captions are normally interpretive rather than descriptive: "They orient viewers to similarities, contrasts, and other relevancies; . . . they supply metaphors, extrinsic connections, and genealogies which instruct viewers' understanding of what they are being shown" (Lynch and Edgerton 202). In contrast, Mary Putnam Jacobi's use of what was for her a new technology of the visible was less assured than her use of text or demonstration; the textual deictic is multiplied and repeated. In fact, these images are among the least interesting representations of the body that Jacobi used: wooden and flat, they are redundantly and insistently interpreted by the accompanying text. The hallmarks of Jacobi's visual practices—abstraction, representation of change, relation to other images—are missing. The picture presents a version of the stained and foregrounded microscopic image; it shows what, under certain circumstances, we might see ourselves.

Jacobi found much more interesting images that represented broad forces and abstract relations. One instance of her use of such images is recorded in her remarkable essay, "The Practical Study of Biology," originally an address to the Massachusetts Medical Society's annual dinner in 1889. After arguing that a medical student must be changed in "his whole mind" so as to "insensibly . . . blend with the phenomena they can profoundly contemplate" (461), Jacobi offers a personal anecdote. So unusual is this gesture for Jacobi that her introduction to the story is uncharacteristically diffident and awkward: "I should like, Mr. Chairman, to mention an incident that occurred to myself in the course of a very simple laboratory experiment" (462), as she was examining the circulation in a frog's lungs.

> I happened to so focus my lens that all the outlines of the capillaries and blood corpuscles disappeared, leaving visible only the spaces between the epithelial cells. Nevertheless there remained a vision of the streaming movement of the invisible blood through the ramified spaces. The streaming was so rapid, so energetic, so ceaseless, it seemed as if it were pure motion or force divorced from the accidents of matter. The microscopic shred of tissue from the insignificant animal seemed for the moment to give a glimpse of a mighty vision of endless life, streaming with infinite energy into the minutest particles of an infinite universe. (462)

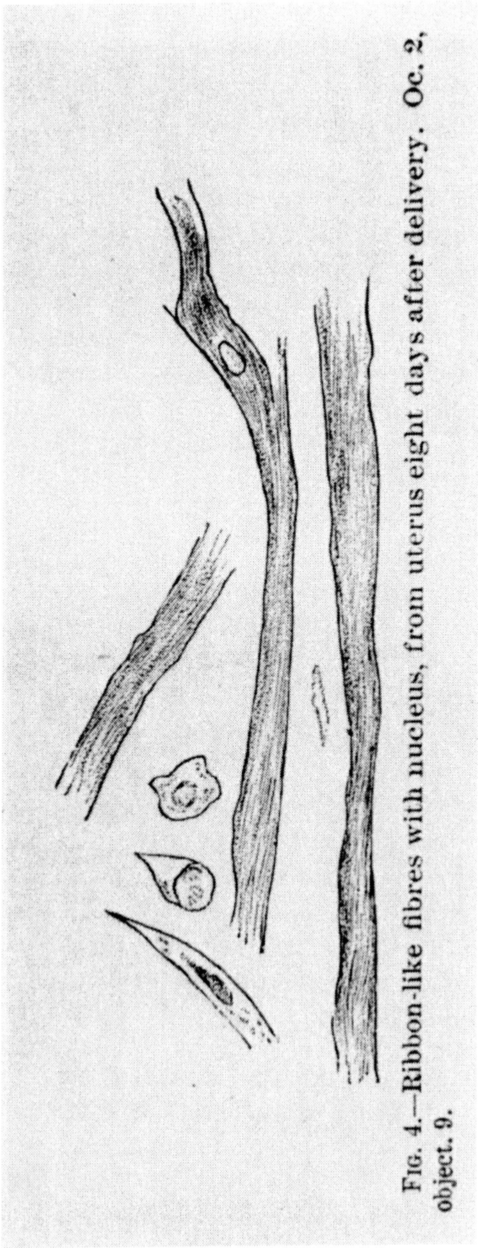

FIG. 4.—Ribbon-like fibres with nucleus, from uterus eight days after delivery. Oc. 2, object. 9.

Figure 3. "Ribbon-like fibres with nucleus, from uterus eight days after delivery"

Jacobi found this perception "indescribably powerful." No wonder. The ghostly image of the hidden, moving, and clearly indicated blood represented for her the intellectual energies that had animated her work: an overarching theory ("mighty vision of endless life") joined to detailed, concrete, and precisely located physiological structures ("spaces between the epithelial cells"), which were, after all, not material objects, but gaps between them. Such an image could speak of nothing but force, motion, will. She repeatedly reproduced this figure for her students: "Since then I have confronted students with this same impression," offering it deictically as "the horizons towards which they were henceforth to keep their eyes directed" (462).

For Jacobi, neither the surface nor the interior was the domain of truth. Truth was mobile; truth inhabited the space between the spectacular image and the awed spectator. The medical truth that Jacobi sought in these verbal images and speaking pictures was a truth about the tempo and structure of complex bodily processes, particularly as they were actively constructed by human beings in displays and experiments. While her experiments in visual representation were modest, the logic behind them was individual, startling, and premonitory. These experiments open to knowledge a body that has been transformed, whether by treatment or disease. It is that transformation which is the object of Jacobi's desire—it was perhaps the deadness of the rat, rather than the visible structure of its heart, that so excited her interest. And she was compelled by dynamic transformations, both in their relation to the normal state of the organism and in their relations to other images, other descriptions. Jacobi's images join a babble of scientific voices and pictures that debate the effects of nitrate of silver, the relation between arterial pressure in the brain and blood volume, and the interactions of atropine and belladonna. Whatever specific physical process these images, verbal or visual, represent, their ultimate reference for Jacobi was to that "endless life" that so fascinated her, a force that was neither a visible object nor an idealization.

PART TWO

Confronting the Public and the Private in Written Language

6

THE COLLECTIVE PRIVACY OF ACADEMIC LANGUAGE

David Bleich

PROBLEMS WITH ACADEMIC LANGUAGE

This essay considers the following thought: in the history of the academy, only one sense of privacy has existed, the collective privacy of the male group. As a social institution, the university and other academies have been, over the past eight centuries, groups of men, separated from the rest of society, bound together by a language few others in society knew, and, except in extreme cases, exempt from civil laws and constraints that applied to nonacademic citizens. The groups of men were privileged by their occupation of learning—reading, repeating, and interpreting texts again and again so as to contribute to the development of civil and sacred laws, principles, morals, and to the training of physicians. People who emerged from the academy did not hold power, but advised those, such as churchmen and governors, who did. This arrangement, strong and stable in itself, drew considerable strength from prevailing unconsciousness of, and resignation to, the principle of the androcentric rule of society.

This history is related to fundamental language problems we continue to face: (1) the complaints about academic writing as obscure; (2) the treatment of writing pedagogy as a relatively unimportant propaedeutic subject; and (3) the censorship of personal, subjective, and intersubjective genres. My path of presentation is first to note briefly the sense of the foregoing complaints, then to characterize the history of the university and how it may have led to the complaints, and then to consider in more detail how to think about them.

Inherent Obscurity

There have been complaints lately about the obscurity of academic work, especially its language. The 1996 Sokal hoax, in which gibberish was mistaken by a respected scholarly journal for serious academic work, brought this complaint to the fore (see Sokal). But as Alain de Botton has written, the same complaint was made by Rabelais in the sixteenth century and by many before and after him: academics were "writing needlessly obscure books, ignoring simple truths, teaching nothing of value and abusing the respect of the population." I stipulate the truth of the complaint and ask why academic work, and especially its language, has seemed so antisocial for so long. Sometimes the complaints have been so intense that Gerald Graff had to write in *PMLA,* the principal professional journal of English and language teachers, that "academic difficulty" was a myth and that succinct instructions regarding stylistic adjustments in writing can be given to critics and scholars to dispel the appearance of obscurity (1041). However, those familiar with academic treatises know that obscurity is not just in appearance, and that many academic texts are *needlessly* difficult and not comprehensible to most people, even those who are well educated.

The Degrading of Rhetoric and Composition

The field of rhetoric and composition, characteristically open to a variety of approaches, was on its way to becoming a forceful, active, and new sort of discipline, involved in both literacy and rhetoric, and expanding its interests to genres found in many parts of society. Abruptly, however, it has been constrained toward obsolete goals: teaching undergraduates to write "for their other courses." Large, complex, intellectually sophisticated writing/graduate programs were reduced and placed under the stewardship of either staff reporting to deans or English faculty believing in the "service" role of writing pedagogy, as Frances Condon has described:

> Comp/Rhet professionals in that Department (people whose work stands out in the discipline of Composition and Rhetoric as being of extraordinary, pivotal value . . .) were systematically attacked, vilified and disenfranchised. Under the guise of "complicating" understanding and developing more "rigorous" curriculum, members of the [English] Department hailing from other "sub" disciplines in English Studies imposed a vision of Comp/Rhet that, for all its pretension to cutting edge theory, reconstituted traditional, top down writing instruction and consigned Composition and Rhetoric as a discipline to a service and skills model, eliminated a visionary undergraduate writing program that was years in the making, and eviscerated an extraordinary doctoral program. (WPA Listserv, November 29, 2001)

Such development, apparently mysterious, is perhaps less so in the context of the history of the university, of which more shortly.

Discomfort with Genres of Subjectivity

In postsecondary English, "reader response" criticism has gained some currency, but few related this style of criticism to teaching (see Bleich; Flynn; Steig), and even fewer saw it as a broad approach to the subject of language and literature. As feminist criticism grew in scope and reference, "life writing," autobiography, autoethnography, and genre mixing in academic writing became accepted formal practices. More people understood why "the personal is political," and this understanding helped to produce a broader spectrum of genres from the private to the individual, to the collective, to the universal public. There are extant new genres that tackle the heretofore taboo "personal" and "private" experiences of scholars who are members of a wide variety of groups in society. Patricia Williams, Robin Tolmach Lakoff, Naomi Scheman in the fields of law, linguistics, and philosophy, respectively, have written personal, mixed-genre essays that bear directly on how they conceive their principal subject matters (see also Holdstein and Bleich). The resistance to the latter effect is what I consider in this essay as the key to the emotional and social paralysis of academic writing. Truly subjective styles are "feminized" in the pejorative sense.

THE UNIVERSITAS AND ITS SOCIAL PLACEMENT

Charles Homer Haskins, in his useful volume *The Rise of Universities* (1923), outlines Hastings Rashdall's earlier observation that the Western university has been a remarkably stable institution, unchanging in its basic relation to the secular and religious governments of society. Mainly, the university is a *protected* society of masters and scholars. Until modern times, its main protection came from the Roman Church, but various local and national governments also protected it. Today it is protected by national governments in Europe and by state governments and corporations in America. What, actually, is being protected?

The history of the (oldest) universities of Bologna, Paris, and Oxford demonstrates the rationale of university protection. As some may erroneously infer today, "university" does not allude to something like "universal knowledge," but to a living social arrangement of male students and teachers. The term *universitas* is cognate with the present-day term *union,* as in labor union. In twelfth-century Bologna, Paris, and Oxford, the masters and scholars needed *rent* protection. As a group, these men from all over Europe were gauged as foreigners—"nations" in the historical literature—and sometimes in response to their disruptive carousing habits, they could not exist stably enough to pursue their studies, which were liberal arts, law, theology, or medicine. Thus, in the middle of the twelfth century in Bologna and Paris, and at the beginning of the thirteenth century in Oxford, the governments and, mainly, the Roman Church, stepped in to secure from the local landlords *rent agreements* for the housing of students and masters. Usually oversight went considerably beyond just housing. In return the *universitas*—the group of students and masters—was *protected* and came more directly under the dominion of the church. This agreement also led to the students and masters occupying the same space, which, in turn, developed into the "college," the place where all both lived and worked. In the fourteenth and fifteenth centuries, universities were founded throughout Europe on this model of sponsorship (see De Ridder-Symoens).Though all students had preliminary study of the trivium, the principal advanced university subjects were civil and canon law (both based on Roman law), theology, and medicine. The church had established in the various universities sites of training that ensured its own continued dominion in society. As is the case today, however, men of various other interests were admitted to the university: there were high levels of secular interest in all the universities. Bologna was a center of civil law, Paris a center of theology, Oxford a center of theology and philosophy. The history of Oxford University is particularly interesting in that its early forms were concerned with secular civil law, especially its practice, but when the *universitas* needed protection, theology become the main subject (see Aston). Because of the "deal"—the sponsorship of the university as a whole—that guaranteed the training of future church leaders, prospective secular leaders were also welcomed as trainees. The ties between these two types of students ultimately led, in the rebellious American colonies, to the principle of separation of church and state. Yet, as was the case in medieval Europe, today in America most religiously sponsored universities make it their business to admit a variety of students; the separation is not complete.

Until the nineteenth century, it was essential to know Latin to enter the university. All lectures were delivered in Latin from the twelfth to the sixteenth centuries, and most were delivered in Latin from the sixteenth to the eighteenth centuries. Students were certified as bachelors and masters by going through a Latin disputation—a debate with a master. The lectures themselves (lecture means reading), most of which were termed "ordinary" lectures, were oral readings of the main texts, always in Latin. The lecturers sometimes commented on these texts. Access to the texts themselves was limited, especially before printing, and so there was a strong oral component to the processes of learning. The trivium—rhetoric, grammar, and logic—was comprised of the elementary subjects which were meant to cultivate the students' proficiency in Latin. The study of rhetoric had at least two main functions: to learn how to conduct oneself orally in order to win certification and to master the established Latin texts about rhetoric, such as those of Cicero and Quintilian. Given that the early universities' studies of law and theology were aimed to create learned church leaders, it seems clear that the trivium was essential as a tool or a path to the main university subjects—canon and civil law as derived from Roman law, theology, and medicine. Latin was thus the "language of knowledge," which meant something like this: real, formal, or "official" knowledge had to be articulated in Latin. However, even this statement is misleading. I want to emphasize that Latin was the language of status and power, and it was more important to know Latin in the sense of being proficient in it than it was to know anything else about it. The use of Latin was tied to the essential functions of church, to essential language in medicine and law, and to essential acts of crowns and dukedoms. The great majority of citizens did not know Latin, and it was, in practice, a "secret" or collectively private language spoken only by a privileged class of men. All authority, including the authority of knowledge, was articulated in Latin. To know Latin was to be a member of a privileged, exclusive male society, which, by virtue of its special knowledge of Latin, could regulate admission to membership.

One of the more important language events of Renaissance humanism was the discovery and study of vernacular literatures, enhanced by printing; vernaculars and printing became part of the academic scene together. Vernacular writing and literary language became, like Latin had been, something to be mastered rather than studied in a critical style. In any event, because the universities remained protected institutions, the subject matters *most important to the protectors* were the main subjects. This meant that literature was less important than law and theology, whose practitioners were not very interested in humanism and its tendency toward encouraging an individual-centered sense of morality, not to mention access to the knowledge of a variety of languages, a knowledge that would put outsiders in position to challenge established practices. As a result of these dangers, language as an aspect of society was not a subject, but specific languages had to be mastered in order to read the texts written in those languages. The subject of language had weight only because knowledge of languages, and especially Latin, was the path of access to the positions afforded for university graduates. Before printing, learning meant going through the difficult process of mastering texts that one could not own or read easily. Just before but also considerably after printing, it was the texts themselves, more than their language, that had to be learned. The "skills and service" status of rhetoric and the liberal arts thus dates back to the founding of universities as we know them and is the result of the principal university subjects serving the interests of the protectors of the universities.

From the twelfth through the fifteenth centuries, the curricula remained stable: the three main subjects preceded by the liberal arts. When in the fourteenth and fifteenth centuries the advocates of humanism studied vernacular literatures and brought them into the university, this period represented, perhaps, the point of greatest respect achieved by the humanities and the study of language in the university. Humanists were what we might call "cutting edge," and for a while they helped to open up the atmosphere and the scope of scholarly work on language and literature in universities. A case in point is that of the fifteenth-century Italian professor of rhetoric, the humanist Lorenzo Valla (1406–57). He has been characterized by modern scholars as being more expert in Greek than most of his contemporaries and as dedicated, more than other humanists, to advocating the greater importance of rhetoric and ordinary language over scholastic philosophy. Jerrold Seigel writes that Valla wanted to "model philosophical discourse on the language of business or politics . . . [and] align [his] conclusions with all the usual notions of common sense" (166). If philosophers try to "refine common language or criticize common ideas of morality, Valla's answer was ready: 'Let the people respond that the rules of speech and all decisions about it lie with them'" (167). Gradually, even in the use of the vernacular, a wide split developed between the language of the academy and speakers of the vernacular, reminiscent of the split between Latin users and everyone else before the humanistic influence. Charles Trinkaus, referring to Luciano Barozzi's 1891 opinion, characterized Valla as "nearer to modern positivist and statistical methods than to rationalism[;] . . . like the positivist philosophers Valla was concerned with human liberty" (154). Similarly, Seigel writes:

> Valla denied that [syllogistic logic] could ever aid in the pursuit of knowledge. One could not decide about the truth or falsehood of simple statements by any logical test, but only by means of some independently acquired knowledge. . . . He made it quite clear that he did not believe reason, by itself, could add to this knowledge. . . . He did not think that dialectic [i.e., disputation, the means used to certify masters in the university] was any more rigorous a procedure than rhetoric. (167)

Valla had an unusual (for the time) respect for ordinary language, and in that regard his stance has something in common with Wittgenstein and other twentieth-century philosophers like Austin and Bakhtin, who began taking natural language use very seriously. According to Walter Ruegg, Valla studied "spoken discourse" and interpreted authors in terms of "his understanding of language and his situation" (456). He was one of the earliest annotators of the New Testament. He "analyzed the Latin language as a living expression of the changing self-understanding of human beings" (457). He tried to create a logic derived from the grammar of ordinary speech. One may describe his approach as "contextualist," as he clearly responded to language as something living in a variety of social situations. Ruegg describes how Valla's reaching out beyond the faculty of arts came "into conflict with the other faculties":

> As a result of such expansion, Valla had to flee from his professorship in Pavia because of the physical danger arising from his violent persecution at the hands of the members of the faculty of law; in Rome he was protected from the attacks of theologians only because he enjoyed the favor of the pope. (457)

Valla was considered dangerous because his subject, rhetoric, when pursued freely, implicated other subject matters. This amounted to an academic heresy, an overstepping of boundaries. The momentum of the Renaissance was carried forward by the discovery of new texts and by the increasing ease of reproducing existing texts. Should a scholar of rhetoric follow the manifest implications of the subject, all texts in all subjects were eligible for critical study. Those scholars most comprehending of grammar, logic, and rhetoric and who had the most languages at their disposal were in the best position to recast the received texts in new lights. Valla's views on the importance of language did not prevail and still do not today: universities still behave as if full engagement in the study of language as it affects other subjects and as it releases disenfranchised populations is not in their interest.

During the Enlightenment of eighteenth-century England, we might guess that language study would be even more liberated than it was in the Italian Renaissance. But the opposite is the case, as described by Miriam Brody in *Manly Writing*. In the eighteenth century, following from the prestige of a science whose picture of the universe was deemed proof of the existence of God, "philosophers" did try to establish standard spoken and written forms and to affirm the superiority of one privileged dialect over others, but "the people" were unable to follow Valla's recommendation to decide on these rules. Traditional androcentrism established certain values that were sought in students and promoted in textbooks. Once again, as when Latin was the standard that limited access, the so-called King's English rendered language as a subject once more compulsorily and myopically propaedeutic: it was separated from the other subjects that depended on it, and it was confined to the status of a preliminary tool.

THE COLLECTIVE PRIVACY

These remarks are meant to open a discussion of how the history of the university helps to explain its social psychology as we live through it today. The three aspects of academic language I cited above—obscurity, the skills and service role of rhetoric and composition, and the eschewing of personal, affective genres—emerge from the collective masculine psychology that has developed in the university. In part this psychology is related to military values inherited from Roman law, passed on through the church, and then instituted by the church as it took over sponsorship of universities. However, monarchies functioned under the same male group psychology. It is not a great leap to say that this psychology marks a wide variety of male groups in society, such as athletic teams, legislative bodies, police forces, businesses, professional organizations, and so forth.

We know very few institutions, in fact, that do not function using this same androcentric social psychology. Our interest has been in how this psychology affects the use of language in the university. The instances I cited above are symptoms of mores, behaviors, and values that did, of course, precede the university and then were put to new uses as this institution formed in the twelfth century.

The key elements of masculine-exclusive social psychology are hierarchical government and leadership, competition, stoicism in the face of pain, concealment of weakness and vulnerability, and the use of language in the service of these principles.

Inherent Obscurity

This amounts to the agreement to use an "underlying code of the professorial message," a language that appears to students and to the public to be a secret code, as suggested by Pierre Bourdieu in his reflection on academic discourse in the university. As already noted, the first university code was Latin, the language one had to know to be admitted to the university (Bourdieu, Passeron, and de Saint Martin 5). When vernaculars were/are used, jargon and related specialized vocabularies become the underlying code. The perspective of members of the university had been that the subject matters themselves were extremely distant from the interests of the population. Yet this could not be the case if the subjects were law, theology, and medicine, since everyone was affected by the law, the church, and the need to stay well: the subjects taught in universities have always mattered to the rest of the population, a situation that justified their pursuit in the first place. It is only that the *language of these subjects* could not be acquired by the public, which, as a result, had no access to the university or to the means by which the subjects affected society. In this way, the language of academics maintains its separation from the public, using the false explanation that the subjects themselves are remote from public interest. Socially motivated study became antisocial in the university.

The case of Martha Nussbaum and Judith Butler could be seen as a challenge to the view I am advancing. Nussbaum, in her hard-hitting critique of Judith Butler, observed that Butler may have overtaken the "extremely French idea that the intellectual does politics by speaking seditiously, and that this is a significant type of political action" (38). Derrida's writings tend to bear out Nussbaum's claim: American academics, influenced by French post-structuralism via the Yale critics, imagine they are taking political action by speaking in obscure ways, using an arcane vocabulary, and making strong, anthropomorphic claims about the social action of abstract ideas. Certainly, Judith Butler has a clear political purpose in her books, and her writing is cited repeatedly for its needless obscurity. Both women are members of the academy and have acceded to its most honored positions. Thus, when a dispute is carried out exclusively among women, it might be said, the traditional agon continues and therefore may not be identified as "male." I don't think this argument can be made, however, as the academy itself is still being protected by the almost exclusively male corporations and legislatures functioning under traditional hierarchical rules. As Carolyn Heilbrun has recently detailed, for her to be accepted at all into the academy, she had to find a way to learn from her male role models yet create a new identity for herself. She learned from her male teachers how *not* to be obscure in her writing and scholarship:

> "Jargon" was their [Lionel Trilling's and Jacques Barzun's] favorite pejorative term. Its misuse arose from the inclusion in prose for a general audience of the specific, technical terms of a particular discipline. When it came to writing, even all those years before the incomprehensible "theory" took over, Barzun and Trilling taught us how to write without shame or condescension for an audience as intelligent as we, though not perhaps as professionally trained. (12)

I bring this case up because it may seem as opposed to my point as the case of Nussbaum and Butler, yet it is to be explained with reference to the same consideration. In her book, Heilbrun spends many pages documenting, not merely reporting, the profound misogyny of all three of her teachers—Fadiman, Trilling, and Barzun—and the ways in which, buried in their own minds but emerging through various modes of speech and judgments of literature, was the assumption that she (their student) did not really belong in the academy. Thus, while her teachers had socially generous views about writing and language—views that still obviously do not prevail—they participated actively in the traditional animus to keep the academy an all-male society. Perhaps Nussbaum's and Butler's work enters a society that is, as it listens to Heilbrun, available to their voices. Yet both figures are strong feminist advocates who, as is clear from their work, are moving uphill in the same cause that

Heilbrun describes: *changing the academy*. They exemplify the "master's tools" debate articulated by Audre Lorde. Butler tried to use the tools; Nussbaum, like Heilbrun, tried to change the tools and to use similar tools for different purposes. Yet all three are using both their language and their discipline to change the academy, to change the character of the university. Even though these three women have found a respected place in the academy, it is still run according to traditional male social psychology: women and others previously excluded from the university must follow the mores of the men who have run it for centuries: hierarchical leadership, competition, stoicism, the concealment of vulnerability, and the use of language in the service of these values. Academic obscurity has still not been revoked.

The Degrading of Rhetoric and Composition

The discipline of rhetoric and composition, with its population of more than half women and its strong interest in pedagogy, has attempted to change the approach to language in the academy. Members of this discipline have studied the history of rhetoric and have worked many more hours than other members of the academy observing students' uses of language in a wide variety of contexts and genres. Also more than other disciplines, it has recognized the daily action of pedagogy: the ongoing need to pay attention to each student and to return to the students through the process of developing their thoughts. In several programs in the United States, the discipline has come close to a point that it could indeed help change the academy and its use of language. In fact, at this time, a writing teacher, Andrea Lunsford, has presented an initiative to the MLA to change the "adversarial academy" to a "collaborative" academy. But what Frances Condon described as happening in one department has happened repeatedly in other departments in major universities: when the program became important and influential, it was dismantled. In the past decade, several progressive, accomplished writing programs that have gone considerably beyond the narrow conception of academic writing have been "put out of business" for reasons that are not obvious, given their indisputable success. The only clear facts are that these programs had momentum, were training writing teachers to be imaginative, creative, inventive, and active, and that they all had faculty directors who were moved to other jobs, while parties without professional stake in the subject were given the task of running the programs.

The most widely publicized instance of this development occurred when the University of Texas writing program was abruptly suspended by the school administration after the Department of English permitted the teaching of writing to take place through the study of court decisions about civil rights. In this series of events, faculty members proposed to study and teach a specific language—that of the law—with its specific vocabulary and habits of use and as it was applied to a specific set of court cases that were of highest importance to the social health of this society. It would be hard to imagine a way better than this one to teach the use of language, and it was adopted with the voted support of over 85% of the faculty in a large department in a major university. Yet the dean peremptorily intervened, the program was canceled, and the faculty member who led it got another appointment at a different university. Is this much different from the fate of Lorenzo Valla? In one way it is: the faculty member whose initiative it was is female. Could this have been yet another manifestation of what Heilbrun experienced at Columbia in the 1950s? It seems similar to me. Linda Brodkey was not fired: she had tenure, but her position at the University of Texas was no longer tenable, and she left. Will someone say she was "driven" out, as Snowball was from Animal Farm? Yes, but then it will be affirmed that she left of her own accord, which, of course, she did. If writing programs and departments of rhetoric and composition grow normally, that is, just as other departments grow and develop, they move into the position of Lorenzo Valla: the close, careful, and disciplined study of language leads inevitably to the study of the language of all disciplines, and this language matters. But the sponsorship of today's university has an overwhelming stake in not disturbing the key disciplines that produce wealth and maintain authority; sponsors have a stake in teaching language in such a way—skills and service—that supports what they sponsor, and that is happening today as it happened in the previous eight centuries of stable university functioning. Corporate sponsors need compliant managers and workers as much as the church and the crowns did.

Discomfort with Genres of Subjectivity

The male academy is not uncomfortable with all genres of subjectivity, only those genres that, if permitted to flourish, would expose the limitations of academic thinking. The roots of this discomfort have been outlined repeatedly by Walter Ong. He is an advocate of Learned Latin and attributes the edifice of modern science to this language and the discipline it had taken to learn it. Science, he writes, "follows from scholastic experience" (*Orality* 114). He associates Learned Latin with writing itself, which he distinguishes from "orality," the zone in which we experience "the emotion-charged depths of the mother tongue" (*Orality* 114). He advocates the fundamental trope of modern science—"separating the knower from the known" (105)—and presents Learned Latin as one of the key factors in establishing this axiom of scientific inquiry. He does not conceal his identification of all of these developments as characteristically male and at one point, traces back male agonism to the womb where, he suggests, male children develop in opposition to the female environment (*Fighting* 64-65). The value of Ong's work is that he takes no pains to mitigate his argument: to him, it is self-evident that male development and its natural movement into the practices of Learned Latin through the church and the university are responsible for civilization as we know it. We may probably grant this argument, oddly enough, except for one key point: how natural could such a process have been, given the well-documented systematic, purposeful exclusion of women from this engine of civilization?

Ong presents literacy as we teach and use it as having derived from the "Christian clerical culture" that David Noble documents as having repeatedly, regularly, and often with malice excluded women and opposed their access to equal citizenship. Certainly women were prevented and discouraged from becoming literate. Ong rightly characterizes this culture as promoting Stoicism and adopting the stance of "male puberty rites" (Orality and Literacy 113) in which the initiate must show that he can "take it." Learned Latin helped to censor the "emotion-charged depths of the mother tongue" (Orality and Literacy 114) while the community that worked up and molded the privileged knowledge of this language separated emotion radically from formal study, setting the stage for the "separation of the knower from the known," a common axiom of scientific work. As a result of this radical separation and with students' involvement in Latin (learning it for the purposes of certification through debate), life outside the university acquired exaggerated and antisocial characteristics. Inside the university, intense pressure built up on the men to succeed and prove themselves; outside, their adolescent wildness was tolerated, overlooked, and understood to be the result of "boys will be boys" (Rashdall1: 4). Yet both inside and outside the academy, the men's behavior was antisocial—fiercely clubby and hierarchical in the university and then in the church, yet subversively and hypocritically undisciplined in civilian life, protected in part by the law and in part by the church itself.

Jason Berry's recent book, *Lead Us Not into Temptation,* suggests the great effort made by the church to conceal, rather than end, such behaviors. The academic antagonism to feeling and subjectivity may thus be traced in part to the learning, status, use, and protection of Learned Latin and to the military discipline usually used to teach it: beatings, as reported by Augustine and many after him (this is a somewhat unusual, yet nevertheless plausible, conclusion). The entrance of women in large numbers into the university coincides with the passing of corporal punishment and has opened up the range of genres and language registers in which scholarly work may be published. Personal and subjective writing itself has taken forms beyond the simple "confessional," the one genre in which formal autobiography existed not too long ago. Now personal, subjective, and emotional writing is clearly and carefully linked to a series of collectively held issues having to do with social equality, human rights, disclosure of systematic secrecies such as sexuality and domestic violence (see Freedman, Frey, and Zauhar; Daly).We do not know at this time whether these new genres will have the effect of introducing the willingness to face and understand private and subjective experience in the different phases of scholarship. As anthropologists have been discussing recently, there are "issues" when scholars introduce themselves into a distant society in order to study it. And there are "issues" when students decide that yes, they can come out in their classrooms and that they can write and share narratives of parental sexual abuse, beatings, and alcoholism, as ways of learning that writing means writing about things that matter, things that will affect and touch others.

THEREFORE

In any event, academic language can no longer claim a collective privacy, though it is not surprising that genres of social disclosure and the critique of scientific language have been attacked and censored (see Gross and Levitt; Sokal and Bricmont). They are still not welcomed in writing programs or considered to be part of the study of language. There is still considerable resistance to the initiatives taken by Lorenzo Valla: the use of the knowledge of language to consider how all disciplines present their authoritative claims for knowledge and understanding. Indeed, the value of "privacy" is often defended with citations from the U.S. Constitution, and many members of the academy, referring to themselves as "intellectuals" (Michael) seem unaware of how fluently this term announces a radical separation of "us" from "them"; the term "public intellectual" attempts to preserve a private sense of individual superiority for members of the academy in the process of claiming to want to reach a general public.

The problem of academic language cannot be isolated from the problems of society that have produced it. On the other hand, the traditional mores of academic language can no longer be assumed to be necessary. There are no longer any justifications for not letting the language speak of all the constituencies now entering the university and acknowledging that the received uniformities of academic usage are as inimical to the spread of understanding as the androcentric rule of society.

7

THE ESSAYIST IN—AND BEHIND—THE ESSAY

Vested Writers, Invested Readers

Lynn Z. Bloom

VOICE-OVER: *Our telephone was tapped during the eight years it took to write and publish Doctor Spock: Biography of a Conservative Radical—my hopeful contribution to ending the Vietnam War. When I'd pick up the receiver to dial out, I'd hear mysterious clicks, breathing—sometimes even panting, but never a voice. Sometimes the line would go dead. I have never again experienced the sense of a palpitating but silent presence on the other end of the line except for a brief stay in Bucharest during the depths of the Ceausescu regime. Our approved Intourist hotel was so close to a thicket of radio relay towers that the spies could have peeped through the window, but they evidently preferred the phone. It rang at random hours of the day and night to deliver breathing and static. No voice, not even in a language I couldn't understand.*

THE PRODIGIOUS PRESENCE OF SUPERSTAR ESSAYISTS

This chapter will demonstrate that the work of superstar canonical essayists is qualitatively different from that of many other essayists (including many canonical essayists of lesser luminosity) in one significant respect—the intensely felt presence of the essayist within the essay. This ethos is comprised of the author's ethical and intellectual stance toward the subject—and perhaps the world—and manifested in the essayist's characteristic voice and literary style. These constitute the author's persona, distinctive and ongoing, sustained from one work to the next. Verisimilitude notwithstanding, the essayist behind the essay is not necessarily the character, the *I*, "the singular first person" who appears in the essay. This essayist-in-the-essay, apparently artless and transparent, is actually a work of art to which readers—even those sophisticated enough to know the character represented is a carefully constructed artifact—react as if it were the real person whom they know and—usually—

love. Indeed, personal essays that successfully reach audiences year after year, generation after generation, demonstrate that a writer's private presence in the essay is most effectively transmitted through a distinct public persona. As Scott Russell Sanders, himself a canonical essayist, observes in "The Singular First Person": "Brassy or shy, center stage or hanging back in the wings, the author's persona commands our attention. For the length of an essay, or a book of essays, we respond to that persona as we would to a friend caught up in a rapturous monologue" (194).

The appendix to this chapter, "Discovering the Essay Canon," explains the research method by which I established the existence of an essay canon and identified the canonical essayists and their canonical essays—those most widely anthologized in readers used in first-year American college composition courses from 1946 to 1996. Readers are collections of essays and other nonfiction works—speeches (Lincoln's Gettysburg Address), fables (Thurber's "Fables for Our Time"), satires ("A Modest Proposal," for instance, is a patently fictional work that is usually treated as nonfiction), and letters (although Martin Luther King, Jr.'s "Letter from Birmingham Jail" is in letter format, I would argue that it is, in fact, an essay)—that are regarded as essays for pedagogical purposes.

Extremely popular canonical essays, those by the twenty superstars with 480 reprints or more, satisfy the felt sense that they have not only transcended time, if not culture, but that the canon could not exist without them. Virtually all of these writers (except two authors of documents that are not essays, Thomas Jefferson as first author of the Declaration of Independence and Plato as author of "The Allegory of the Cave") convey a powerful sense of a human being within and behind the writing that many other perfectly competent nonfiction writers—including many canonical essayists of lesser ranking—exhibit less memorably or not at all, even when they are writing on subjects of comparable significance. These are the canonical superstars, like the rich whom Fitzgerald allegedly told Hemingway are "different from you and me."

George Orwell heads the list, with 1,785 reprints of such essays as "Politics and the English Language" and "Shooting an Elephant", his work is included in virtually every reader published during the second half of the twentieth century. E. B. White, with 1,340 reprints—including "Once More to the Lake" and "The Ring of Time"—is a close second. Then come: 3) Joan Didion, 1,095 reprints; 4) Lewis Thomas, 1,020; 5)

Henry David Thoreau, 900; 6) Virginia Woolf, 885; 7) Jonathan Swift, 865; 8) Martin Luther King, Jr., 825; 9) James Thurber, 790; 10) Mark Twain, 715; 11) Annie Dillard, 680; 12) Thomas Jefferson, 660; 13) Russell Baker, 630; 14) Loren Eiseley, 605; 15) E. M. Forster, 590; 16) Maya Angelou, 565; 17) Ellen Goodman, 560; 18) James Baldwin, 510; 19) Richard Rodriguez, 495; and 20) Plato, 480.

(A parenthetical observation to keep in mind to contrast with the canonical superstars. At the bottom of the canon list are twenty authors with 100–10 reprints apiece: Hannah Arendt, Michael Arlen, Sigmund Freud, Dick Gregory, Sidney J. Harris, Jane Jacobs, Alfred Kazin, X. J. Kennedy, Robin Lakoff, Ashley Montagu, Gloria Naylor, Chief Seattle, Eric Sevareid, George Bernard Shaw, Gail Sheehy, William Stafford, John Steinbeck, Alvin Toffler, Gore Vidal, and Edmund Wilson. Try this test. What works of these authors come to mind? Many have reputations as writers of novels, poetry, drama, psychiatric treatises, urban analysis, or theology, and it is likely you would identify their best-known works first. If you can think of essays or longer pieces of nonfiction written by any of these authors, what works are these? I surmise that if readers do associate a specific authorial presence or persona with each or any of these writers, it will be the presence that emanates from their best-known works in the genres and fields where their reputations lie—fiction for Naylor, drama for Shaw, poetry for Stafford—rather than through their essays.)

"THE SINGULAR FIRST PERSON": THE AUTHORIAL PRESENCE OF SUPERSTAR ESSAYISTS

Simply—and subjectively—put, for an essayist to become a canonical superstar, teachers—and by extrapolation, their students—have to love the performance. Readers respond vigorously to the work and thus to the author whose presence emerges in and through the writing. By and large, they love the writer they come to know as a more or less constant presence from one canonical favorite to another: the George Orwell of "Shooting an Elephant," "Marrakech," and "Politics and the English Language"; the E. B. White who emerges in and through "Once More to the Lake," "The Death of a Pig," and "Walden"; the Joan Didion of "Why I Write," "On Keeping a Notebook," and "Some Dreamers of the Golden Dream." Yet when the narrator of a superstar essay elicits loathing, as the monstrously bland narrator of Swift's "Modest Proposal" is calculated to do, readers are expected to recognize and respect the ethical distance between the actual author and his created character (even though some naive readers elide the two). For better or for worse, as Scott Russell Sanders explains: "It is the *singularity* of the first person—its warts and crochets and turn of voice" (196)—to which readers respond as if that first person were a real person.

Essayists themselves are under no illusions about the illusory characters they create, nor about why they do so. The author's self-presentation as simple and unadorned is as old as the genre, invented by Montaigne, who artfully began the tradition of artlessness, as well. He slyly explains "To the Reader" of *Essays*: "I want to be seen here in my simple, natural, ordinary fashion, without straining or artifice; for it is myself that I portray. My defects will here be read to the life, and also my natural form." Custom permitting, Montaigne says he would "very gladly have portrayed [himself] here entire and wholly naked" (qtd. in Sanders 195).

Contemporary canonical superstars have addressed this subject in a comparable vein. Thoreau opens *Walden*—of which textbook excerpts are treated as essay—by observing: "In most books, the *I*, or first person, is omitted; in this it will be retained; that, in respect to egotism, is the main difference. We commonly do not remember that it is, after all, always the first person that is speaking [whether or not the pronoun is there to send that signal]." Adds Thoreau: "I should not talk so much about myself if there were anybody else whom I knew as well" (3). E. B. White introduces his own selected *Essays* by acknowledging that although the essayist "can pull on any sort of shirt, be any sort of person, according to his mood or his subject matter—philosopher, scold, jester, raconteur, confidant, pundit, devil's advocate, enthusiast," he must tell the absolute truth. Lest readers suspect that this multiplicity of roles might lead to artifice and role-playing, White—drawing again on the example of Montaigne, who "had the gift of natural candour"—confidently asserts that the essayist "cannot indulge himself in deceit or in concealment, for he will be found out in no time" (vii-viii). Although George Orwell in "Why I Write"—a literary manifesto written near the end of the author's short life—concludes that "one can write nothing readable unless one constantly struggles to efface one's own personality," he acknowledges that all writers—members of a small class of "gifted, willful people who are determined to live their own lives to the end"—are driven by "sheer egoism." Ego motivates the "desire to seem clever, to be talked about, to be remembered after death." Essay writers also share three other motives: "(2) Esthetic enthusiasm . . . [;] (3) Historical impulse . . . to find out true facts and store them up for the use of posterity [; and] (4) Political purpose . . . [that is,] desire to push the world in a certain direction" (316). And in her version of "Why I Write," Joan Didion, acknowledging that she stole the title from Orwell, gets right to the point—the egoistic emphasis of the "*I, I, I*" sounds in the title: "In many ways writing is the act of saying I, of imposing oneself upon other people, of saying *listen to me, see it my way, change your mind*" (44).

Such pronouncements could easily lead readers to expect that superstar canonical essayists are writing autobiography, itself a highly constructed artifact despite autobiographers' protestations of truthfulness (see Gusdorf; Mandel; Howarth). However, the only autobiographers among the top twenty are Maya Angelou (virtually all her "essays" are editorially selected excerpts from *I Know Why the Caged Bird Sings*) and Richard Rodriguez, with chapters or excerpts of chapters from the autobiographical *Hunger of Memory: The Education of Richard Rodriguez*. Indeed, although the essays' readers could glean occasional "facts" about the lives of the canonical superstars, these are insufficient to present even a fragmentary sketch of the writer's life. For instance, in "Once More to the Lake," White tells us about the time the narrator and his unnamed son spent an idyllic week at an unnamed lake in Maine, doing a variety of activities (boating, fishing, swimming) that White himself had enjoyed as a boy vacationing at the same lake. But however ample or minimal, such autobiographical information is beside the point. The essayist's point of view—as signaled by the "*I, I, I*"—is the focal point of authorial presence, as Scott Russell Sanders explains in "The Singular First Person" and Gordon Harvey elaborates on in "Presence in the Essay."

After modestly claiming that the essayist, in comparison with poets, playwrights, and novelists, "must be content in his self-imposed role of second-class citizen," E. B. White admits that "some people find the essay the last resort of the egoist, a much too self-conscious and self-serving form for their taste; they think that it is presumptuous of a writer to assume that his little excursions or his small observations will interest the reader." Acknowledging the "justice in their complaint," White adds, "I have always been aware that I am by nature self-absorbed and egotistical; to write of myself to the extent I have done indicates a too great attention to my own life, not enough to the lives of others" (vii-viii). Not so, explains Sanders, for contrary to the autobiographer's practice of looking inward, the superstar essayists are looking outward on the creation that is the world. As White says in "The Ring of Time": "As a writing man or secretary, I have always felt charged with the safekeeping of all unexpected items of worldly or unworldly enchantment, as though I might be held personally responsible if even a small one were to be lost" (143). These superstars know that, as Sanders says of his own essays: "The public does not give a hoot about my private life." He adds: "I choose to write about my experience not because it is mine, but because it seems to me a door through which others might pass" (197–98).

Indeed, the perspective of the first person singular that dominates the essay is that of the essayist who opens doors to others' common experience. (That all essayists are embedded in constraints of class, ethnicity, gender, physical and emotional functioning, age, time, and culture is today's truism; that no writer can claim universal connections with a universal audience does not negate the fact that the work does establish a great many significant relationships.) This perspective establishes the authorial presence within the world of each individual essay that creates the bond with the readers, the ethos, that persists from one essay to another. It should be noted that presence (amplified below) is a more robust concept than voice, even as addressed in Carl Leggo's comprehensive list of ninety-nine "Questions I Need to Ask before I Advise My Students to Write in Their Own Voices" (ranging from "What is there of desire in voice?" to "Is voice like a thumbprint—unique?" [145–50]) as elaborated on in Peter Elbow's sophisticated discussion of "audible voice or intonation in writing," "dramatic voice in writing," "recognizable or distinctive voice in writing," and "voice with authority" xxiv–xxxiii). When Elbow addresses the last item on his list, "resonant voice or presence," he finds "trouble—the swamp" because this concept embeds questions of authorial sincerity, authenticity, and relationship to the "real character" of the "actual author" beyond the text (xxxiii–xlii). The answer, he says, lies in Aristotle's *Rhetoric,* in which he "clearly implies what common sense tells us: we are not persuaded by the implied author as such—that is, by the creation of a dramatic voice that sounds trustworthy; we are only persuaded if we believe that dramatic voice is the voice of the actual speaker or author" (xlii). (Elbow elaborates: "We don't buy a used car from someone just because we admire their dramatic skill in creating a fictional trustworthy voice. If ethos is nothing *but* implied author, it loses all power of persuasion.") This presence constitutes the sense of the essayist *in* the essay; the more powerful the sense of presence, the more likely the essayist is to be a superstar.

It is this sense of presence that Gordon Harvey anatomizes in "Presence in the Essay." In an explanation that reinforces the observations of White and Sanders, he says:

> If a piece of autobiographical writing *is* an essay, it has already moved beyond private confession or memoir to some shareable idea, for which the personal experience works as evidence. This move from experience to idea, and then, through painful revision, from a dull idea and simple, narrative structure to an interesting idea and structure, bringing general insights out in the particulars and erasing narcissism, is precisely the great challenge and the great value of the personal essay as a Freshman Writing assignment—this and the broadened sense it gives of what can count as evidence for ideas. (648)

The "personal" in essays is not necessarily "represented by autobiographical anecdote and image or by explicit self-analysis and introspection," but rather by authorial presence. Presence, Harvey says, "is the concept we invoke when we feel life in writing, when we feel an individual invested in a subject and freely directing the essay—not surrendering control to a discipline's conventions, or to a party line, or to easy sentiments and structures, or to stock phrases" (650).

In general, readers don't know or care much about the essayist behind the essay except to assume that figure to be intellectually and ethically congruent with the writer whose perspective appears in public. By and large this assumption is warranted to the extent that the author's ethos—disposition, character, and fundamental values—is stable in person and in print. And this assumption holds true even when readers know that an author such as Virginia Woolf is writing on her more cheerful days rather than from depression, or that George Orwell's unverifiable accounts of "A Hanging" and "Shooting an Elephant" do not depend on "factual, historical veracity" but on fidelity to the generic experience of colonial officers in Burma (Crick 85, 95–96, 112).

VOICE-OVER: *During the course of my research, Dr. Spock and four others were prosecuted by the federal government for conspiring to encourage students to resist the draft during the Vietnam War. The FBI agents who testified were to a man rigidly erect in posture and testimony, literalists all—with no acknowledgment of the figurative that pervades the language their wiretappers would have overheard—metaphor, hyperbole, understatement. What someone said or wrote, they meant. Thus "Oh, I'd like to kill her" could be construed as an intent to commit murder, rather than a comment of exasperation.*

"ONCE MORE TO THE LAKE" AS AN EXAMPLE OF AUTHORIAL PRESENCE

Harvey goes on to explain the process and technical means by which essays, including academic writing, can "be *informed* by personal experience without injecting personal *information*" or even the personal pronoun, "a matter of felt life in the writing rather than anecdote or self-analysis" (649). Although presence is "everywhere" in an essay, it is particularly apparent in the six aspects of the essay that Harvey identifies, which I will analyze here as they are manifested in "Once More to the Lake," using male pronouns to accommodate the male author.

Harvey's first aspect is (1) *motive.* Usually in the introduction the writer establishes, for himself and his readers, why the subject is "interesting enough to pursue," "why it isn't simply obvious, why there's a mystery to unfold"—in brief, why the essay needs to be written (Harvey 650). At the outset White announces that throughout his childhood his family spent every August at a lake in Maine: "none of us ever thought there was any place in the world like [it]." Although I have "since become a salt water man," says White, "there are days when the restlessness of the tides and the fearful cold of the sea water and the incessant wind that blows . . . make me wish for the placidity of a lake in the woods" like the one of the childhood summers (197). To recapture this "sacred" time and place, he returns to the same lake with his son, and the story begins. The element of the quest is subdued but omnipresent: can a father reexperience the past and transmit this legacy, and its meanings, to his son?

The second aspect Harvey identifies is (2) *development.* Presence, says Harvey, "is manifest, along with pleasure, sometimes wonder and even passion, in a willingness to pursue a topic through twists and turns: to see in it, and follow it through, its various aspects and complications and sub-ideas, which not just anybody would think of or predict." The real issue "isn't between orderly and disorderly development, or between linear and nonlinear; it's between dull, mechanical order and complex, alert order, whose creation and control manifest presence" (650–51). White signals this alertness in the second paragraph, when he explains the associative nature of the juxtaposition of past and present that he proffers throughout the essay: "It is strange how much you can remember about places [like the lake, "this unique, this holy spot"] once you allow your mind to return into the grooves that lead back. You remember one thing, and that suddenly reminds you of another thing." He reaffirms this, with a surprise—as much to himself as to the readers—in the fourth paragraph: "I began to sustain the illusion that [my young son] was I, and therefore, by simple transposition, that I was my father. . . . I seemed to be living a dual existence. I would be in the middle of some simple act . . . and suddenly it would be not I but my father who was saying the words or making the gesture" (198).

White's fifth paragraph illustrates all of the remaining characteristics Harvey describes concurrently: (3) *"Control of quotation* [when the writer is responding to other texts] *and detail"*—through original metaphors, similes, metonymic details that indicate "the feeling of a mind engaged in the subject at hand," not grandstanding razzle-dazzle; *"An awareness of cliché and what doesn't need saying,"* witty allusions to readers' shared knowledge and experiences; *broadenings* of the subject ("It's a mistake," says Harvey, to think that particulars only "particularize," when in fact they can broaden out the discussion, perhaps drawing on "the essayist's experiential grasp of human behavior, of how life tends to go"); and *judgments and reasons,* "Giving specific reasons for one's general impressions . . . happens also to be its most personal aspect" (651–52).

White's fifth paragraph illustrates all of the above characteristics concurrently. To establish the convergence of past and present, White repeats "the same" in detail upon detail of going fishing the first morning: "the same damp moss" covers the worms in the bait can; "the small waves were the same"—original detail—"chucking the rowboat under the chin"; and "the boat was the same boat, the same color green and the ribs broken in the same places, and under the floorboards the same freshwater leavings." A dragonfly lights on the tip of his rod, convincing him "beyond any doubt that everything was as it always had been, that the years were a mirage and that there had been no years." Despite the comfortable familiarity of these phenomena, White uses no cliches. Nor does he spell out his interpretations, trusting that if he presents appropriate information his readers will understand the music as well as the words. Indeed, he broadens the subject even as he embeds his interpretations in the telling details: "I looked at the boy [whose name does not matter], who was silently watching his fly, and it was my hands that held his rod, my eyes watching. I felt dizzy and didn't know which rod I was at the end of" (198–99). White's presence here is far more profound than a voice; it is an active, engaged mind in motion, even in the stillness of the event.

The essay, originally published in the *New Yorker* in August 1941, re-created for its sophisticated, urban audience the rhythms and events of a summertime-out-of-time "pattern of life indelible, the fadeproof lake, the woods unshatterable, the pasture with the sweetfern and the juniper forever and ever, summer without end" (White 200). Whether or not White's readers have ever gone to the woods (with their overtone of Thoreau's *Walden*, where one could live "deliberately"), White invites them there, to that special segment of the universe in the last tranquil summer before the cataclysm of World War II, where grandfather and father and son blend in an indissoluble union. This essay has withstood sixty years of intervening shifts in reading (and to a lesser extent teaching), and some critical bashing from post-structuralist, postmodern, neo-Marxist, feminist, multiethnic and a plethora of other critical perspectives. Its survival attests to its resonance in human terms for generations of readers—women as well as men—who value the essay's real subject, the human connections White celebrates. Moreover, it is pedagogically versatile and can be taught for its narrative, implied argument, comparison and contrast, illustration, characterization, tone, structure (of sentence, paragraph, and whole work), and pace, as well as this myriad of themes.

The actual person of E. B. White, the existential human being, is irrelevant to the authorial presence conveyed within the body of his work. Readers' response to the intensely felt presence of the author in this essay carries over to their reading of White's other widely reprinted essays as well; the process is the same for all other canonical superstars, among them Orwell, Didion, Thoreau, Virginia Woolf, Martin Luther King, Jr., Thurber, and Twain. This sense of authorial presence, when coupled with other features of teachable texts identified above (such as intellectual relevance, accessibility, and length) is predictive of future canonical superstars as well. These are the contemporary belletristic writers whose essays are beginning to appear in textbooks in significant numbers, essayists whom some critical readers already refer to as "canonical" because of the felt sense that their presence is indispensable. Tomorrow's superstar shoo-ins (some of whom are already on the canonical list) include Sherman Alexie, Diane Ackerman, Gloria

Anzaldúa, Dave Eggers, Anne Fadiman, Henry Louis Gates, Jr., Jamaica Kincaid, Scott Russell Sanders, Shelby Steele, Gary Soto, Amy Tan, David Foster Wallace, and Jhumpa Lahiri, if only she'd write more essays.

VOICE-OVER: *Here's what the FBI eavesdroppers in Cleveland, Indianapolis, St. Louis would have heard: Colloquies in disembodied voices. Conversations with academic colleagues, editors, and students about work-in-progress. Arrangements with neighbors about car pools, play groups, peace marches, integration efforts, and the elementary school's annual geranium sale (run, of course, by the Blooms). One babysitter's routine calls—on the job—to her bookie.*

After my initial call to Dr. Spock—"I've recently finished my Michigan doctoral dissertation on literary biography and now I'd like to write a real biography—of you"—we talked only in person. Whether the FBI ever provided a context for the fragments of lives they overheard, ever sought to assemble whole presences from the auditory mosaic that tumbled into their tapes, I do not know. Literalists would leave out the laughter, the fun and effort of the process, the exhilaration born of the hope that this writer—myself—an author behind the author of America's best-known baby book—would and could change the world.

ISSUES IN TEACHING CANONICAL ESSAYISTS

Teachers who distrust personal-sounding writing in the classroom respond to such texts—particularly student papers—with suspicion and distrust, and perhaps with readings more literal than the writing warrants. The authorial presence sends the wrong message in an academic universe, they say, making little allowance for the literary artistry—shaping characters, establishing a voice and an individual style—that they reward in fiction and poetry (see Bartholomae "Inventing"; Bizzell "Cognition"). Not so. The essayist's human presence raises ethical problems (for innocent or forgetful readers) and possibilities for teaching writing and for reinvigorated academic writing that I have space to discuss only briefly.

Ethical Considerations

Author-evacuated texts, conventional academic articles, appear objective, impartial, as William H. Gass says in "Emerson and the Essay," "complete and straightforward and footnoted and useful and certain" and "unassailable," and are therefore "a veritable Michelin of misdirection" (25). Author-saturated texts may be equally misleading. Readers expect honesty, openness, intimacy; a writer as personal-sounding as Orwell or Didion or White is trusted to tell the truth, the whole truth, and nothing but the truth. This trust in the personal is paramount, in spite of what teachers as well as authors know about the aesthetic necessity—and latitude—in shaping characters, setting scenes, representing dialogue, and other features common to both fiction and creative nonfiction. In a variety of circumstances—political, religious, cultural, academic—audiences trust the messenger and so they adopt the message. Thus teachers have an obligation to make it clear that like all forms of literature all essays, however personal or impersonal, are constructs. Wendy Bishop offers teachers "Places to Stand," saying that as a reflective writer-teacher-writer, "I still need a place to write from, a writer's identity; as a teacher, I need to ask students to question the self they are constructing in their physical texts and in the actual classroom" (22). Harvey provides practical advice in "Presence in the Essay" on how teachers can teach their students to create such constructs by employing the features of presence he has explicated (649–53) and that I have used above in analyzing "Once More to the Lake."

Pedagogical Influence

Personal presence gives essayist superstars, like canonical authors in other genres, significance in the field disproportionate to their numbers. Although they are not the rock stars of the belletristic world, because their essays have been reprinted so widely, their influence has the potential for being profound. Yet we can ask whether these essayists have really affected the way the millions of student readers in the past fifty years have seen the world. Have these essayists caused their readers to think and act on the subjects their works address—civil and human rights, education, culture and multiculturalism, science and technology, writing and the arts? Is the superstar influence actually as profound as its potential?

As many textbooks reveal, students are obliged to read essays as prose models to emulate, even in process-oriented courses. In courses focusing on critical thinking, argumentation, or disciplinary issues, students are expected to read critically, take an intellectual stand, and enter into the agonistic language and dialectical postures of the academy. But most of the superstars' work is reflective, interpretive instead; it invites readers to enter the writer's world, look around, deepen their understanding, and come to their own interpretations and conclusions about that world.

Some of these interpretations could, however, lead to social action—even to civil disobedience or more extreme activity—for a number of the essays by canonical superstars are revolutionary. These include Swift's "Modest Proposal"; Orwell's "Politics and the English Language," "Shooting an Elephant," and "Marrakech"; Thoreau's "Civil Disobedience"; Martin Luther King, Jr.'s "Letter from Birmingham Jail"; and the Declaration of Independence. Yet Americans—teachers and students alike—tend to respond to these as historical documents, rather than as incitements to social action (see Bloom, "Essay Canon" 419–22). If essays such as these will make the students more thoughtful, morally better people (perhaps in emulation of the author's presence) or move them to noble or socially responsible action, it is hard to discern such effects in any given composition class. It is impossible to find any empirical research on the subject other than individual teachers' claims to success, such as Bruce Herzberg's "Community Service and Critical Teaching." To recontextualize any essay, no matter how inspiring or incendiary, in a textbook and a school setting is for most college students to blunt the keen edge of the excitement—intellectual, political, aesthetic—that inspired the author to write it in the first place.

Teachers should expect to expend some effort to override the anesthetic effects of anthologization, to help transform students from passive readers of entombed works, however canonical, to active responders to living words, the lively presences within and behind the essays they read. If, for example, students read "Shooting an Elephant" only as a course requirement or as a personal essay—in this case, an episode of a junior colonial officer's humiliation before Burmese "coolies" long ago and far away—they miss the point. If they read it in isolation from other canonical works of civil disobedience they miss the point. Teachers can help students understand a work's importance in its original and its current contexts—political, social, intellectual, aesthetic. Thereby teachers can reinvigorate significant essays by encouraging students to make meaningful connections—among the past and present implications of a given work and among works on related topics (say, issues of civil disobedience, human rights, or multiculturalism). As such works come alive to the students, so will their meaning and their invitations (implicit and explicit) to think—and to act, to change the world. This transformative potential of literature is one of the foundational principles of Kurt Spellmeyer's forthcoming *The Arts of Living: Remaking the Humanities for the Twenty-first Century.*

Reinvigorating the Genre

If more teachers wrote essays or academic articles with presence that acknowledged their authorial investment, they would be better able to teach students not only the craft but the art. Until recently, composition studies scholars took the ideas—and indeed the personae—of academic essayists with presence, such as Peter Elbow, Donald Murray, Mike Rose, and Nancy Sommers—to heart but dismissed or trivialized the genre in which they wrote as too obvious, too easy, too confessional: "U.S. composition teachers have created a school genre that can exist only in an expressivist composition classroom" (Dixon 257). However, now that more academics have begun to try such writing themselves, they have realized how hard it is, in the absence of a predictable form and conventional academic language, to present profound ideas simply, with elegance and apparent ease. It is even harder to create a credible persona of the sort that appears with regularity in such publications as the *American Scholar, Creative Nonfiction, Writing on the Edge, Fourth Genre,* and the serial volumes of *Best American Essays,* among others. Yet they are also experiencing the rewards; while conventional academic articles engender citations, personal essays inspire fan mail, dissertation chapters, invitations to parties—and republication.

As writers of the genre, teachers and other essayists can with greater authority show students ways to convey the presence that can transform their own worlds and their relationship to their readers from distance and abstraction to immediacy and engagement. As writers of personal-sounding essays, teachers could speak with authority about the inevitable disparity between the private person behind the work and ways to translate salient elements of self-characterization to the public document. They could have students try to consciously control features such as motive, voice, degree and nature of investment in the subject, with an awareness that what beats on the page is the vitality of the writer's vision, not the bleeding heart of the writer behind the work.

VOICE-OVER: *In 1993 the Massachusetts Civil Liberties Union Foundation honored the five defendants of the 1968 conspiracy trial, Dr. Spock included, at its annual Bill of Rights Dinner. In attendance was John Wall, who had prosecuted the government's case twenty-five years earlier. Tight-lipped and remote during the trial, he was now genial, beaming as he introduced himself to me. "I read your book and I loved it." He added, "When I saw Dr. Spock and the others in person, and came to know them through their presence in the courtroom, I grew to admire their ethics and their courage in speaking out and being willing to go to jail—for life if necessary—to defend the principles our country is founded on. The [FBI] agents just didn't get that on the tapes."*

APPENDIX

DISCOVERING THE ESSAY CANON

The Research Method and the Evidence

Several years ago I casually asked, "What essays do people read today? And where do they read them?" The short answer to a lengthy five-year research process is this: those Americans who read essays at all find them reprinted in composition anthologies (a.k.a. readers) intended for freshman writing courses. Indeed, the twentieth-century American essay canon is unique among literary canons, for it is primarily a teaching canon rather than a critical canon. Thus it differs from the canons of poetry and fiction of any era, and even from that of nineteenth-century essays, in the way it is formed, transmitted, and changed. The poetry canon, for instance, as Golding (*From Outlaw to Classic*) and Rasula (*The American Poetry Wax Museum*) demonstrate, is created by an establishment of fellow poets who promote each other's work. They publish each other's poetry in the little magazines and poetry anthologies they edit; they award each other prizes in contests they judge, appoint each other to judging panels, elect each other to prestigious literary societies. They translate and comment on each other's work, interview each other for publication, invite each other to give readings and to teach at writer's workshops (Golding 70–110; Rasula 415–69). Novelists' works—potentially far more lucrative than poetry—tend to be promoted initially by publishers, then by critics who, as Barbara Herrnstein Smith explains, judge, review, interpret, rank-order, evaluate and reevaluate them. The critics' esteem has traditionally influenced professors, who then create a teaching canon by putting these authors on reading lists, teaching them in their courses, and including them in the literary anthologies they edit (42–53). However, while the teaching canon is but one way for fiction and poetry to become mainstream, it is the only venue for essays to become canonical in the twentieth and twenty-first century.

This has not always been the case. In the nineteenth century, the works of essayists such as Lamb, Ruskin, Carlyle, Mill, Arnold, Emerson, and Holmes arrived in the literary canon through the same cultural processes as novels and poetry—their admission enhanced by a reading public that would "purchase, preserve, display, quote, cite, translate, perform" imitate, and discuss them (see Smith 42–43). But for a variety of reasons (see McQuade; Connors; Bloom, "Essay Canon"; Bloom, "Once More"), in the twentieth century the essay became relegated to a school genre, its status reduced to that of the unreal, unreasonable "five-paragraph theme." At this turn of the millennium, despite the distinctive literary presence of essayistic critics such as Susan Sontag and William H. Gass, Americans have no tradition of buying single-authored collections of what they regard as *essays.* Sometimes such collections get reviewed, but except for the AWP and a few less prestigious creative nonfiction prizes, they are seldom the objects of promotion by other essayists, acknowledgment by critics, or extended treatment by biographers of the authors, such as Orwell (see Root). Thus although compilations of essays (on science, travel, sports, religion, food, and general subjects—sometimes regarded as *creative nonfiction*) are now being published, only the teaching canon ensures the endurance and widespread reading of essayists in our time. No matter where an essay first appeared—whether in the *New Yorker* or in a little magazine or on a newspaper's op-ed page, if it is to survive in the hearts and minds of the reading public, it must be reprinted time after time in a textbook reader, where it has the chance to reach a significant number of America's three million first-year college students. As Rasula observes: "Anthologies . . . are the steroids of canon-building" (481). Consequently, the authors of those essays that appear consistently in these readers become canonical.

To determine who were the canonical essayists, I decided to examine the most influential readers, reasoning that the most widely read authors would appear repeatedly in the most widely adopted collections—all books published in four or more editions over a fifty-year span, from the end of World War II to the present. These turned out to comprise fifty-eight titles published in 325 volumes, an 18.6% sample of the total number of readers published during this period, the most robust titles of the total number of 1,600-plus books that could be identified. A database of their complete tables of contents—21,000 items—includes some 4,300 essayists, the authors of the 9,000 titles reprinted. Of these, the works of only 175 authors have been reprinted more than 100 times, a scant 4% of the total number of authors but nearly half of the total reprints. These 175 authors—from Agee to Zinsser—are the canonical essayists. Note that because I'm using a sample approximating

20% of the total number of books available, the numbers in my published canon tables (Bloom,"Essay Canon" 426–28; Bloom, "Once More" 35) have to be multiplied by five to obtain a more exact estimate of the actual number of reprints. The figures I am citing here represent that multiplier.

All essays in a teaching canon, irrespective of authorial presence or voice, need to have the following characteristics that make them teachable. The essay needs to be *intellectually appropriate* for the course, in this case first-year composition (a.k.a. Freshman English). It has to fit the subject(s), level of difficulty, and orientation—social, political, philosophical—to reading and learning the course promotes, without being so immediately topical that it will quickly go out of date. It has to appeal to the teacher, for overt good reasons (is it intellectually challenging? aesthetically engaging?) and covert bad ones (can it stimulate a good discussion even if the teacher hasn't read it beforehand?). It has to be reasonably accessible to the students, with or without a lot of explanation in class.

In addition, a canonical essay must exemplify various *formal features.* It must either be short enough (usually under 5,000 words) to be discussed in one or two class periods or capable of being excerpted without undue violence to attain that length. A canonical essay should be well written, a good model of organization, style, and vocabulary as well as of one or more rhetorical modes, such as argument or description; the more versatile essays exemplify a multitude of rhetorical and stylistic techniques, as we have seen in the case of "Once More to the Lake." Additional influences on canonicity include the *author's reputation* (a plus) and the essay's *cost* (a potential minus to canonical status because every popular—and therefore pricey—author erodes an editor's royalties; unknown writers are much cheaper).

8

UPON THE PUBLIC STAGE

How Professionalization Shapes Accounts of Composing in the Academy

Cheryl Geisler

In the late-nineteenth century, concepts of public activity were reshaped by the emergence of the modern professions. Before the second half of the nineteenth century, the term *profession* was reserved almost exclusively for the three classic professions inherited from the Anglo-Saxon tradition and largely restricted to members of the upper class: law, medicine, and the clergy. By the end of the century, however, the rise of the modern professions had transformed this upper-class solidarity based on social ties into a middle-class solidarity based on ties of occupation (Collins).

As occupation-based alliances formed to protect professional privilege, professions became players on the public stage in two senses. First, professional associations assumed numerous roles, both formal and informal, in shaping the regulatory conditions under which their members worked (Freidson). Second, individual members of professions assumed the role of public representative of the profession itself, taking on the burden of public trust by virtue of professional training and oversight. The actions of individual professionals, for good or for ill, were no longer a strictly private matter but reflected, as a matter of public record, on the entire profession.

The professionalization process entailed not simply the emergence of a new set of privileged occupations but also a redefinition of individuals as *professionals* with lifelong "careers" (Larson). In the academy, this redefinition of the private self as public professional played itself out on the stage of publication. Through texts, individuals created the ethos of professional participation—invoking professional values, declaring their own allegiance, and "making a contribution to knowledge" that substantiated the profession's claim to privilege.

In this chapter, I explore the dynamics by which writers construct professionalized selves during composing in the academy. My basic question is "What story do participants construct in their accounts of composing?" In particular, how do they understand themselves and others as players on the public stage of the professions?

BACKGROUND

The link between literacy and professional identity has been well established by two decades of research on writing in the disciplines. Learning to write in school, for example, not only requires one to acquire specialized knowledge and vocabulary but also to rearrange one's sense of self and relationship to others (Berkenkotter, Huckin, and Ackerman; Haas; Prior). Writing in the professions also has consequences for identity and relationships (Bucciarelli; Susan Katz; Myers; Winsor). Perhaps as a result, the transition from one setting to the other is often fraught with confusion and conflict (Clark and Doheny-Farina; Geisler, Rogers, and Haller). Educational efforts to make the transition easier have had limited success (Dannels; Freedman, Adam, and Smart).

In the academy, identity issues are shaped by the great divide between expert and layperson (Geisler, *Academic*), a legacy of the professionalization movement, which sets the academic professional apart from and above the general public. Through long training, the academic professional is expected to transcend the common misunderstandings of the laity and to generate the specialized knowledge that enables other professions to work for society's improvement. The general public becomes both a source of misconception to be corrected and a market for those corrections. For external validation, the academic professional looks instead to the discipline.

In academic texts, the effects of professionalization are most obvious in the citation practices that began to emerge in the second half of the nineteenth century and still dominate academic writing today. In research article introductions, the "gap" opened up through a literature review (Swales and Najjar) often originates in a public misconception about the topic that the disciplinary community has been trying to redress through a program of research or scholarship. Citations to specific individuals are seldom to members of the general public but to members within the disciplinary community, and progress is defined as disciplinary progress.

THE STUDY

In this chapter, I extend work done previously with two individuals writing academic argument with different degrees of professionalization (Geisler, *Academic*; Penrose and Geisler): Janet, a college freshman who had not taken an introductory philosophy course, and Roger, a Ph.D. candidate nearing completion of his degree in philosophy. These two worked for over a month on a writing project that led to the construction of an original argument about the issue of paternalism in philosophical ethics.

Extensive analysis of the protocols these participants produced as they worked has been reported elsewhere (Geisler, *Academic*). From looking at these protocols, we know several things about Janet and Roger. First, they both completed their task by moving through the same set of activities: Reading, Reflecting, Outlining, Writing/Revising. Second, Roger was more specialized in what he was trying to accomplish within these activities than Janet appeared to be. He interacted with other authors' texts only in the early activities and did not refer to them later; he thought through just a few specific cases of paternalism, and he did this thinking almost exclusively during the activity of reflecting. Janet pursued things differently. She interacted with other authors' texts throughout her working time; she thought about many more and varied cases than Roger, and she did this thinking throughout her working time. These differences were suggestive of an increasing specialization in Roger's work, and they could with some logic be linked to Roger's greater participation in the profession of academic philosophy.

The protocol analysis alone has not, however, given us a firm grasp on the actual mechanism by which these participants were seeing—or not seeing—themselves as public figures in organizing their private efforts at composing. To pursue this issue, I have analyzed the interviews each participant gave following each working session—a total of ten for Roger and twenty-two for Janet. Since my focus was on accounts of past actions, sections of interviews were selected in which participants spoke about the work they had accomplished so far. By and large, these responses were in answer to one of the following questions (Geisler, *Academic* appendix C):

- At what point did you stop in your last session?
- Can you describe the process you went through?

- What problems did you encounter in your last session?
- Why did you stop your last session?

Using techniques for the analysis of verbal data (Geisler, *Analyzing*), I examined these accounts for differences in the ways in which Janet and Roger characterized public action and how this characterization played out as they moved through the composing process. The specific analytic procedures I used were as follows: I segmented the accounts into clauses, each with its own inflected verb. I selected from these clauses those with human agents. I eliminated from analysis any clauses that dealt with paternalistic situations ("the doctor interfered with the patient's rights"), with the situation of the interview or study ("I ran out of tape yesterday"), or with repetitive back-channel expressions ("you know?"). I then coded the remaining clauses as expression action in either the private or the public realm. If the clause was in the public domain, I looked at the agents of the actions and the actions themselves. Further descriptions of the coding procedures and their results can be found in the discussions that follow. All of the differences to be discussed were found significant using the Chi-square test for homogeneity (Geisler, *Analyzing*).

THE LAYERING OF PRIVATE AND PUBLIC

In their accounts of themselves and their work, both Janet and Roger tipped the balance of their accounts more to the private than to the public. Some of these private accounts were descriptions of managing the work process itself: "I *stopped* at the end of the section." Others were part of descriptions of literate actions: "I was just *reading* it / and *taking* . . . some *notes* / and *jotting notes down* next to the paragraphs . . . in the margins in the booklet / as I was *reading* it."And many of them were accounts of thinking itself: "what I *thought* to be important . . . / just what I want to *remember.*" Such private accounts attempted to give the interviewer access to the private cognition of the participants. Neither Janet nor Roger assumed we could infer these actions from the texts they had written; they needed to be explained.

On this base of private action, both Janet and Roger layered accounts of action in public. That is, they both attributed actions to themselves and others in ways that could be directly observable. A few of these actions took place in the world: "Jamie [a friend] and I *talked about* this at great length." Most of them took place in text: "Komrad [an author] *is talking about* a blanket justification." These public accounts of action in text attempted to give the interviewer an understanding of what the author of a text was doing, to characterize its accomplishment.

Although both Janet and Roger tipped the balance of their accounts to the private, the nature of this balance and the way it played out over the time of their work was significantly distinct according to a Chi-square analysis, where the sum of Chi-squares was 38.09 with 1 degree of freedom and significance at $p<.001$. To begin with, Roger's accounts drew nearly as often from the public realm (45%) as from the private realm (55%), whereas Janet's accounts were predominately private (72%). Figures 1 and 2 indicate how these different balances played out over time.

For Janet, accounts of public action spread in an even layer over a large base of private activity throughout the accounts that she told of her composing. For Roger, however, accounts of public action pile up in the middle period of his work, beginning at the close of reading and continuing in the period of reflection that preceded outlining or writing/revising.

PLAYERS ON THE PUBLIC STAGE

The Authorial "I"

For both Janet and Roger, the most common human agent in their accounts of public action was "I." This authorial "I" was one who spoke in text: "*I'd* just like say that in my introduction . . . say something about that . . ."; an "I" who discussed things: "*I* have already discussed . . . Ms. Carter's straight consent approach . . . actual consent approach . . ."; an "I" who engaged in critique: "*I* made three criticisms of her." In the public realm, then, this authorial "I" was the animator of the text, the agent who moved through it and, with it, accomplishing his or her purpose.

Others

The world of Janet and Roger's public accounts contained others, however. Not unexpectedly, a great many of these others were the authors they were reading: "*he* [Childress]'s the one with the simple-minded one [definition] . . . just crossing anybody's will about anything." Some were the friends they talked to about the project: "I started talking to this kid

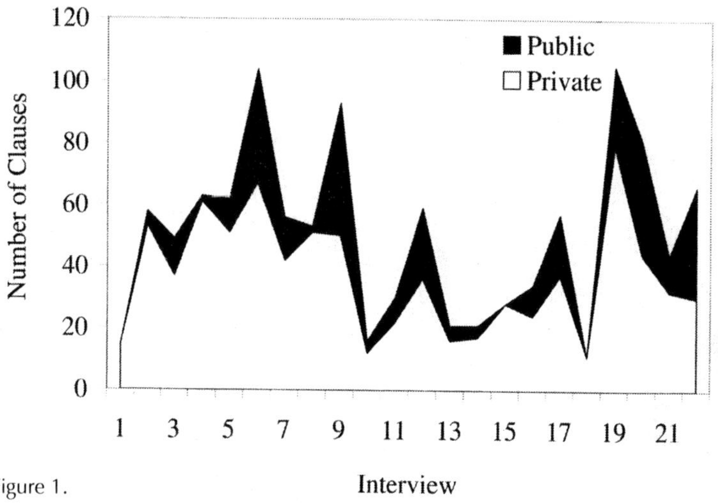

Figure 1.

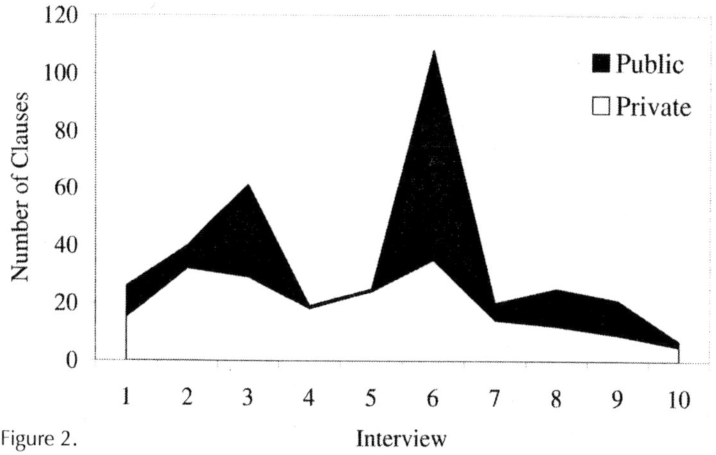

Figure 2.

/ I knew from my hometown / and *he* told me / on the side of his school work, *he*'s reading all these books on psychoanalysis and psychology."

Others were agents from the reference group they took as their base community. For Janet, these were agents in school such as her composition instructor: "Like one time, *he* asked us to write down / how much time we spent on a rough draft." For Roger, these disciplinary representatives included the "we" who reads: "*we* don't get the next move"; the "we" who deals with issues: "*we're* dealing with justification now / *we've* gotten out of the definition business"; and the "you" who considers cases: "but when *you* consider cases involving some blood transfusion . . . kidney transplants . . . and whatnot . . ." These other agents, the authors they were reading, the friends they were talking to, and the members of the communities that formed their reference groups, were the agents with whom they saw themselves interacting on the public stage.

The Dance of "I" and Others

In keeping with the general tendency of Janet to work in private, the majority of the actions she accounted for were her own even when she moved onto the public stage. This pattern was significantly different from Roger's pattern of agency, according to a Chi-square analysis, where the sum of Chi-squares was 52.73 with 3 degrees of freedom and significance at $p<.001$. Both Janet and Roger referred to the authors they were reading and the friends they were talking to with about the same relative frequency (28% and 8–9% respectively). For Janet, a small percentage of her remaining agents came from her school reference group (9%), while the majority was attributed to her authorial "I" (54%). For Roger, however, the use of the authorial "I" was much less common, replaced by the disciplinary "we" or "you" about one-third of the time, leaving the "I" with a bit less than one-third of the public agents (30%).

As the graph in figure 4 indicates, Roger's references to his disciplinary reference group played itself out over time in much the same way that his public accounts did in general. Most of them piled up in the period that closed his reading and continued through reflection. Other agents had more delimited appearances on the public stage. Friends came on stage early and then dropped out entirely. Authors were a presence through session 6, after which they nearly disappeared. The authorial "I" only played a major part from session 6 onward.

The dance of figures on the public stage was significantly different for Janet (see figure 3). Authors appeared throughout. The authorial "I" didn't appear until the middle sessions, making a second major appearance at the end. School and friends seem to have served in a complementary role: they came on stage when "I" was absent; they left the stage when "I" returned.

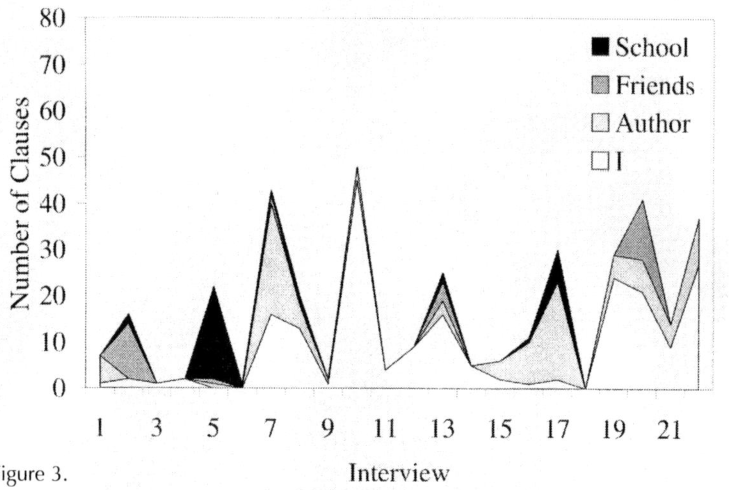

Figure 3.

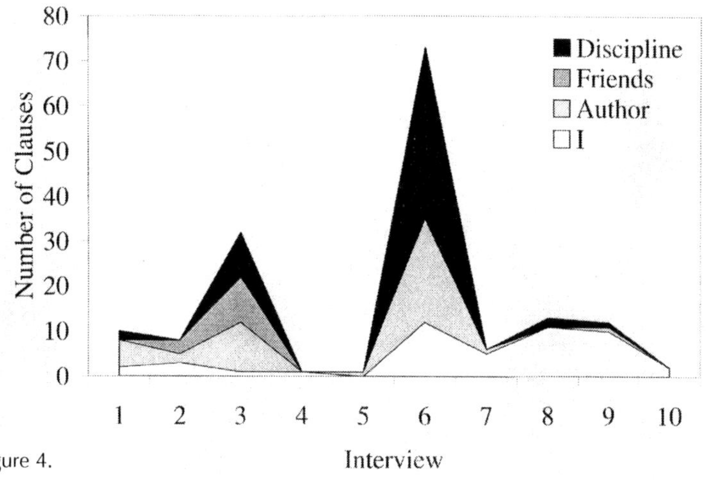

Figure 4.

ACTION ON THE PUBLIC STAGE

In their accounts, Janet and Roger portrayed significantly different kinds of actions on the public stage, according to a Chi-square analysis, where the sum of Chi-squares was 137.33 with 4 degrees of freedom and significance at $p<.001$. By and large, Janet concerned herself with what was "said" (54%) and how things were "orchestrated" (32%) and to a lesser extent with what was "claimed" (11%). Roger had a comparable level of interest in "orchestration" (26%) but significantly less interest in "saying" (11%) and more in "claiming" (48%). He was also interested in "considering" ideas (8%), an action in which Janet took no interest. [Note: some totals exceed 100% due to rounding.] In the following discussion, we look at each of these actions in turn. Complete definitions and examples can be found in the appendix.

Saying Things

Actions "to say" are foundational verbs of articulation. Some of them were literal: "Jamie and I *talked about* this at great length." But most were metaphorical, describing giving voice in text: "that I . . . I *said* was impurely paternalistic." "Say" was the preferred action for Janet who used it in more than half (54%) of her public accounts. Figure 5 suggests that she used it both to describe her own actions and the actions of the authors that she read, and that "saying" occurred in accounts throughout her sessions. Roger portrayed himself and authors as "saying" things a lot less often (11%). Figure 6 suggests that, for Roger, "saying" was a minor part of periods of generally high activity on the public stage.

Orchestration

Actions "to orchestrate" involved managing the arrangement of text. This often included actions of putting things in or leaving them out: "I *put* as my definition"; actions whereby ideas were elaborated: "somebody *was developing an account* in terms of rights"; actions by which the agent moved around in text: "maybe I should just *move on to* the next section"; actions that did something with an author: "I *did* Komrad . . . before I *got to* Childress"; and actions that did something with an example: "and then I tried to *give an example*." All of these actions of orchestration involved the text, concerned themselves with arrangement and elaboration, and set aside the issue of belief. Orchestration was a major concern of both Janet (32%) and Roger (26%), without significant difference between them in how they played out over time.

Making Claims

Actions "to claim" involved the public expression of belief. This included actions of believing: "I *disagree* strongly"; actions of argumentation: "and she does this by *wording her definition* in such a way as to involve some kind of interference with . . . the subject by the paternalist"; actions that lead to the accomplishment of work in text: "they . . . made something up"; and actions that provide elements of an argument: "so

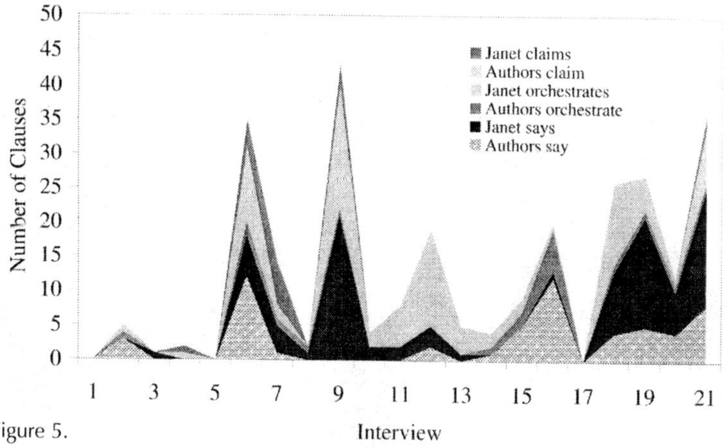

Figure 5.

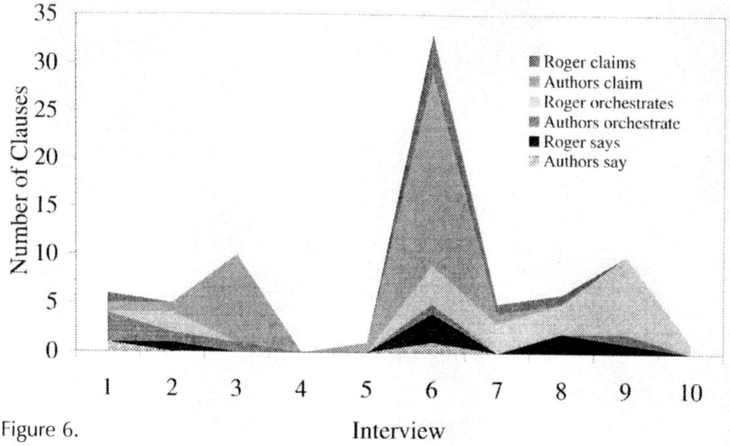

Figure 6.

you have to *provide* piecemeal *justification* of whatever." Verbs of "claiming" go beyond simply "saying" by implying the expression of belief in text; they are foundational to the activity of argumentation. "Claim" was the preferred mode of action for Roger, who used it nearly half of the time (48%) in his public accounts. Interestingly, for the most part, it is others rather than Roger who make claims, perhaps because he has associated most of the claims with which he would agree with disciplinary agents. By contrast, the relative frequency of "to claim" in Janet's work was low (11%). For Janet, claiming was not something that she or her authors did very often.

Discussion

Actions "to discuss" involved interacting with others: "and he was telling me / about a *debate* he *had.*" Unlike actions "to say" discussed below, actions of discussion imply the presence of other interlocutors. Surprisingly, discussion played a relatively minor role in the accounts of both Janet (4%) and Roger (7%). Neither one seemed to see others, particularly authors, as interlocutors with whom they interacted.

Consideration

Finally, actions "to consider" involve thinking publicly about an idea: "imagine a case." Verbs of consideration invite others into a process of thinking that otherwise would be done in private. "Consider" was not very common in Roger's accounts (8%), but was entirely absent from Janet's. Thus, it was only for Roger that verbs of cognition moved onto the public stage to be shared with others.

HOW PROFESSIONALIZATION SHAPES THE PUBLIC STAGE

What can we say about the public stage across which both Janet and Roger play out their accounts of composing? For Roger, the public stage emerged in the activity of reflection through which others (authors, friends, and the discipline) used the actions of argumentation ("to claim") and cognition ("consider") in the service of developing the position that Roger's authorial "I" emerged to claim as his own by the closing act. For Janet, early scenes on the public stage were dominated by the "saying" of others (authors, friends, and school); in the middle scenes, the authorial "I" began to "say" things for itself; and in the closing scenes, both "I" and others were on stage together, still "saying" for the grand finale.

Professionalization has shaped the accounts of both Janet and Roger, though from quite different perspectives. For Janet, the story of paternalism is a story told from the perspective of the layperson who attends to the public stage in order to hear what others have said about the topic and then orchestrate some of those things into a text for her own readers. For Roger, the story of paternalism is told from the perspective of the expert who projects a series of claims onto the voices of the discipline in an effort to create a position for himself.

While it might be tempting to see Roger's accounts of composing simply as a contrast to Janet's, we can also understand them as developmental in several ways. To begin with, it's important to note what they have in common. Both base their accounts on a solid layer of private work. Both interact with authors, friends, and their particular reference group. Both concern themselves with the orchestration of text and somewhat less with discussion with others.

Furthermore, the differences between them, though striking, are not surprising. Roger's disciplinary reference group can be understood as an extension of the school-based reference group that Janet used, though its role has grown tremendously. His authorial "I", rather than simply disappearing, seems to have been transformed into a disciplinary "we" that has now taken over much of its work. His "claiming" can also be understood as an extension of Janet's weaker "to say"; in fact, the relative frequency of "say" declines in Roger's work (54% to 11%) in direct proportion to his increase in the use of "claim" (11% to 48%). And finally, his use of actions "to consider" is not wholly without precedent in Janet's work; what may have happened is that cognitive actions moved out of the private realm where they are found for Janet and onto Roger's public stage. The accounts that Janet and Roger offered thus show them to represent, at the same time, two sides of the great divide that separates the laity and the public and two ends of a developmental spectrum through which academic expertise develops out of school literacy.

It is important to recognize, however, that the sense of "public" for Janet and Roger is much reduced compared to the visions of public that shaped the oratorical tradition before professionalization (Clark and Halloran). Janet's public is a public trained to listen to what the experts "say," not to think about it. Roger's public is his discipline, which, through the give-and-take of argumentation, develops the knowledge that the Janets of the world are waiting to hear; they do not expect to hear from her.

It might be tempting to consider Janet as a representative of an alternative way of knowing (Belenky et al.), one who, under an epistemological stance often more frequently associated with women, seeks to build community and extend knowledge, rather than "do battle" in argumentation. In academic philosophy, the division between professional and layperson is fraught with issues of gender. Men dominate the field and the gender bias in the kind of ethical thinking with which Janet and Roger were dealing has been questioned by feminist philosophers (Noddings). Janet's epistemology does not, however, so much represent an alternative to Roger's as its complement. That is, Janet's stance is dependent upon the Rogers of the world; she cedes knowledge-making power to the players on the public stage while she is content to remain in the audience. Thus, if Janet's way of knowing has been shaped by gender, it has not yet been transformed by it—at least, in some of the ways called for by feminist critics.

In fact, much has been written in critique of the model of professional expertise that we have seen underlying these accounts of composing. Many concerned with the public sphere have decried the impoverishment of the public forum and its replacement with disciplinary expertise (Bender; Farrell; Phillips). Many in the academy have renounced the foundationalist assumptions shoring up disciplinary claims to expertise (Bauman) and have begun to explore alternative relationships to the public and to members of other disciplines. What this analysis has suggested is the ways in which professionalization has shaped the very language with which we account for our work, the daily stories we and our students tell of our progress in the academy, the stories through which we shape our identities. What will be interesting in the coming years is to see is how such programs of reform reshape our language, the identities that underlie it, and the scope of academic action on the public stage.

APPENDIX

VERBAL CATEGORIES AND DEFINITIONS

Category	*Definition*	*Verbs found in interviews*
Say	To say or give voice to	Articulate, mention, remark, say, talk, talk about, tell
Orchestrate	To orchestrate or manage the arrangement of ideas, including	
	To include	Bring in, drop, get in, have that, include, incorporate, leave out, limit, put, put in, shove, spend, stick in, take in, take out, throw in, throw out, use, write in
	To elaborate	Call attention to, deal with, describe, develop account, emphasize, expand, explain, give feeling, go into depth, list, make variations, relate, repeat, skim, skip, stick to, summarize
	To move	Come, finish, get out of, get to, go along, go back, go from, go on, go through, move into, move on, move toward, pass on, start, step back
	To use an author	Be imbedded in, do author, quote, use author
	To use example	Bring up examples, give example, have examples, make case work, make use of example, use
Claim	To claim or express an opinion or develop an argument, including	
	To believe publicly	Agree, be against, believe, be with, disagree, justify, regard as, subscribe to, suppose, take, think
	To claim	Argue, call, claim, come up with, define, give definition, have as, have point, make criticism, make statement, make up, point out, show, take a stand, waive, word definition, write
	To accomplish	Cook definition, do, do something, have flaw, make much of, make plausible, move toward definition, prime to do

	To provide an argument	Accommodate belief, appeal, apply defense, give definition, need justification, offer definitions, provide, provide justification, supply definition, supply justification, take definition, want argument
Discuss	To discuss or interact with others	Address critic, ask, discuss, have a conversation, have a debate, have discussion, love to hear
Consider	To think about publicly	Allude to, consider, do with, find features, get move, imagine, look for definition, make of it, parse

9

ETHICAL DELIBERATION AND TRUST IN DIVERSE-GROUP COLLABORATION

Geoffrey A. Cross

Public interaction can expose private beliefs. In deliberating a public policy, discussants may have to reveal personal values or privately held information. This disclosure can make them vulnerable because some people in positions of authority are not trustworthy recipients of sensitive information and may punish dissensus. How does one determine when to reveal personal values or proprietary information in public settings? The answer to this question has important implications for solving problems—particularly ethical problems—when writing and speaking in collaborative groups. For instance, if group members are reluctant to reveal differing private values, how can they work publicly to resolve an ethical dilemma?

The question of when to reveal private beliefs in public settings is of particular relevance today. Survey researchers report that while ethics indicators are improving and a majority of employees are positive about ethical standards in their organizations, one out of three American workers in 1999–2000 observed behaviors that violated either the law or their organizations' ethical standards. One-third of the survey respondents also said that if they reported their observations, they would be treated as "troublemakers by management or snitches by their coworkers" (Daigneqult). Although managers play a significant role in setting the norms of ethical behavior by example (Pettit, Vaught, and Pulley), flattened organizational hierarchies have distributed more responsibility for ethical policies across individuals and teams (Sanders, "Technical" 111). More companies today have developed ethical standards than in 1994 (Daigneqult), yet an examination of forty codes of companies recruiting at Cornell University revealed that such written codes provide little guidance to employees regarding potential ethical dilemmas (Stevens 79). This finding is consistent with those reported in three other studies conducted within the last twenty-five years (White and

Montgomery; Cressey and Moore; Matthews); researchers here found that written ethical codes are focused upon legalities and profits rather than "community, personal character issues, or values" (Stevens 79).

In collaborative writing groups, different people are brought to teams chiefly to share their different viewpoints and resources. With such diversity, conflict is nearly inevitable. As Clark notes, we need to value differences so that groups can cooperate as equals—"competing viewpoints must be recognized and attended to" (Clark, "Professional Ethics" 38, cited in Sanders 111). Although everyone may not get his or her way in the end, research suggests that groups that engage in substantive conflict (conflict over ideas) are more productive than groups that try to smooth over differences (Burnett; Karis; Putnam). Yet "affective conflict," conflict involving personal or emotional issues, has been found to be disruptive to the group's goal (Cross, *Collaboration*; Falk; Guetzkow and Gyr). Private conviction with its accompanying emotions, however, cannot always be neatly separated from public action.

Habermas has advanced an approach to ethics that addresses the problem of stakeholders with diverse values in public deliberation (McCarthy, *Critical*). Instead of relying upon principles that are not universally acknowledged, this approach requires that the group provisionally arrive at a governing set of common interests and rationally settle moral issues by using a method of argumentation and analysis of argument that is closely related to Toulmin's.

The goal of this approach is agreement that the group outcome has been arrived at fairly. To enter into ethical dialogue, participants must adhere to several ground rules. Group members must hold the premise that the best argument will prevail, even though this triumph of reason may not occur. Members must start with this assumption or their search for the best solution is invalidated. To achieve consensual action, participants also have to assume that the other group members know what they are doing and why, that their beliefs and goals are intentional, and that they can support them with reasons if necessary. Group members must assume this even though it often may not be true. Another prerequisite is that discussants choose language that will allow them to discuss the subject precisely and as much as possible without biases such as sexism or ethnic prejudice. Such language is crucial to ethical deliberation, as Rentz and Debs have noted.

Having established the necessary attitude of participants toward the dialogue and toward each other, group members must next consider the nature of the statements in the arguments. For a statement to be valid, it must meet the following standards:

1. The statement must be comprehensible.
2. The statement must have true content.
3. The speaker must express his or her intentions truthfully.
4. The utterance must be right in the light of the existing norms of the group.

Norms are "binding reciprocal expectations of behavior" (McCarthy, *Critical* 313). An easy way to capture the function of norms in arguments is to see them as "warrants," as proposed in Toulmin's argumentative scheme. Norms are backed, in Toulmin's sense of "backing," by their essential role in satisfying generally accepted needs that are related to the issue at hand. So for all collaborators there is "something in it for them" in adhering to the norms. An example of a norm might be the ground rule "silence means dissent." If one agrees with the point at issue, one says why. If not, one reveals one's position. The ostensible advantage for all here is that competing viewpoints are expressed.

Of course, to set up these norms for group participation so that following them becomes mutually beneficial, people must be capable in the situation of "nondeceptive recognition of common needs and interests in the light of adequate knowledge of existing and effectible conditions, likely consequences, and so forth" (McCarthy, *Critical* 315). Habermas asserts that we need the condition of the "ideal speech act" for his method to work—that is, unlimited discussion that is free from open domination, strategic competition, and/or communication problems caused by self deception (McCarthy, *Critical* 306). Therein lies a part of the rub: to speak the truth in dialogue and reveal our true intentions we make ourselves vulnerable. How forthright can people be when responding to authority? Results of the survey cited earlier suggest that a significant number of actions in the workplace are unethical and/or illegal. If superiors and/or peers abuse their positions of authority and mistrust is logical, then taking the rational approach to a "consensus ethics" outlined earlier is not wise.

Consensus and logic per se are not enough to assure ethical outcomes in deliberation. A problem with Habermas's reliance upon logic, pointed out by Couture (190), is that in an extreme case a circumscribed, pragmatic logic may override ethics, as Steven Katz has shown in his evaluation of the rhetoric of a technical document recommending the improvement of portable gas chambers during the Holocaust. The recommendations in the document, if followed, would make the gas chambers more efficient, but here logic and efficiency only advance the monstrous. Another factor supporting the Holocaust was consensual judgment—what Popper called "juridical positivism"—or mistaking norms for facts (*Open Society*, 4th ed. 71). Just because a group of people find something is acceptable or "true" does not make it so: the Nazis' holocaust, egregiously wrong, was accepted by many. With this example in mind, we must be careful about accepting any group's consensus as "truth." Yet, we must also be aware that a diverse group, that is, one with divergent and conflicting values, may still assess something truly. Most countries and their inhabitants agree that there are crimes against humanity that can be identified; thus, there are underlying values of right and wrong that we all share at some level that may be ignored or voted out but not erased. A diverse group of individuals may be able to speak their minds and illuminate the subject in full relief because of their multiple perspectives. Group diversity can, in fact, be insurance against the juridical positivistic groupthink that destroyed both the Nazis and their divergent victims.

So aside from avoiding obvious breaches in ethics, an organization should not demand agreement but instead thrive on constructive dissensus, productive "collaborative fighting" (Cross, *Collaboration* 133). But for conflict to produce more than a pugilistic catharsis, for it to achieve mutual understanding depends, as Habermas notes, upon "a capacity for learning, both at the cultural and political level" (*Between Facts*, 324). Sometimes a cross-functional group includes members of such different departmental/disciplinary cultures that members find it difficult to create a common mental model and translations are needed before deliberation can be productive (Cross, *Forming*). More important than translation across divergent groups is the political climate established for collaboration: people have to trust the organization they are in sufficiently that they do not fear losing face when speaking out and learning from one another. In short, the organization where they work must be in touch with core values of humanity.

The conditions for trust that I have described are straightforward, but they are not always apparent in real situations: what does one do when it is unclear whether we should extend trust or not? Let's consider a hypothetical "real-world" situation. People are working on a business plan in a company that has recently acquired another company. The finance professionals in the acquired company are reluctant to collaborate on the plan—to share their techniques and knowledge of operations with the finance people in the parent company—because they fear that they will become expendable once their knowledge is no longer theirs only. Not only are they reluctant to work on an intercompany business plan, they also are thinking about getting their former president (now a vice president of the parent corporation) to lobby against this plan, employing the rationale that the parent company doesn't need to micromanage them. In working together on the intercompany plan, should they try to come up with a common set of ground rules, perhaps considering rules such as "what we say won't be used to replace us?"

The outcome is quite uncertain: on the one hand, perhaps the acquiring company will indeed fire the acquired financial professionals, but on the other hand, perhaps they will bring them into the company more substantially, promote them, otherwise empower them, and financially reward them. Should the acquired employees trust the acquirers enough to reveal intentions? Or even enough to reveal their distrust by recommending ground rules that prohibit knowledge transfer leading to the firing of those who shared their knowledge? Is Habermas's approach applicable here? The essential problem that this example illustrates is that trust is needed for collaboration to work, but it is not always clear to individuals whether they can safely extend trust. To help solve such dilemmas, we first need to define what is meant by *trust.*

Baier observes that trust is a cooperative activity in which we assist one another in the care of goods or, I would add, people for whom we are responsible. To be specific, allowing someone else to take care of our goods (or people for whom we are responsible) is trust. Because we cannot alone take care of everything valuable to us, we all must trust or rely upon others to some extent. As Baier notes, trust changes the power relations between people, causing the truster to depend upon the trustee, risking disappointment, betrayal and/or harm to self. A good deal of responsibility is thus given to the trustee, who may or may not accept this responsibility, explicitly by refusing the role requested, or tacitly by accepting the role but not fulfilling the responsibilities. Problems with trust often result from power imbalances, imbalances that occur in many of our personal and professional relationships. Power imbalances in the workplace become amplified for those people who trust authority too readily, adding the vulnerability of trust to the vulnerability of the subordinate position. Those in positions of power must guard against unintentionally taking advantage of trusting subordinates, as Potter notes (unpublished manuscript).

It is not surprising, as H. J. N. Horsburgh has identified, that, on the one hand, full trust can be extended to one person just for a particular situation, and, on the other hand, extended to another person absolutely (353). In many situations what occurs is not trust but reliance: we are uncertain what the person will do but trust them to some degree anyway (Potter).

When should we *not* entrust someone else with our intentions and needs or accept their trust? As Baier notes, it is when people have motives and loyalties that conflict fiercely with ours. These conflicting motives and loyalties may be the result of conflicting organizational goals, or they may reflect individual priorities. For example, Maccoby has identified "jungle fighters" as workers who in their lust for empires not only always try to best their competition but also eliminate them from the organization. Because of the possibility of untrustworthy acquisitors—to come back to our workplace example—the acquired company may want to probe the acquiring company to find out its leadership's motives. Logic suggests that we also probably should not extend trust to people who have betrayed trust in the past, even though they do not have conflicting motives, loyalties, or ethical codes. A company can adopt very impressive ethical codes, but they will not be engaged if employees do not have integrity, that is, the moral will to act on these ethical principles. In the case of the employees in our example, the acquired employees should scrutinize the acquiring individual employees' track records in dealings with others. Such scrutiny may reveal whether they can be predicted to act with integrity.

When the institution of which any group is part is corrupt, it would be unwise to extend its representatives full trust. Aristotle asserted that we are by nature political, and how good we are is determined by how good our institutions are. I would think that Thoreau, Gandhi, and King would disagree to an extent, but institutions clearly influence people's behavior, as is indicated by even these nonconformists' attacks on institutions. To apply this principle to our example, the acquired finance employees should go beyond scrutinizing the ethical behavior of a few individuals and check out the acquiring institution's track record in dealings with the acquired company and with others.

Habermas points out that in cases where we cannot extend trust, typically we choose to break off communication, resort to force, or engage in strategic competition (perhaps less euphemistically known as "bureaucratic infighting") (McCarthy, *Critical* 289). Thus, it is not surprising, as Potter tells us, that chronic distrust can be demoralizing, divisive, and contagious in organizations. When groups with diverse identities, values, and goals interface in a company, distrust may dominate, undermining cooperation, self-respect, and moral action. Widespread distrust is a major problem because, as was pointed out before, trusting some people is necessary since we cannot care for all that we are responsible for all the time.

Having noted now when distrust is appropriate, when is it most favorable to extend trust? I propose these conditions:

1. When the trustee cares about what I care about—shared norms are already operative.
2. When the trustee loves us (perhaps not *always* the case in every workplace).
3. When the trustee places a high priority on being trustworthy.
4. When the trustee's past actions have indicated trustworthiness.
5. When the trustee has a genuine interest in others' successes.

While these conditions for trustworthiness are fairly clear, often we do not know people well enough to tell if they will or can meet them, so we begin with some reliance and take baby steps toward full trust. This approach exemplifies what Wiggins calls the temporal aspect of trust: trust is often a quality and a process that develops over time. Trust resembles induction; the degree of trust develops as data accrues to the one considering extending trust.

How may we agree and get anything done in an American society of increasing diversity? Rather than try to overtly engage universal principles that all members may not acknowledge, collaborators can try to agree upon Habermassian operating rules that provide ethical direction. But individuals need to determine if the atmosphere is appropriate for this kind of rational consensus building—by gathering information about the motives, loyalties, values, and integrity of both the potential collaborators and the sponsoring institution or institutions. When we cannot tell whether to extend trust to reveal private values or privileged information in public, it may be prudent to extend trust gradually. For instance, in our example, employees in the acquired company might choose to work on only a part of the business plan with the acquiring company. If trust is not merited, individuals should, it would seem, use other strategies to defend themselves.

Rather than taking baby steps in every unsure situation and frequently lapsing into unconditional bureaucratic warfare resulting from poor communication and trigger-happiness, there is probably also a time for leading by extending trust and fully discussing ethical problems. As Potter notes, if we value responsibility and responsiveness to others, we need to—within our abilities—encourage moral actions in ourselves and others to enlarge the sphere of the moral. Because being trustworthy is a praiseworthy quality, being trusted can build a group member's self-image and trustworthiness. Knowing that one is being trusted can increase one's desire to be trustworthy (Potter).

If one wishes to achieve a moral world, one may need in some cases to "act as if" it existed, leading by example, acting in good faith even in some cases with people whose trustworthiness is questionable. To paraphrase Antoine de Saint Exupery, one cannot just be a dweller in a moral community; one must be a contributor too. To Saint Exupery, this contribution allows one to understand others: "I can be bound to no men except to whom I give. I can understand no men except those to whom I am bound" (120).

As Ruskin and Saint Exupery have noted, the devotion to a moral humanity and sacrifice of a diverse group of people has given the great cathedrals of Europe their idiosyncratic majesty. These triumphs of group effort were produced by the community's entrusting labor, goods, visions, and lives. A common trust drives successful collaboration, even more than the remuneration for achieving the group goal because, to paraphrase an adage, when you are up to your belt in bureaucratic alligators, it's hard to remember your purpose was to drain the swamp. Destructive infighting keeps groups from achieving their goals. Through a rational extension of trust where warranted and through risking trust in some situations where a positive outcome is less sure, the collaborative group has a chance to deal with ethical issues and otherwise flourish. Without a common understanding/trust, group diversity becomes a multidimensional barrier. Diversity without underlying trust is an empty surrealism: a surrealism without the unifying power of the subconscious.

The appeal to our sense of virtue or ethos, as Aristotle said, may be the most persuasive appeal of all. To motivate group members to achieve the synergy possible through a common understanding, we must at times risk going beyond the Habermassian rational—the logos of collaboration—into the ethos—the spirit—of collaboration. Enacting trust in these situations risks the private for the improvement of both the private and public, which in the end are but two sides of the same life.

PART THREE

Public and Private Identities in Popular and Mass Communication

10

IDENTITY AND THE INTERNET

The Telling Case of Amazon.com's Top Fifty Reviewers

Douglas Hesse

Shortly after the publication of his memoir *A Heartbreaking Work of Staggering Genius,* Dave Eggers announced a contest whose rules were simple: 1) post a review of the book on the Amazon.com Web site that 2) awards the book five stars (the top rating) and 3) bears no resemblance to the book itself ("McSweeney's"). Within a week the Amazon site for *A Heartbreaking Work* featured several cleverly wrought evaluations of how the book treated strategies for hanging sheetrock, the Netherlands/Bhutan trade imbalance, or the relative merits of crotchet versus spot welding, all of them headed with five stars. Clearly not appreciating the spirit of the contest, the Amazon.com Webmasters took down the whole lot shortly thereafter, and the 400-some reviews that accumulated by the fall of 2001 had little of the whimsy and decidedly fewer top ratings.

In devising the contest, Eggers parodied several conventions: the socially acceptable ways for authors to promote their own books, the genre of book review, the reviewer's stance and function, book-rating systems, the Amazon.com reviewing/marketing nexus, and the status of Web communication itself. Like all good parodies, this one unveils interesting questions about its subject, and I pursue a few of them in this chapter. The published review has historically been reserved for scholars or otherwise sanctioned (and usually remunerated) reviewers. What constitutes the reviewing impulse and, by direct extension, the impulse to write, especially when neither money nor career is at stake? If it's partly an impulse for self-expression/creation in a public forum, how is identity manifested in the reviewing space? What role does the medium itself play? And how does this clarify broader questions of "the personal" in writing whose direct subject is not the experience of the writers themselves?

Before considering those questions, let me review some facts. As most readers will know, Amazon.com invites site visitors to review products sold there, not only books, videos, and music but also items ranging from scanners to chain saws. Following a description of the product and, regularly, an "Editorial Review" written by Amazon.com or taken from publications or the publishers/manufacturers themselves, reader reviews appear. Each begins with a rating from one star to five, provides a bit of information about the reviewer (with a link to more information), and then offers comments ranging from a short blurb to several hundred words. Readers are prompted to "Write an online review" via a link that compels them formally to log in to Amazon.com's site; one does not review without providing credit card information, among other things.

But having the reviews written, posted, and entered into calculations (one learns the average reviewer rating for each product) is scarcely the end of it, for Amazon.com compiles statistics for each reviewer and, in fact, ranks them. For several months in 2001, the top reviewer was Harriet Klausner, a retired acquisitions librarian from Pennsylvania, married, with a twenty-one-year-old son. Ms. Klausner, who has four cats and two dogs (a cairn and a pom), had written 2,768 reviews for Amazon.com by Thanksgiving. That was 1,011 more than the number two reviewer, Donald Wayne Mitchell, an "organizational process improvement and strategy consultant" who is, among other things, heading a "noncommercial project to make it possible for everyone in the world to make progress at 20 times the normal rate." We know these things about Ms. Klausner and Mr. Mitchell because they (like thousands of other reviewers) tell us, in personal profiles that are linked through their reviews or, more conveniently, through a "Top Reviewers" page that Amazon.com maintains. Given their transitory nature, Web pages are notoriously problematic citations. The Amazon.com "Top Reviewers" pages are triply so. By definition, they change. A reviewer with a certain rating one month may have a different one the next. Further, reviewers are permitted to modify at any time the information they provide through the personal profiles. Finally, new reviews for individual products continually are written, and at least occasionally, Amazon expunges submissions. In writing this chapter, I selected several reviewers and reviews for analysis in early October of 2001. On November 17, 2001, I revisited those pages on the Amazon.com Web site and printed a few hundred screens' worth, including at least three pages from each of the reviewers mentioned in the chapter. (Researchers or other readers who need to consult these pages and who find that they have changed on the Web may contact me for copies of archived materials. For more information on the reviewing process, see "Reviewers FAQ." <http://www.amazon.com/exec/obidos/subst/community/reviewers-faq.html>.) In addition to including a personal statement, the reviewer's "About Me" space reprints several of his or her reviews, notes the "featured review categories" in which they work (Ms. Klausner reviews in over fifty categories), and lists the reviewer's "favorite people," which in this case rather means "virtual favorites": other Amazon.com reviewers. More on them later.

My point is that Amazon.com has developed an elaborate technology for keeping track of thousands of writers and hundreds of thousands of reviews, and it is worth considering what this technology represents, both for the company and for at least some writers who are clearly motivated to compete in the system. A badge icon appears alongside each piece by the Top Reviewers, indicating their status as in the Top 1,000, Top 500, Top 100, Top 50, Top 10, or #1. Reviewers' motivations are undoubtedly diverse, from writing as a hobby, to writing as an ego exercise, to writing as a way to influence, however subtly, American material and intellectual culture. Amazon.com's motivations for including reviews are undoubtedly diverse, too, from providing helpful advice, to creating an additional marketing mechanism (and also a data source for market research), to keeping people longer on the Web site, to highlighting the "Internetness" of online shopping by importing features reminiscent of chat rooms and Listservs. But just as the free territories of the Web promised in the early 1990s have been colonized, claimed, and regulated, so has Amazon.com's review space. Whatever other incentives exist for rating reviews, the practice creates a corporate ethos of being helpful and adding value, supplementing the words themselves with one measure of the reputations of their authors. The whole system of blurbs and ratings mimics, after a fashion, the academic publishing system.

The ratings are generated through both quantity and quality measures. Site browsers vote whether a published review was helpful, and the more helpful votes, the higher the reviewer rating. At work, then, is a crude form of peer review. But it is a numbers game, too. Obviously, the more items that one reviews, the more readers are likely to see and be

TABLE 1. AMAZON.COM REVIEWERS CONSIDERED FOR THIS ESSAY

Rank	*Reviewer Name*	*Number of Reviews*	*Information from personal profile.*
1	Harriet Klausner	2780	Former acquisitions librarian and current pet owner.
2	Donald Wayne Mitchell	1757	Organizational consultant and business book author.
3	Frank Behrens	476	Retired junior high teacher.
4	Michael Woznicki	542	Technical instructor and reviewer of electronics.
5	Lawrance M. Bernabo	2008	"Irony is the master trope of the universe." (His entire submitted personal information.)
6	Angel Lee	360	Recently started a rubber stamp company in Cleveland.
7	Barron Laycock (Labradorman)	481	Admires Francis McInerny (see #10) and disdains other reviewers' numbers games.
8	Robert Morris	477	Business consultant who creates content for many websites.
9	Rebecca@Seasoned with Love.com	792	Personality type is INFJ; working on a cook book.
10	Francis J. McInerney	515	Has stopped posting; encourages Laycock (see #7) to keep writing.
11	Rebecca	584	Sixteen years old and likes fantasy, science fiction, and horror.
12	Petersmaclean	486	Holds diplomas in business management, and wishes all could live in harmony, free of abuse.

able to vote on them. By the same token, if one reviews relatively fewer popular items, the latest Harry Potter book, for example, one will be exposed to a broader readership than if one reviews relatively more but less popular items, such as the latest Oxford University Press book. (However, just to complicate this further, a Harry Potter review is easily lost among hundreds and may go unread and unvoted—unless, of course, it is flagged by a top reviewer badge that makes it stand out.)

This complex reviewing apparatus suggests a number of interesting analyses. Selecting a corpus for closer study, I chose, first, the top twelve reviewers on Amazon.com's list, next the ten reviewers from the top fifty who wrote the fewest reviews, and finally the remaining five reviewers who wrote the most but are not among the top ten. I selected people

Fewest reviews in Top 50

26	Turgay Bugdacigil	133	Turkish-based human resources manager. Reviews only five star business books.
27	Doug Vaughn	234	I program computers for profit because they afford no ambiguity. I read books for pleasure because they do.
32	Marc Ruby	219	A pleasantly rounded, somewhat middle-aged member of the male subset.
36	maniacmedia	182	Actor and graphic artist.
37	Alex Leslie	221	Reviews tools and books. Graduate of Peekskill High. Former pilot.
38	Toolpig	180	Reviews tools and hardware. Carpenter and father of two.
40	Laura Haggarty	229	Likes most things often labeled new age.
43	Nick Gonnella	231	Account manager in the publishing industry.
43	Friendly Spirit	163	Quaker, Mother, Booklover.
45	G. Merritt	205	Provides no personal information.

Others with > 800 reviews

28	Jason	849	Grew up listening to 70's and 80's rock and still likes it best.
31	Thomas Magnum	1094	Provides no personal information.
39	Maximillian Muhammad	3187	Lists several hundred favorite musicians.
47	Brian D. Rubendall	892	Average Joe type who loves any book that tells a great story.
50	Bernard Chandler	949	Helps by putting ISBN numbers in his reviews.

who wrote the fewest reviews because they necessarily had a high percentage of their works deemed "helpful." I selected those who wrote the most reviews because a comparatively low percentage of their writings were judged worthy or they were so obscure as to go unread. Table 1 presents an overview of the group.

HOW REVIEWERS TALK ABOUT THEMSELVES

Amazon.com's "About Me" space allows reviewers to introduce themselves directly to readers. One might expect autobiographical information, but practices in the list range from reviewers who provide no information at all, to those who have only disembodied slogans ("Irony is the master trope of the universe," from #5 Bernabo), to those who present what amounts to a résumé (sometimes even in the third person, as with #26 Bugdacigil), to those who share personal details at levels beyond Christmas letters (#38 Toolpig, whose daughter Missy loves butterflies).

There are three basic topics in the personal profiles: occupation, personal life, and reviewing itself. Some writers cover all, others only one. Reviewers appear most likely to dwell on their work when it has some connection to the kind of reviewing they do. Mitchell (#2), Morris (#8), and Bugdacigil (#26), for example, write extensively about business-related books, and they themselves work as managers and consultants. For them and others (such as Lee, #6), reviewing constitutes nearly a form of marketing, of generating whatever name recognition accrues to this kind of visibility on Amazon.com. When reviewers choose to include information about their occupations—and about half of this group did—they tend to put it first, which is hardly surprising given Americans' general tendencies to introduce themselves in casual conversations by asking or telling "what they do," meaning how they earn a living.

Most reviewers include some discussion of reviewing itself, and this topic subdivides into three areas. First is "why I review," and the customary answer is to help others. Some confess reviewing because they enjoy writing, but apparently this reason comes across as egocentric; it is more palatable to avow liking books or reading, the implication being that you can best serve by writing about them. To claim an interest in writing per se counters the site's ostensible service to reading. The second subtopic of reviewing deals with "how I review." Several writers talk about the kinds of products they treat. A few explain either why their ratings are consistently high or low (Vaughn #27, for example, says he usually doesn't finish and therefore review books that are bad), and fewer still describe their processes (as in Chandler's [#50] explaining that he includes the ISBN numbers in his reviews so people can find the books more easily). The last subtopic is a kind of metadiscourse on reviewing itself, often with references to Amazon.com and to reviewing practices there, especially ones deemed suspect.

The most interesting example of this last is an exchange between Laycock (#7) and McInerney (#10). Laycock writes, "It is with great sadness that I read about Francis' [McInerney] decision to no longer post reviews" and cites his own dismay that quality plays no role in reviewer ratings and his contempt for "one paragraph throwaway reviews of obscure DVD and VHS releases" that can thrust a reviewer into the top ten. McInerney responds: "Barron, I have taken this long to reply as your thoughts caught me unprepared. Your words mean a great deal, and I thank you." He then goes on to comment on the proliferation of reviews. Beyond the "there-goes-the-neighborhood" nostalgia evocative of, say, Stanley Fish fretting about the demise of *PMLA*, and beyond the direct evidence that at least some Top Reviewers keenly follow their status, what is striking here is the use of the "Personal Profile" space for direct exchanges; after all, this is not a Listserv or a chat room.

While most reviewers do not directly converse with each other, many do intimately address their readers. Rebecca@seasonedwithlove.com (nickname: "cookingrl," #9) starts her profile with an epigram, the first eight lines of Shakespeare's Sonnet 116 ("Let me not to the marriage of true minds/Admit impediments"), which she attributes to *Brush Up Your Shakespeare.* She tells us that she lives in Washington, is thinking about adopting a kitten, loves castles and towers, has published two recipes, and has an INFJ personality type. This mode enters her reviews, too. In comments on J. Budziszewki's *The Revenge of Conscience* (a review that five of six people found helpful), she describes the author as "someone who became almost an angel to me."

Another Rebecca (nickname: "rebby," #11) is less effusive, both in her profile and her nearly six hundred entries. Sixteen years old and homeschooled, she lists among her favorite series *Dear America* and *Star Wars: The New Jedi Order*, and her reviews scatter through fantasy, horror, science fiction, and historical fiction. Her persona is considerably more guarded than Rebecca@seasonedwithlove.com's, or to put it another way, more closely matching traditional conventions of the review, down to the reviewer's bio.

Even more guarded, though at the opposite end of the self-disclosure spectrum, is Marc Ruby (nickname: marcruby, #32). If, in Walker Gibson's taxonomy, Rebecca is a "tough" speaker and Rebecca@seasonedwithlove.com a "sweet" one, then Ruby is a "stuffy" one. His profile begins: "I am a pleasantly rounded, somewhat middle-aged member of the male subset of the human species. Normally even tempered, I am subject to pique when I find someone who doesn't like my reviews (or who doesn't appreciate how nice it is to have someone around who is right all the time)." His reviews have a similarly überpolished style that closely matches published conventions. (Consider: "Jim Butcher has clearly created one of the strangest wizards in detective fiction. Actually he is a wizard/gumshoe with the kind of do-gooder streak that is a cinch to cause trouble.") In both style and content, these three reviewers suggest the X and Y coordinates of self-presentation on the "About Me" pages: the amount of personal information disclosed and the degree of intimacy or formality with readers.

REVIEWING AND THE CONSTRUCTION OF IDENTITY

The diversity of the reviewers' "About Me" statements leaves unanswered the question "why do they write?" As I noted, several foreground business interests to the point of writing as (self) marketing. These reviewers are relatively few, as are those who openly come out for making the world a better place. More frequent are the writers who modestly want to guide other customers. My own first experience with the Amazon.com reviews came as I researched buying the entire run of *National Geographic* on thirty-one CDs, only to be eloquently convinced by reviewers that poor technical quality made it a bad investment. Finally, however, marketing, altruism, or direct advice accounts for only part of the drive to review. Rather, and this is especially true for the Top Fifty Reviewers, there is the motive for self-expression or creation.

In one of the best concise definitions of the personal essay, Edward Hoagland defined the genre as existing on a line between "what I think and what I am" (46). The *identity* pole is typically figured by autobiographical elements in the essay. To the extent that the "About Me" sections or the reviews themselves contain such elements, they make explicit this essayistic impulse. A traditional way to account rhetorically for self-disclosure is to consider it as an ethos-constructing strategy. A traditional theoretical account would label it the situating of knowledge, the making present of the writer's subjectivity and situation in order to contextualize her or his interpretation. No doubt both are part of these reviews. But as Robert Connors noted, epideictic rhetoric (and surely the review has as its ostensible impulse praise or blame) is a rhetoric of display, finally a display of the self (30). Consider Friendly Spirit's admission that "I loved Kathleen [a character in Nuala O'Faolain's novel *My Dream of You*] because she is so much like me—a cynical romantic (can there be such a thing), ever hopeful and yet practical, imperfect, packed with mistakes and flaws, some painfully obvious to others, some painful to herself, and yet ultimately lovably human." Such expressions are common across the reviews and across the personal statements, but they are hardly universal.

Even when writers don't narrate their experiences, the very nature of these reviews invites self-fashioning. Understanding this claim involves understanding the genre and discursive nature of these reviews in relation to other Internet textual practices, existing somewhere between a newsgroup or Listserv posting and a Web page. The Amazon review, or rather the complex of reviews by a single author, has a closer affinity to the Web page, especially as the writer produces more reviews and achieves a top ranking.

Various theorists have explored ways that Web pages serve substantially to construct and assert identity. As Nina Wakeford notes, the subject of a personal home page is the author him- or herself, with the central organizing question being "Who am I?" (34). Charles Cheung explains that while many home pages answer this question "directly" by including specific autobiographical information, others do so indirectly through the nature of the information and links included. Chances are fairly slim that any personal home page gets found on the Web through general Web searches (Cheung 47–48). Yet this may not be a barrier. As Jennifer Petersen explains: "Audience plays an integral, and interesting, role in these self-representations. Whether or not the sites have many (or any) readers, the very public nature of the representation presupposes an audience; the self-representations are geared toward the (envisioned) audience" (161).

In the strictest sense, Amazon.com reviews do not constitute home pages for the reviewer. The reviews, after all, are assimilated into the Borglike site that Amazon.com manages, reviewers creating neither the physical appearance nor linkages of their contributions. Yet to a large degree, they do individually and collectively control content, and through the rating competition, they even control an aspect of the design. Each posted and read review potentially juggles the rating order, with implications especially for what shows up on the Top Reviewer's opening page. Further, since every posted review has a link to "About

Me," "About Me" takes on characteristics of a home page, space that can be used toward various ends, as my quick review above indicated. Finally, once readers are on the "About Me" page, they can link to other reviews that the writer has published, so that each new review adds another incremental element to the reviewer's constructed identity, all organized by "About Me"—and by Amazon.com's apparatus.

I suggest this is quite a new way to construct identity, one dependent on the intersection of several genres and discursive practices: the review itself but also Web pages, newsgroups, journals, and Listservs. For traditional reviews, a book's being published or a product released creates the epideictic occasion for writing. Usually limited by space (though the reviewer's fame buys extra acreage), writers figure themselves primarily through relating the book under discussion to other books, the references outlining their verbal identities. In print publications, the relatively scarce spaces for people to write to strangers are generally assigned. In Amazon.com's space, reviews are elected, and there are no external space limitations that I can discern, though surely if one tried to upload, say, a novel into the review space, the site's Webmasters would sanction it as they did the Eggers reviews.

Unlike the traditional review, and borrowing a genre feature from Web pages, Amazon.com reviews can be linked through the writer's "About Me" page, with some of them further including a URL to other author pages (though Amazon.com doesn't make these links active). There are additional Weblike features, most notably the "Friends and Favorites" area. Reviewers can create a list of "Favorite People," "other Amazon.com shoppers, friends, and favorite reviewers that you like and trust." Whenever someone you designate a "favorite" writes a review, Amazon.com sends it to you. A step beyond "Favorite People" are "Amazon Friends" (formerly designated as "Trusted Friends"), people who "have permission to see a private view of your About You area," including not only personal information about the reviewer but also items from his or her "Shared Purchases Page." This last is a list that you choose to share of the items you have bought from Amazon.com. Fascinating as it would certainly be to analyze the appeals and marketing strategies of these features, there is no space in this chapter. I will simply note the five strands of identity creation available to reviewers: what you say about yourself, what you read, what you say about your reading, who you like, and what you buy.

None of this information really pertains to the very occasional Amazon.com reviewer, but all these elements come into play for the Top Fifty Reviewers. Traditional personal Web pages are hit-and-miss affairs in terms of whether anyone ever reads them. The structured marketing space of Amazon.com paradoxically offers a pretext for being discovered that traditional pages do not, and the more one insinuates oneself into that space, the better one's chance of being found. If *hits* mark the degree to which one is *present* in virtual space (much as citation indexes mark one's influence within some academic disciplines), then more is better—and more hits mean more links to "About Me." The drive to (re)produce oneself textually in the world (and there is not room here to explore how that drive is both socially constructed and biologically impelled) is an end to itself, and Amazon.com provides one means to it. That means differs from other self-fashioning Internet genres such as the online diary or blog. A blog, shortened from Web log, is "a web page made up of usually short, frequently updated posts that are arranged chronologically—like a what's new page or a journal, [whose] content and purposes . . . varies greatly—from links and commentary about other web sites, to news about a company/person/idea, to diaries, photos, poetry, mini-essays, project updates, even fiction" (Blogger). (For an interesting example, see the diary diligently kept at http://www.slithytove.net.) Unlike the single-author spaces of diaries and blogs, the Amazon.com site depends on congeries of writers interacting, producing not only reviews but ratings and rankings.

Christine Hine explains how Internet users are engaged in configuring one another, but the idea of "user" is complicated here beyond the conventional subject position of information consumer. Most business advice on Internet marketing focuses on knowledge as exchanged between suppliers and consumers. Of seven strategies summarized by Davenport and Jarvenpaa, only one explains how to "design electronic communities for knowledge exchange" (151), although a seller risks much through this strategy, including losing control of the message space, as in the case of the spurious Eggers reviews. In the face of postmodernity's proliferation of information sources and abjuring of final authority, James M. Slevin observes:

> [Internet readers and writers] actively seek to forge commitment and mutuality with others in an attempt to restrict the experiences they have to sample

> in order to develop a coherent self-identity. . . . Individuals are thus routinely engaged in accessing information which often stems from distant sources, and in making information available to distant others in an attempt to unify and make sense of their own involvement and the involvement of others. (25)

While grounded in commitment and mutuality, Amazon.com's "Top Reviewers" site multiplies rather than restricts writer experiences. "Coherent self-identity" comes substantially through the sheer number of writings produced, sometimes to such extreme ends as #39 Maximillian Muhammad's 3,187 reviews and his "About Me" statement seeming to list every musician he could possibly name. It is telling that most Top Reviewers mark coherence through an "About Me" page that serves as the nexus (as cogito? as strategic persona? as reptilian brain core?) for their scattered reviews. It is perhaps more telling that some reviewers decline any personal statement—though Amazon.com does it for them by reporting their basic data (number of reviews and ratings, review categories, and so forth).

BEYOND AMAZON.COM: SCHOLARSHIP AS OCCASION FOR THE PERSONAL

An early commonplace, since challenged in theory and practice, was that the Internet would provide open spaces for radically democratic presentations of information and ideas. It is telling that developers chose *browser* to name the software for negotiating the Web, for implied in the name is a relatively undirected mode of use. Early advice for developing Web pages emphasized providing readers links through which they could seamlessly follow associations to unexpected places. However, Web use has evolved much differently, toward more purposive *searching*, away from more serendipitous browsing.

The transition has had subtle implications for how writers imagine and place themselves on the Web. Browsing readers may happen across your home page, vivifying a virtual you. Searching readers likely will not. Writers therefore have to find or create occasions that will attract readers. Topics or products are such occasions. In creating the reader reviews superstructure, Amazon.com almost certainly didn't have the main goal of offering a pretext for writers to construct and extend textual selves, nor would I assert that reviewers self-consciously intend to do so. But this Web site enables just that.

In doing so, it functions in ways similar to academic journals. To varying degrees, both reviewers and academicians share the goal of interpreting and evaluating texts with the aim of influencing others. But the advancement of knowledge is hardly the only or even most important motive. With direct consequences for merit, tenure, and promotion, professors have to establish textual selves within the discourses of their disciplines. Obviously, except for those seeking marketing angles, Amazon.com reviewers don't have this imperative. Still, the dynamic is instructively similar, as writers in both situations need official spaces to which readers turn.

But there is more, and it has to do with manifestations of the personal in the academic. Three common, entwined rationales for autobiographical elements in academic discourse are rhetorical, epistemological, and political. Writers include personal materials for reasons of ethos and pathos or for Burkean identification. Or writers do so to mark the contingencies of knowledge: who I am filters what I perceive and how I understand it. Or by dramatizing experiences that represent or evoke certain subject positions, writers call attention to groups that must be taken into account. All three strategies are no doubt true. But as a list they are incomplete.

We ought not overlook the plainer desire to put ourselves textually into the world, our interpretations and ideas, yes, but also some fuller identity. Those autobiographical elements collectively recognized as "the personal in the scholarly" are metonymic of this broader desire. Just as reviewing gives Amazon.com writers a pretext to write themselves where personally unknown readers might read, so does academic publishing. Yes, to advance knowledge and a career. But also to establish a self. Scholarship's "About Me" equivalent has traditionally been the author's bio, its personal home page the curriculum vitae. Because print lacks hyperlinks, "About Me" has been stealthily making its way into printed texts themselves. In standing the conventional order on its head (the scholarly serving the personal rather than vice versa, personal identity being the ends rather than the means), I confess exaggerating for effect. But only to a certain extent, perhaps one similar to Richard Miller's assertion that ours is now "a world where all writing—from the achingly personal confession to the finely tuned literary exercise to the resolutely indifferent bureaucratic memo—competes on a level playing field for our attention." He concludes: "The world is now awash in writing that no one reads" (49).

In such writing times, when the circle of readers we know personally is too small to accommodate the selves some of us would put forth, we look for bigger circles. As decades of vanity press books and, more recently, Web pages make clear, individuals widen those spheres themselves, especially when texts proliferate, and bookmarking, not browsing, becomes the preferred user mode. Finally, it is the space that editors, publishers, and even retailers control that is our best hope for readers. But it isn't enough to fill this space with mere information. In his provocative analysis of life-writing's role in an age of "data fatigue or data nausea" (146), especially as caused by the Internet, Charles Baxter muses that "the memoir is memory's revenge upon info-glut" (151). To write oneself into the information—or against it—is an act of self-constitution not only for the writer but also the reader. The burgeoning enrollment in MFA writing programs, especially the thirty-five new ones in creative nonfiction that have sprung up in the past half dozen years, is but one sign of a cultural push to expression through writing. Another, more mundane, is the thousands of Amazon.com reviewers and a vast realm of discourse—perhaps less about books than about me.

11

THE INFLUENCE OF EXPANDED ACCESS TO MASS COMMUNICATION ON PUBLIC EXPRESSION

The Rise of Representatives of the Personal

David S. Kaufer

The concept of a *public* is contested territory. We can't even decide on a preferred part of speech. Noun or adjective? Is the public an entity in search of properties? Or a property in search of entities? When we think of public in the entity sense, we usually think of it as a mass of citizens. A politician says, "The public is behind me," meaning that there is constituent backing. But how much backing? The difficulty in answering this question is that public, as entity, is a mass, not a count, noun. It is more like air than sheep. You can count the sheep in the field. But counting air? Of course, you can count people in a poll. Unfortunately, publics are not people polled. Our tradition of Whig liberalism celebrates politicians who make unpopular decisions, who speak to a public that includes excluded voices, future generations, and not just the voters that pollsters sample.

In American public address, *publics* as entities reference the speaker's perception of his or her backing—the public is behind me—when charging into a rhetorical situation or the barriers he or she must cross—what the public needs to understand—to address a situation effectively (see Cramer for a discussion of how the public is used within art controversies). Within both discourse conventions, the public as entity fills in rhetorical slots rather than draws out specific references to persons.

My interest in this chapter is more the adjectival sense of public, particularly as a modifier of the noun *expression*. What is public expression and what properties does it confer to ordinary expression? With Brian Butler, I have already addressed this question at some length (Kaufer and Butler) but will briefly summarize our answers here. Public expression is expression that meets the speaker's goal of on-the-record predictiveness. By virtue of being predictive and on the record, a speaker is able to claim standing as a representative of a community's felt condition. The notions of on the record, predictiveness, and representativeness reinforce different sides of the same basic speech attributes. On-the-record expression means that the speaker permits the audience to hold his or her utterances to future review. The speaker going on the record allows audiences to archive his or her present expression and compare it for consistency with his or her future statements. Predictiveness refers to the speaker's self-imposed constraints in granting the audience this permission. It puts the speaker under pressure for constancy from past to future. Unlike promising, which obligates future action to a specific other, on-the-record predictiveness creates only a presumption, to nonspecific others, of constancy from present to future. Representativeness refers to the reasons why the audience claims these rights over the speaker and why the speaker feels bound by them. The speaker's words are meant to stand in, be a mouthpiece for, the audience's interests. The audience thus has a natural interest in the speaker's on-the-record predictiveness. A public speaker can say, "We will spend the surplus on social security" on the record and then contradict that statement months or years later ("We will spend the surplus on war with terrorists"). The speaker has not broken a personal promise. Still, the speaker must account for the inconsistency even if the shift from present to future is perfectly justified. That is the burden of public expression.

The term *public expression* is now often used interchangeably with *mass expression.* This practice is understandable but also a mistake. The adjective *mass* references the mathematical ratio of speaker to audience. The Greek amphitheater allowed for the one-to-many communication marking the tradition of oratory and public address. But a child babbling in a crowded amphitheater, though not forfeiting the environment of mass expression, never claims the title of public speaker in the sense of mouthpiece for others.

Extensions in mass expression wrought by technology correlate with changes in public expression. However, if we blur the two concepts, we lose any possibility of understanding their mutual influence or their joint and separate influence on new media. In the next section, I will turn my attention to the influence of the new media on mass expression, putting us in a better position to understand how public expression may be changing as well.

NEW MEDIA AND THE OPENING OF ACCESS TO MASS EXPRESSION

New media have significantly opened access to individuals seeking to participate in mass expression. In traditional rhetoric, the many of mass expression had to fit into a single space, sharing propinquity growing out of shared proximity. Under new media assumptions, the disruption of proximity also weakened the assumption of propinquity. This is not because, with enhanced technological support, communication precludes strong ties between speakers and audiences. It is because with such support, communication no longer requires such strong ties between sender and receiver (Kaufer and Carley). The many of mass expression need share nothing but a remote wire. No assumptions need be made about social or spatial ties as a requirement of communication. Contemporary rhetoric (Farrell; Harris; C. Miller, "Idea") has, for this reason, focused on communities of divergent backgrounds, interests (Zappen, Gurak, and Doheny-Farina), and discourses (Bakhtin), where the right to speak (and be heard or read) is open to negotiation and interpretation.

Barriers have also lowered with respect to the entitlements required to participate in mass expression. In traditional rhetoric, participation relied upon speaker entitlements that gave access to a forum. These entitlements were accumulated in life as a precondition for public expression. A speaker's ethos in classical rhetoric was achieved, artistically, in the speech. But the speaker still relied upon claiming a material status in life (viz., lawyer, legislator) as a condition for displaying ethos in art. The speaker's capacity to create public expression was measured by the (prior) power to assemble a mass audience.

Under new media assumptions, by contrast, expression is taken for granted, irrespective of entitlements accumulated in life. Community groups, on- and off-line, participate in special interest discussions, where speakers self-select based on an expressed interest in a forum to speak. Whether the expression rises to public discourse is an act of legitimation left up to the community (Eberly). The competition to hold attention as a public discourse is fierce, as private interaction can exist in a cacophony of voices. The situation resembles that described by Zappen, Gurak, and Doheny-Farina: "seventeen 'voices' from different places all 'speaking' at once in the same 'place' and 'speaking' in fragments rather than complete discourses" (400).

Mass expression, many-to-many communication, can as easily involve the instant messaging of teens as subsidized political speech. Modern technology severs the ancient tie between mass communication and institutional infrastructure. For reasons to be applauded, many contemporary rhetoricians have raised questions about how the lowering of barriers to mass expression can lead to collective democratic action. These questions involve delicate balances describable in many overlapping ways: balancing the communitarianism of collective action with individual rights and privacy; balancing the prudence to listen only to what is worthy with the egalitarianism to say (and listen to) what is available to hear, balancing deliberateness with the speed of spontaneous expression. The delicacies of these balances have occupied many rhetorical theorists investigating contemporary assumptions (Gurak; C. Miller; Harris, "Idea").

Nonetheless, the outstanding problem this literature has yet to answer—and for which I confess no answer—is how to leap from the quantitative expansion of mass communication to the qualitative improvement of public communication in the sense of representative speech. Because an expansion of mass communication tempts, without guaranteeing, an expansion and improvement of public discourse, the path of one to the other becomes all the more problematic.

Conundrums Posed by the Technological Access to Mass Expression

When access to mass communication is so abundant today, even in the absence of strong ties, what do speakers and listeners readily share that still defines a community of interest in need of representatives? What makes your private expression representative of my own and others' thoughts and beliefs? When, in the absence of so much shared physical context, does speaking *about* (ordinary reference) also become speaking *for* (public discourse)? What makes the expression that comes from my mouth worthy of shared attention—that is, worthy, necessarily, of my attention and the attention of others? When the many-to-many communities of interest to enter are so numerous, how does a single speaker or a single listener hold attention with any one?

While these questions are fundamental and predate technology, the fact that technology now (in principle) grants anyone both a printing press and a microphone to the world makes these questions especially pressing today. As technology makes speech universally assessable in principle, it becomes necessary to seek other grounds, beyond cultural privilege, that make it public and representative. What are those grounds?

Representatives of the Personal: Personal Identity as a Rising Public Trope

My own lead on this question is to follow Elbow, Billig, Ritivoi, and other writers in rhetoric who, in various ways, have noticed that the personal has become an increasingly central trope of contemporary rhetorical behavior. In traditional rhetoric, a speaker seeking representative power had to have an ongoing story of identity to be predictive from past to future. A shaper of ethos, the identity story girded the speaker's call to judgment or action in a world of shared proximity. In contemporary rhetoric, marked increasingly by long-distance mass expression and weakened social ties and attention, the identity story has found its way more and more into the foreground of public expression. Because of the impact of contemporary mass expression, the common denominator left for us to notice and share, as a rhetorical resource, may be our very personhood. As a public trope, personhood is not just referencing a single life but telling life stories that claim to speak for others, to win adherents about a life that is worth learning from if not imitating.

A CASE STUDY: THE *NEW YORK TIMES'S WRITERS ON WRITING* SERIES

For the rest of this chapter, I use a case study to briefly illustrate my point, both of the rise of personal life stories as a rhetorical trope and their popularity in the culture. I analyze the *Writers on Writing Series,* published by the *New York Times* since 1997. The column regularly appears every other Monday on page 1 of section E of the *Times.* The series was the brainchild of the *Times*'s culture editor, John Darnton. A Pulitzer winner for fiction and a Polk Award winner for journalism, Darnton reports that he had struggled with his first novel and found himself endlessly curious to know the secrets of successful writers. He thus devised the *Writers on Writing* series to satisfy his own and what he expected to be the literate reader's curiosity about writing. At the time I was completing my analysis (July 2001), the series had accumulated some fifty-seven contributions, each between 1,300 and 2,000 words (see the appendix to this chapter). In the early summer of 2001, the *Times* also published a hardcover book edited and introduced by Darnton, containing the first forty-one entries.

The *Times*'s series contributors feel under no pressure to create, or to spur the creation of, public discourse. They explain their personal craft through their subjective eyes. They speak only as individuals. They do not try to communicate truths from the authority of the other contributors. The authors never cross-reference one another. But, as I show, there are still traces of a collective perceptiveness and bids to win adherents about preferred life stories relative to learning or teaching writing.

The *Times*'s Series Viewed as Personal Expression

Rather than encouraging the analyst in search of a tidy synthesis of public discourses, the assumptions of the contributors about literacy seem as individualistic and quirky as they are in the profession of English. I shall map out here, in more detail, the divided attention of the series, viewed as multiple individual expressions.

Some contributors in the series see the Western literary tradition as the sine qua non of literacy. The education of the writer, according to these contributors, properly includes Shakespeare, Wordsworth, Defoe (Goodman), Proust (Epstein), Joyce (Turow), Woolf, Eliot, and Pound (Howard), along with citizenship within an elite "Republic of Letters" (Bellow). Others emphasize a linguist's eye and ear for everyday language (Erdich; Salter), spoken and written, beyond the narrowly literary. Still others insist that writers of today need to understand writing as a form of media studies, noting that the visual media of the twentieth-century have profoundly influenced our current sense of the literary (Doctorow). Other contributors praise the dogged archival skills that draw writers not only to dusty library shelves but also to basements, attics, and garage sales (Proulx). Still others feature the teaching (Bernays; Delbanco) or study (Wolitzer; Vonnegut) of writing as an intellectual pursuit of its own.

The education of the writer portrayed in the series is wide-ranging and diverse. Yet the writer's formal education is only part of the divergence at issue. The series' contributors also have many divergent things to say about the life experiences shaping writers and their writing. Illness and suffering are notorious for cutting short a writing career. But some contributors single out these same factors as helping to inspire writing success (Hoffman; Stern). Other contributors emphasize the importance of the writer cultivating a cultural awareness of politics, history, and class

(Koning; Paretsky). In some contributions, this takes the form of urging writers to unearth from the culture interpretations that are poorly understood, misunderstood, or unknown among majorities. The Native American Ojibwe language taught Louise Erdrich how to notice relationships in nature that English conceals. Close observation of his dog, Colter, taught Rick Bass that the summons to hunt is a natural calling that others, perhaps less sensitive observers of their own pets, have too frequently failed to notice. The lack of explicit sex in so-called serious literature tantalized Barbara Kingsolver to explore, and break, this taboo in her own work.

The series' writers make clear that writers are nourished by personal obsessions. Yet, here again, the obsessions are diverse and fit no uniform pattern. Writers are obsessed with putting an order on life's disorder (Leavitt), with lives they wish to know (Howard), lives they wish to escape (Banks), and lives they wish to transform (Aciman). They are obsessed with current events in the popular culture (Hiassen) and with the characters they meet in daily life (Shields; Miller). The obsession intensifies when the characters are drawn from their own families (Aciman; Tan; Kincaid; Robinson). And, overall, the obsession spills over into a sense of love for the characters and the worlds they see coming alive on the page (Smiley).

Finally, the series calls attention to the fact that the sublime art of writing is always dependent on the mundane daily sustenance of the writer. Although writers need high-minded objects of attention to wield their craft, they also need the bare necessities, necessities that writers, one of history's most fragile occupational workers, seldom take for granted. Besides an income, these necessities involve a shelter to write in, tools to write with, and methods to write from.

There exists much variability about favorite shelters, tools, and methods. With respect to shelter, the writer must have a habitat. The habitat may be a room adjoining the kitchen (Rosen), a coal room in the basement (Haruf), or an attic with an old typewriter (Chute). It may be "the same chair" at "the same hour" (Mosley) or simply a "little room" (Kincaid). It may not be a permanent but an occasional habitat, like a table in a library surrounded by shelves of books (Goodman). The habitat need not be stationary nor even enclosed. It may involve moving feet, the writer as runner (Oates; Kincaid). Wordsworth, Coleridge, Shelley,

Thoreau, and Dickens regarded their long walks as part of their literary habitat (Oates).

The writer too must have equipment, whether a computer (Mosley) or a Waterman pen with black enamel and gold trim (Gordon). And the writer must have technique. It may be consulting one's internal muse (Smiley), turning off one's internal critic (Goodman), entering a reverie (Mosley), nocturnal dreaming (Fleming), or rereading what has been written before (Sontag). It may require turning on Bach's *Christ unser Herr zum Jordan kam* as background music to get going each morning (White). It may even require watching TV and goofing off, accumulating enough life experiences to decide when enough can be harvested to resume writing once again (Ford).

The *Times*'s series calls up a set of divided themes surrounding the nature of literacy and its fundamental relationship to language, the literary, culture, class, media, politics, and everyday ritual. I want to be careful to distinguish *divided* objects of attention from *divisive* objects of attention. The attention of this series is deeply divided but not divisive. Most contributors enter different topics. And when they do enter the same topic, they seldom make observations that question the truth of other observations. The spirit of the series is pluralistic and nonagonistic, even when true disagreements are broached.

The *Times*'s Contributors Viewed as Representatives of the Personal

I would now like to examine the *Times*'s series from the other side of the private-public duality. We will now read for an interest in providing public representatives of the personal, models of a writer's personal life that can represent, speak for, and win the adherence of certain readers.

As a rhetorical theorist, I am struck by the fact that the series marks a common solicitation for roughly comparable accounts (about writing) and is addressed to a roughly common rhetorical situation: The *Times*'s series invites market-proven authors to talk about their craft. What are the possibilities of responding to this rhetorical situation? In light of the fact that each respondent must produce a text of a relatively similar length and format (a short feature article), can we say something systematic about the choice points and the actual choices that underlie the rich variety of responses we can read? Let us then turn in more depth to the rhetorical situation the *New York Times* has defined and to the structure of the responses the *Times* has thus far elicited.

The writers invited to participate in the *Times*'s series are emblems of artistic and commercial success in letters. This is not insignificant to the mass readership of the *Times*. Textbook publishers put out hundreds of dry books on writing each year that never draw the mass reader. What draws *Times* readers to the *Writers on Writing* series is the ethos of the writers. Each of the contributors boasts success in a field where odds for success approximate the lottery. The mass-market reader is likely to construe the invitation to successful writers to discuss writing as also an invitation to discuss beating the odds. Like devoted concertgoers who come to hear a favorite artist's underground notes and back stories, readers of the *Times*'s series are drawn to understand the accounts of those who, against great odds, have "made it."

While aspiring artists might be expected to focus on a future still hoped for, established artists are challenged to address the startling fact of success when success is rare. The writers' accounts in this way are accounts of agency. Given the nonrandom barriers standing in the way of market success, readers will not accept an account that bases success solely on random accident. They will seek to find agency in the writers' accounts even if the writers themselves are reluctant to provide it. A writer claiming to be the beneficiary of dumb luck or a friendly muse will invigorate the mass reader to look for how the writer nevertheless managed, below the radar, to rein in luck or court the muse. No matter how much an account focuses on how a writer "fell into" success, mass-market readers, seeking agent-based explanations, will keep a watchful eye on what the writer relied upon to *make* his or her own success. The mass-market reader looks to the *Times*'s series for positive role models of writers, not simply arid explanations of writing.

One need not take my word to accept this analysis of the mass-market reader of fiction. Rosellen Brown reports running into such readers all the time, who complain to her when her characters are complex human beings rather than role models imagined for self-improvement books. She describes one encounter with a female lawyer who had hated one of her characters, also a female lawyer. The reader complained to her, saying:

> "Well, look, I'm a lawyer, too, and a woman, like your character, but"—and her expression became urgent as if she had clamped her hand to my arm—"the book was no help to me. It didn't tell me how I should live my life." (Brown, as cited in appendix)

In addition to seeking potential role models, the mass-market reader also seeks out themes or lessons as specific points to learn from and follow. The image of the mass-market reader hungry for "themes" does not originate with me, but with Diane Johnson, who observes that the "themes" of a text are something readers of fiction are much keener to look for than authors are to spoon out. To illustrate the point, Johnson remembers the following tale:

> In Seattle a man asked me what the theme of rescued cats and dogs in my books meant. I had to think about that, because I hadn't really noticed them there. Freud would say those cats and dogs are children, but that doesn't seem quite right to me. (Johnson, as cited in appendix)

Johnson cautions that a novelist too invested in themes may end up with a novel weighted down with more ideas than can be investigated through action. She suggests that themes are a reader's device for holding in memory some of the various layers of a layered text. Themes do readers more good than writers.

Returning to our rhetorical analysis, let us suppose that readers are drawn to the *Times*' s series in part for role models and lessons about writing. Let us further suppose that the contributors to the series accepted the invitation to participate with some knowledge of this mass-market expectation. Each writer, that is, knows he or she has been selected as an example of success and has been asked to write for an audience that is likely to be interested in picking up some of the secrets behind that success. Each contributor may have chosen, of course, to meet this expectation to a greater or less extent. But the fact that the expectation lurks in the background of the invitation probably had some constraining effect on all the contributions.

The writers of the *Times*'s series needed to adapt their writing to a common occasion and expectations. From the patchwork of texts we reviewed in the earlier part of this essay, we will be able to discern how the authors work systematically to portray themselves as public representatives of the personal.

The invitation to participate in this first person series is based on reputation. The writers know that readers want to learn about an "I" that has built a successful career from past to present. To let readers in on their secrets, the writers of the series will want to help readers consolidate their past and present selves into a single career image.

CONCLUSION

From traditional to contemporary rhetoric, we have witnessed a dramatic growth of the ordinary individual's access to a mass audience. This growth has spawned much conjecture about the relationship between increased individual access to technology and changes in public address, the language making bids to represent others and to form groups. I have restated the evidence that our increased access through technology has weakened the ties between ourselves as individuals and has further weakened our attention to one another's messages. I have conjectured that these weakenings themselves account for an increased focus on personal life stories in our public discourse. No matter where in the culture we are situated and no matter how fragmented our affiliations and attention, we are still persons invested in life stories that are told to us from the point of view of those we perceive as role models. In the second part of the chapter, I used the *New York Times*'s *Writers on Writing* series as a case study to explore and to try to explain the popularity of this contemporary form of rhetorical behavior. For those of us grappling with the problem of defining democratic collective action in the face of the new technologies, we may be advised to start with the assumption that speakers and their audiences have, at least and perhaps at most, selves in common to bring to a public sphere of representation.

APPENDIX

THE *WRITERS ON WRITING* ARCHIVE USED IN THIS STUDY

Aciman, A. (2000, August 28). A Literary Pilgrim Progresses to the Past. *New York Times.*

Banks, R. (1999, December 6). Time Can Transform the Fantasies of Youth. *New York Times.*

Bass, R. (2000, May 8). To Engage the World More Fully, Follow a Dog. *New York Times.*

Bellow, S. (1999, October 11). Hidden Within Technology's Kingdom, a Republic of Letters. *New York Times.*

Bernays, A. (2000, February 28). Pupils Glimpse an Idea, Teacher Gets a Gold Star. *New York Times.*

Brown, R. (2001, January 1). Characters' Weaknesses Build Fiction's Strengths. *New York Times.*

Cheuse, A. (2001, May 21). Literary Second Acts in American Lives. *New York Times.*

Chute, C. (1999, September 27). How Can You Create Fiction When Reality Comes to Call? *New York Times.*

Delbanco, N. (1999, June 21). From Echoes Emerge Original Voices. *New York Times.*

Divakaruni, C. (2001, February 12). New Insights into the Novel? Try Reading 300. *New York Times.*

Doctorow, E. L. (1999, March 15). Quick Cuts: The Novel Follows Film Into a World of Fewer Words. *New York Times.*

Epstein, L. (2001, June 4). Returning to Proust's World Stirs Remembrance. *New York Times.*

Erdrich, L. (2000, May 22). Two Languages in Mind, but Just One in the Heart. *New York Times.*

Fleming, T. (2000, January 3). Instant Novels? In Your Dreams. *New York Times.*

Ford, R. (1999, November 8). Goofing Off While the Muse Recharges. *New York Times.*

Gen, G. (2000, December 4). Inventing Life Steals Time; Living Life Begs it Back. *New York Times.*

Godwin, G. (2001, January 15). A Novelist Breaches the Border to Nonfiction. *New York Times.*

Goodman, A. (2001, March 12). Calming the Inner Critic and Getting to Work. *New York Times.*

Gordon, M. (1999, July 5). Putting Pen to Paper, but Not Just Any Pen or Just Any Paper. *New York Times.*

Haruf, K. (2000, November 20). To See Your Story Clearly, Start By Pulling the Wool Over Your Eyes. *New York Times.*

Hiassen, C. (2000, April 24). Real Life, That Bizarre and Brazen Plagiarist. *New York Times.*

Hoffman, A. (2000, August 14). Sustained by Fiction While Facing Life's Facts. *New York Times.*

Howard, M. (2000, February 14). The Enduring Commitment of a Faithful Storyteller. *New York Times.*

Johnson, D. (2000, September 11). Pesky Themes Will Emerge When You're Not Looking. *New York Times.*

Just, W. (2000, June 5). Sitting Down a Novelist, Getting Up a Playwright. *New York Times.*

Kincaid, J. (1999, June 7). Those Words That Echo . . . Echo . . . Echo Through Life. *New York Times.*

Kingsolver, B. (2000, March 27). A Forbidden Territory Familiar to All. *New York Times.*

Koning, H. (2000, July 31). Summoning the Mystery and Tragedy, but in a Subterrean Way. *New York Times.*

Leavitt, D. (2000, November 6). Comforting Lessons in Arranging Life's Details. *New York Times.*

Leithauser, B. (2001, April 23). The Glory of a First Book. *New York Times.*

Mamet, D. (2000, January 17). The Humble Genre Novel, Sometimes Full of Genius. *New York Times.*

McBain, E. (1999, March 29). She Was Blond. She Was in Trouble. And She Paid 3 Cents a Word. *New York Times.*

Miller, S. (1999, April 12). Virtual Reality: The Perils of Seeking a Novelist's Facts in Her Fiction. *New York Times.*

Mosley, W. (2000, July 3). For Authors, Fragile Ideas Need Loving Every Day. *New York Times.*

Oates, J. C. (1999, July 18). To Invigorate Literary Mind, Start Moving Literary Feet. *New York Times.*

Paretsky, S. (2000, September 25). A Storyteller Stands Where Justice Confronts Basic Human Needs. *New York Times.*

Piercy, M. (1999, December 20). Life of Prose and Poetry—an Inspiring Combination. *New York Times.*

Proulx, A. (1999, May 10). Inspiration? Head Down the Back Road, and Stop for the Yard Sales. *New York Times.*

Robinson, R. (2000, July 17). If You Invent the Story, You're the First to See How it Ends. *New York Times.*

Rosen, J. (2001, May 7). A Retreat From the World Can Be A Perilous Journey. *New York Times.*

Salter, J. (1999, September 13). Once Upon a Time, Literature. Now What? *New York Times.*

Saroyan, W. (2000, October 9). Starting With a Tree and Finally Getting to the Death of a Brother. *New York Times.*

Shields, C. (2000, April 10). Opting for Invention Over the Injury of Invasion. *New York Times.*

Shields, D. (2001, April 9). Confession Begets Connection. *New York Times.*

Smiley, J. (1999, April 26). The Muse: The Listener Also Instructs. *New York Times.*

Sontag, S. (2000, December 18). Directions: Write, Read, Rewrite. Repeat Steps 2 and 3 as Needed. *New York Times.*

Stern, R. (2001, March 26). Autumnal Accounting Endangers Happiness. *New York Times.*

Tan, A. (2001, February 26). Family Ghosts Hoard Secrets that Bewitch the Living. *New York Times.*

Turow, S. (1999, November 22). An Odyssey That Started With 'Ulysses'. *New York Times.*

Updike, J. (1999, March 1). Questions of Character: There's No Ego as Wounded as a Wounded Alter Ego. *New York Times.*

Vonnegut Jr., K. (1999, May 24). Despite Tough Guys, Life is Not the Only School for Real Novelists. *New York Times.*

Walker, A. (2000, October 23). After 20 years, Meditation Still Conquers Inner Space. *New York Times.*

West, P. (1999, October 25). Planting the Seeds of a Contemplative Life. *New York Times.*

Westlake, D. (2001, January 29). A Pseudonyn Returns From an Alter-Ego Trip, with New Tales to Tell. *New York Times.*

White, E. (2001, June 18). Selecting Music for Writing. *New York Times.*

Wiesel, E. (2000, June 19). A Sacred Magic Can Elevate the Secular Storyteller. *New York Times.*

Wolitzer, H. (2000, January 31). Embarking Together on Solitary Journeys. *New York Times.*

12

PRIVATE WITNESS AND POPULAR IMAGINATION

Marguerite Helmers

Father, don't you see I'm burning?

Cathy Caruth, *Unclaimed Experience*

Beck screamed helplessly as the wind blew his tent doors open, then blew the sleeping bags from his body.

David Breashears, *High Exposure*

On May 10, 1996, a sudden storm stranded several climbers on Mount Everest. By all accounts, the mountain was crowded with over fifty amateur and professional climbers that day. The traffic caused slow movement toward the summit and a bottleneck of climbers at the Hillary Step, the last hurdle before the slope toward the summit. When the clouds lowered, the wind picked up speed, and the temperature dropped. It was already past the safe turnaround time for the climbers, the time that is imposed to avoid the hazards of climactic changes that are common in the mountains. No one knows why, but some climbers continued to ascend. By the time they began to descend, they were lost, blinded, and frozen. Six climbers were dead by the next morning. Two were professional climbers who lead groups of *clients*, the term for paying customers, to the top. Two succumbed to frostbite and lack of oxygen. Two had simply disappeared.

One of the clients on the mountain that day was a Texas pathologist named Beck Weathers. Weathers was an experienced, nonprofessional climber climbing with the New Zealander Rob Hall's team. Like the others in his group, he had paid $65,000 to have a shot at the summit of Everest, the tallest mountain in the world and the legendary icon of dreams. Due to the storm and the incredible events that unfolded over the next day, Weathers became something of an icon himself.

Professional climber and photographer David Breashears notes in *High Exposure*: "If I can be one tenth of what Beck was that day, I will have been a worthy man" (274).

On May 10, on the way to the summit, Weathers had stopped climbing earlier than most of his team. A year and a half earlier, he'd had a radial keratotomy operation on his eyes to correct his nearsightedness. However, he remarks: "At high altitude a cornea thus altered will both flatten and thicken . . . rendering you effectively blind. . . . That is what happened to me about fifteen hundred feet above High Camp in the early morning hours of May 10, 1996" (Weathers 32). The team leader, Rob Hall ordered Beck to remain where he was and wait for the rest of the party until the afternoon descent, when they could return to High Camp together. Weathers did what he was told, but the hours dragged on with no sign of Hall, until in the dark at 6:00 p.m., with six other climbers, he began to descend, roped to guide Neal Beidleman. Within an hour, they were engulfed in a roaring wind and a wall of white clouds. Lost on the mountain, the group huddled together to stay warm. Search parties sent out from High Camp over the night and into the morning rescued five of the seven at this camp. Two clients were so badly frozen that they were left for dead: Yasuko Namba and Beck Weathers. With their faces covered by inches of ice, they were amazingly still breathing, but "were judged so near death as to be beyond help" (Breashears 270). It was an act of triage, part of the mountaineers' code to leave behind those who are so close to death that a high-altitude rescue by physically exhausted and oxygen-depleted climbers would endanger other lives.

Yet Weathers did not die. He opened his eyes, struggled to his feet, and began stumbling forward in the direction he believed was High Camp. He fell repeatedly and began hallucinating:

> Both my hands were completely frozen. My face was destroyed by the cold. I was profoundly hypothermic. I had not eaten in three days, or taken water for two days. I was lost and I was almost completely blind. (Weathers 52)

At camp, someone radioed down the mountain that "the dead guy" had just walked in, like the lurching Frankenstein monster of the old films. Recalled climber Todd Burleson: "This man had no face. It was completely black, solid black, like he had a crust over him. . . . His right arm was bare and frozen over his head. We could not lower it. His skin looked like marble. White stone. No blood in it" (Weathers 54).

Weathers was put into a tent. Climbers at High Camp were told to leave him there and not attempt to bring him back to Base Camp, as he was certain to die anyway. During the night, another storm furiously struck the camp. The wind ripped open the doors of the lightweight shelter and filled the tent with snow. The tent began to collapse around him. Alone in the tent, helpless from the frostbite and exhaustion, he cried out for help, but the wind roared so loudly that no one could hear his cries. At some point, as he fell in and out of consciousness, he was blown from the sleeping bag and left lying on the floor. The next morning, writer and climber Jon Krakauer popped his head into the tent. "What the hell does a person have to do around here to get a little service" Weathers yelled (Weathers 58).

In the book *Unclaimed Experience: Trauma, Narrative, and History*, Cathy Caruth describes "the address of the voice" that "demands a response" (8–9). This is the *cry* of trauma. Caruth recounts Freud's story of a father's dream of a burning child, in which a child dies from a fever and the corpse catches fire from a candle left burning near the body. The father, asleep in the next room, hears the boy calling to him in his sleep, "Father, don't you see I'm burning?" (9). We should understand from this narrative, Caruth tells us, that "one's own trauma is tied up with the trauma of another" (8), that we must listen to the language and the silences of trauma, experience, and the cries of the wound. A trauma, Cathy Caruth posits, is a wound upon the mind, "experienced too soon, too unexpectedly, to be fully known and is therefore not available to consciousness until it imposes itself again" (4). Survivors of trauma must revisit and rewrite the events in order to give themselves a voice in the events.

Weathers's autobiography, *Left for Dead,* is a cry of the wound. It is, in Caruth's words again, a story that relates the crisis of death, but also the crisis of life for, having survived the terrible days on the mountain, Weathers is rescued by helicopter and returned to the United States, where he must reconstruct his body, his life, his profession, and his marriage. Readers of his autobiography are enmeshed in a personal narrative of overcoming the illness of his body and the lifelong mental illness that caused him to seek climbing as a refuge. I focus in this essay on Weathers's memoir because it is part of a larger discourse on high-altitude climbing, real-life adventure stories, and narratives of disaster in remote areas that has appeared as a major publishing trajectory in the last five years. Today, the names of turn-of-the-century explorers Robert Falcon Scott and Ernest Shackleton are almost as familiar as the hard-boiled heroes of the films *Die Hard* and *Hunt for Red October.* Thus, Weathers's book fills a reader's need to know more and vicariously experience more from places that lie beyond the accessible regions of the earth. Significantly, the tales of Shackleton, Scott, and the Everest teams of 1996 are tales of misfortune and disaster. We read their tales as testimony to the endurance of the human spirit, but also as evidence of their pain.

As Michael Bernard-Donals has recently written, the truth of a person's testimony affects historical understanding, just as the witness has been affected by the cultural conditions of retelling. A testimony often relates to events that have been culturally construed to be significant to many people. "It is the point at which the event is lost that writing begins," argues Bernard-Donals (77). The writer "becomes an 'I' over against which the event can also be identified, given attributes, and finally named," entering into the interplay between language and silence that Maurice Blanchot describes as the writing of the disaster. Weathers's autobiography provides an interesting case for study because the facts of his story were widely known prior to his writing. If we follow Bernard-Donals's argument, then, it is up to Weathers to establish his character, rather than the facts, in the narrative. Weathers must take the events known to the public and provide his private reflections on them.

At least five accounts of the "disaster season" were published before Weathers's own work. In May 1996, e-mail dispatches were forwarded home from Everest through the NOVA/PBS Online Adventure (*Expedition '96: Everest Quest*). John Krakauer, a journalist for *Outside Magazine,* was assigned to cover the Everest climb but ended up covering the disaster. His account, *Into Thin Air,* was published in 1997. Anatoli Boukreev, one of the guides assigned to team leader Scott Fischer, published his own account of the disaster titled *The Climb* (1997). David Breashears, on the mountain with four climbers and an IMAX camera crew, published his memories in *High Exposure* (1999). The 1998 IMAX film, *Everest,* that incorporated the May 10 disaster into its story line was filmed by Breashears. These accounts served as indexes for the points of the disaster. Furthermore, Weathers's story was related in the national press, on television, and in the television "docudrama" *Into Thin Air* (1997). Thus, the facts and the general trajectory of the story line are known. Weathers is in the interesting position of writing a response to the disaster. He is a witness as well as a survivor who offers testimony of the event. In Caruth's terms, his own trauma is "tied up with the trauma of another" (8). At the same time, Weathers is somewhat transparent. We gravitate toward his narrative in order to see through to the iconic moment he is representing, satisfying our public need for more information and for personal revelation.

Media critic Joshua Meyrowitz has noted that the easy access to multiple types of *media* in American society, such as books, magazines, newspapers, television, and the Internet, allow access to previously remote or forbidden spaces and experiences. Places such as Mount Everest become demystified because people are familiar with these places through multiple exposures. At the same time that media allow us access to the remote places of human experience, they provide us with access to the interior spaces of the human psyche. Behaviors previously considered "private"—or what Meyrowitz calls "offstage"—become the focus of media. He cites the television program *Entertainment Tonight* as an example of the ways that media present "a wide range of personal expressions in addition to 'objective facts'" (177). Furthermore, Meyrowitz argues, the American audience has developed a "presumption of intimacy" by being exposed to these confessional media (181):

> It now seems more acceptable to write books about the very personal lives of great people, to reveal old secrets, and to betray old confidences. Indeed, memoirs *without* such intimate revelations about the writer or others now seem stuffy and unrealistic. (179)

The premise of this book, *The Private, the Public, and the Published,* is that everything we say and do can be made available to nearly everyone who shares our access to media. Modern technologies—print, voice, and electronic—translate private lives into the objects of public consumption. "Contemporary life increasingly *deprivatizes* stories, displacing ownership from individuals to broader going concerns," write sociologists Jaber Gubrium and James Holstein (180). In this cultural milieu, Weathers's authority as an author is fragmented—and this fragmentation is reflected in his ghost-authored text (the book was written with the assistance of Stephen Michaud), spotted with reflections from his friends in Dallas and his wife, Peach. *Left for Dead* is the story of a wound and its healing, and like the recovery, the book represents the unevenness of healing. There are points of disruption, moments of silence, anger, pain, and humor. Weathers's wound was suffered once in private and then reenacted in public narrative.

Bernard-Donals notes that a traditional view of testimony is that it contributes to the construction of history, transparently providing facts and details to the public (79). The American public has multiple ways to access personal stories, but as we will see, testimony is not a "window through which we see clearly the events themselves" (Bernard-Donals 79). Weathers chose to employ multiple narrators in his autobiographical account of his trauma in order to occupy different points in time and different attitudes toward the events. He intentionally destabilizes the events of May 10, 1996 by placing emphasis on the rescue efforts of May 11, 1996 and the subsequent recovery of his mind, body, and family.

The word *witness* is used as a noun and a verb in the English language. As a noun, it stands for evidence; as the *Oxford English Dictionary* defines it, the oral or written testimony of an event is "an attestation of a fact, event, or statement." As a verb, the word *witness* indicates the active participation of a person who has seen and who can verify, "one who is or was present and is able to testify from personal observation, one present as a spectator and auditor." Steven M. Weine describes witnessing as being able "to see, to know, and to be engaged with an other's experience of traumatization":

> Assuming many different forms, the phenomenon of witnessing occupies a central position in late twentieth-century Western culture. Witnessing encompasses more than the traumatic experiences themselves; it also includes the life that was shattered and the life of the survivor. Witnessing is concerned both with the individual and the collective. It is private, a confession embodying the survivor's spiritual, aesthetic, and moral essences. And it is public, a documentation of historical events and cultural traditions. The witness receives, processes, and transmits survivors' knowledge. Most important, witnessing strives to be consequential—for the witness, the individual survivor, the collective of survivors, and other witnesses to this witnessing. (168)

Weine stresses the importance of collective memory, which is a process of documentation. Yet the act of recording facts and events does not in itself constitute witnessing. The witness must be able to establish credibility, must be permitted a place and time to speak, and the tale must be remembered (Shay 222). In Shoshana Felman's book *Testimony*, Dr. Dori Laub points out that trauma is not *witnessed* until it is inserted into language. Writing and language are essential to recovery from traumatic experiences because they overcome the silence that is "a place of bondage" to the trauma, the oppressors, and the events (58). Narrative also involves an audience, and, as Laub points out, "the listener to trauma comes to be a participant and a co-owner of the traumatic event: through his very listening, he comes to partially experience trauma in himself" (57). Psychologist James Pennebaker has commented on the connection between writing and trauma as well, although Pennebaker disputes that an auditor or audience is necessary for the writer:

> [L]anguage apparently plays a critical role in processing the trauma. One of the critical aspects [of recovery] may be that somehow in the process of writing down their deepest thoughts and feelings about the experience, people get to organize the experience in a very emotional way. . . . Another critical discovery was that it does not seem necessary for people to directly share what they have written with others. . . . I think our work is hinting that as a therapist you need to create an environment where a person feels completely free to reveal what they are thinking and feeling, and allow them to put things together. (King and Holden 359)

Extrapolating to the broadest rhetorical terms, then, the traumatic experience deploys logical and emotional elements that affect teller, tale, and audience. Bernard-Donals warns readers and listeners that the narrative has the power to displace the events of the real into a representation, thereby making the events and their retelling uncanny because there is uncertainty as to their "true nature" (84). In other words, once a narrative of trauma becomes public, it assumes conventional constructions of public discourse that may mask its authentic nature. Laub and Bernard-Donals are both taking Holocaust testimony as their subject, while Pennebaker's subjects were men and women who lost a spouse to suicide or car accidents. It goes without saying that there is a significant difference between Holocaust testimony and a narrative of illness such as Weathers's. No one would willingly place themselves into a situation of extreme brutality and oppression, whereas people quite willingly climb Everest each year. Everest, the physical mountain, is extrapolated into an idea, and the idea feeds fantasies of glory and adventure, the stuff of Kipling and Stevenson, the epic of Man versus the Elements.

From an Aristotelian perspective, the ethos of the speaker or writer influences the reception of the work, although it is equally necessary that the ethos of the listener be trustworthy. Ethos is described by Aristotle as the quality of the speaker's reputation. Ethos is an important—if somewhat intangible—element of rhetorical persuasion that determines how an audience reacts to a speaker. A witness to history must present enough facts to become veritable, and the degree to which he or she is able to reconstruct an authentic chronology of events and provide details of fact that are consistent with other reports is essential. In a study of autobiography and personal narrative that draws on Aristotelian rhetoric, Candace Spigelman notes that "[n]arrating the individual's deliberate choices or attributes of character and connecting them to moral principles help to establish an ethical character with which the audience can identify" (72). Using common emotional appeals as the basis for the narrative results in effects such as tragedy because the bond of sympathy is established between sufferer and auditor (72). I would like to add to Laub's, Bernard-Donals's, Pennebaker's, and Spigelman's conceptions of trauma, narrative, and audience in claiming that the ethos of the witness is also affected by general public attitudes toward the event, such as horror, dismissal, curiosity, or ignorance. Together, the witness and audience construct a third entity, the disaster, in a dialectic between fact and attitude.

Aristotle establishes the basis for studying rhetoric and trauma in his *Rhetoric* and his *Poetics*. In the *Rhetoric*, he notes that a narrator should establish "proof (where proof is needed) that the actions were done, [and a] description of their quality or of their extent" (207). Thus, the witness both represents the facts and offers an evaluation of their importance. Aristotle also points out that a narration "should depict character," continuing: "One such thing is the indication of moral purpose; the quality of purpose indicated determines the quality of character depicted and is itself determined by the end pursued" (209). This observation is surprisingly contemporary when applied to mountaineering literature, for climbers often must address the question of why they risk their lives routinely in the search for high places.

Jon Krakauer, a climber and author, has no answers, but is acutely aware throughout his published work of the moral implications of climbing. In response to the terrible 1986 season on the Himalayan mountain K2 in which thirteen climbers died, Krakauer asks: "Should a civilized society continue to condone, much less celebrate, an activity in which there appears to be a growing acceptance of death as a likely outcome?"

(*Eiger* 161). The climbers' awareness of an audience that seeks a justification for their wanderlust or vivifies itself through its own thirst for danger is reflected in their prose. It occupies a large section of Weathers's own narrative, in which he describes his desire for high places and provides, as a counterpoint, his wife's aggrieved comments on his all too willing abandonment of the family.

In fact, Weathers's justification for his climbing is morally thin, indicating that his main purpose in writing was not to provide larger answers to the public. In his own words, he wanted "recognition" (6), he desired the test "against the ultimate challenge" (4), he "gained hard muscle" and "drank in the moments of genuine pleasure, satisfaction and bonhomie out in the wilds with my fellow climbers" (6). The story that is narrated by Margaret "Peach" Weathers within the pages of the autobiography reveals the consequence of the climb on the family:

> [W]hen Beck left for Mount Everest in March of 1996—he spent our twentieth anniversary there—I decided this was the last time he would run away from us. Beck was living only for his obsessions, and I saw no further hope of making our marriage work. . . . Beck seemed selfishly determined to either kill himself or get himself killed. (69)

Peach is the Greek chorus of the book: she is both the editorial commentator and the exposition. There are points in the narrative that must be accounted for, details of which Beck himself is unaware, and it falls to Peach to provide these details. She is also a witness to the trauma, the one who listened, observed, and was affected by Beck's wounds. In the *Poetics*, Aristotle describes tragedy as "an imitation of an action that is serious, complete, and of a certain magnitude," which "through pity and fear . . . [purges] these emotions" from the spectators (230). Modern narratives of trauma, although they are represented—or "imitated," to use Aristotle's term—in many media, do not purge emotions but rather create secondary traumas that are worked through by the witnesses. Physical pain is individuated and resistant to language, Elaine Scarry tells us, but can be represented discursively, through storytelling. Although that storytelling can often be partial and fragmented, the listener plays an important role in witnessing the story, retelling it, and becoming a "writer" or "author" of the pain itself (Scarry 9). Thus, rhetorically, the story indicates its credibility through the reader's emotional reaction to the events.

Up to this point, I have focused on the rhetorical framework of the survivor's story. Each survivor is situated within a cultural nexus of attitudes and material structures that inform the nature of the trauma and the telling of the events of the disaster. In her analysis of women's rape testimonies, Wendy Hesford discusses how self-representations are negotiated with "prevailing cultural . . . scripts" (197) that sometimes overwrite the individual, or the personal, with dominating attitudes. Hesford asks how stories can be treated as individuated, authentic, and unique, while at the same time she provides a means for political interrogation of the structures that allow disasters to happen. "American mass media tend to focus on victims and perpetrators' psychological states rather than on the sociological, political, and material forces that facilitate and sustain violence," she notes (196). Writing about the deaths on K2 in 1986, for example, Krakauer indicts the publicity surrounding Reinhold Messner's ascent of the Seven Summits without supplemental oxygen as a "distorting" cause of the disasters. Messner himself is a brilliant climber with "uncanny 'mountain sense,'" Krakauer admits, but his amazing ability to ascend the high peaks "may have given unwarranted confidence to many climbers" who believed that Messner was setting new standards for playing "the high-roller's game," rather than recognizing the achievements as the apex of one man's outstanding personal ability (*Eiger* 161–62).

From a similar material perspective, Weathers's narrative must be understood as the story of a privileged white male: he has money, power, mobility, and education. His rescue from Everest was facilitated by the intervention of politicians and doctors who could easily draw on power, money, and time. Within the pages of *Left for Dead*, it falls to Peach to tell the story of the rescue. On May 11, when Beck was still breathing but was covered with ice and abandoned by his teammates, Peach was told that he had died. Hours later, when she was called again with news of his miraculous recovery, she brought together a network of friends and business associates. They began to make phone calls; she reports: "We were not worried about getting Beck off the mountain. We just knew he was in critical condition, and he probably was going to need better medical attention than what was available in Nepal" (75). Weathers's partners called worldwide for medical facilities, locating a medical center staffed with U.S.-trained physicians in Singapore and a frostbite expert in Alaska. They next called Texas senator Kay Bailey Hutchinson, "whom several of us knew" (75), Texas governor George W. Bush, whose daughters went to school with Weathers's daughter, and Senator Tom Daschle (also a friend). As Peach recounts it: "Daschle contacted the State Department, which contacted the embassy in Katmandu, which assigned David Schensted to the matter, which resulted in Madan K. C. risking his life to save Beck's" (76). Beck's brother Dan flew to Katmandu immediately. The high-altitude rescue was not routine. Colonel Madan of the Royal Nepalese Army had never flown a helicopter that high on the mountain before, as the air is so thin at high altitudes that the helicopter cannot function. "However, nobody told Peach about this," Weathers comments. "Assisted by her bunch of North Dallas power moms . . . they proceeded to call everybody in the United States. If you did not personally receive a phone call from my wife or one of her associates in this effort, it was because you weren't home" (61).

In addition, because of his social position, he has access to publishing his story in ways that many victims of violence and trauma do not. Weathers has a voice because of the ways he is culturally encoded: the wealthy white male's power to speak and to represent. Unlike many sufferers, Weathers is not silenced. Rather, he uses the occasion of his trauma in order to advance another culturally coded narrative: that of the journey that leads to an epiphany, a deeper realization of self. On the mountain, stranded by teammates, frozen, in pain, he saw his family standing before him: "My subconscious summoned them into vivid focus, as if they might at any moment speak to me. I knew at that instant, with absolute clarity, that if I did not stand at once, I would spend an eternity on that spot" (51). At the tail end of the book, he comments: "While the story of what occurred during those few days on Everest clearly is of interest, the story of what happened when I got back home and had to rebuild my life—redefine who I was—became the story for me" (289).

It is axiomatic for rhetorical analysis to consider who is authorized to speak in certain cultures. Gubrium and Holstein draw on the insights of Michel Foucault when they ask: "Who is, or is not, entitled, obligated, or invited to offer their stories and under which social, institutional, historical, and material circumstances?" (179). On the mountain, the pool of authorized speakers is determined by money; it is, in other words, a self-selected population of privilege. Krakauer was authorized to represent the event because of his association as a writer for *Outside Magazine.*

Breashears was a well-known documentary photographer. Weathers is permitted to speak because of his money, of course, but he is primarily permitted to speak because of his survival and his prolonged need to be physically and mentally reconstructed. He is aware of the extraordinary circumstances that allowed him to survive and admits to a profound discomfort in seeing Yasuko Namba's family in the hotel after the disaster. Namba, recall, had also been left for dead with Weathers as the storm raged below the summit. She was left to die there. Unlike Weathers, she did not raise herself and walk toward camp, physically imposing herself upon those who had left her alone in the ice and cold. Unlike Weathers, her family was not politically connected enough to authorize a rescue. Seeing Namba's family in Katmandu, Weathers is stilled:

> They very much wanted to know about her and her last moments. I really didn't know what to tell them. I searched for anything that might comfort them. But for one of the very few times in my life, the easy stream of words simply wouldn't come. At some level I felt guilty standing there, alive, when Yasuko was gone. I couldn't even offer meaningful consolation. (82)

In this moment of uncertainty, the two climbers who were once equals on the mountain, Namba and Weathers, are revealed to be profoundly unequal. Their inequality is not based on physical ability or personal aspirations; it is the power of American money and social position that divides them. Following this encounter, Weathers does not moralize. He does not reflect on the cultural causes for the Everest disaster in the way that Krakauer did in *Into Thin Air*. Krakauer searched for the underlying causes for the May 10 disaster, wondering "how could things have gone so haywire?" (264):

> With so many marginally-qualified climbers flocking to Everest these days, a lot of people believe that a tragedy of this magnitude was over-due. But nobody imagined that an expedition led by Rob Hall would be at the center of it. Hall ran the tightest, safest operation on the mountain, bar none. . . . So what happened? How can it be explained, not only to the loved ones left behind, but to a censorious public? (272)

Earlier comments in this essay alone indicate that Krakauer is interested in the relationship of climbing to the greater nonclimbing public. Weathers admits in his epilogue that he has left the analysis to Krakauer and others. He doesn't engage in any musings about his potential complicity in the tragedy. To what extent, then, is this also a material characteristic of his memoir? Hesford finds that feelings of complicity are a characteristic of women's narratives of trauma. For example, Hesford recounts one survivor's story of her rape that includes her ruminations that she was somehow responsible for the violence against her:

> What happened at the door is that I let him in. I knew there was danger, and I didn't follow my intuition. I didn't protect myself. I let him in. For years, I have felt guilty about that. I thought that it was my fault.(200)

In *Left for Dead*, it falls to Peach, in her rhetorical role as chorus, to warn readers against not the physical but the emotional toll of mountain climbing. Perhaps unconsciously drawing on female narrative strategies, Peach sees the dangers to the extended family and not to the individual. Finally, it is worth pointing out that, although the Everest disaster of 1996 was unexpected on May 10, it was a common type of disaster in the mountains. Repeatedly, climbers tell of the need to acknowledge when you must turn around. The mountains are said to send warnings, and it is up to the sensitive to heed them.

Who owns personal stories? Gubrium and Holstein note: "Typically, the personal story is believed to belong to someone: someone's account is his or her story" (178). But ownership is socially organized: "A story may belong to its teller, in one sense, but features of narrative composition and local conditions of storytelling are also proprietary." So much of tragedy and atrocity is communicated visually from remote locations that it is difficult to say what the effects are on viewers. Laub asserts that witnesses are not only those who were there, but those who witness the pain of survivors. In the final section of this essay, I would like to offer some initial thoughts on issues of recent trauma. Who are the witnesses of the September 11 tragedies in the United States?

The events of September 11, 2001 are widely known. On that day, two commercial airplanes slammed into the twin towers of the World Trade Center, sending clouds of fire outward in enormous roiling balls and scattering glass, steel, and paper across the streets of lower Manhattan. Within the next hour, planes would attack the Pentagon, crash into a field in Pennsylvania, and the towers of the World Trade Center would collapse. Many Americans watched this horror unfold in *real time* on their televisions. In fact, witnessing took on new meaning as it divided those who watched live media from those who saw the evening news replays. Yet, the act of remembering the disaster is accessible to everyone through print and electronic media. Within minutes, televised replays of the first plane hitting the first tower were saturating the networks and these spectacular, horrifying images would be replayed again and again in subsequent days and weeks. Newspapers and electronic news media (the Web and the television) began to feature chronologies of the events. It was immediately clear that there were multiple chronologies: there were the chronologies of the terrorists, who had planned the hijackings of the planes years in advance; there were the chronologies of the passengers on the planes, many of whom, the public learned, phoned home to say goodbye to their families; there were the chronologies of the media witnesses, who suffered in ignorance of what was happening and the relationship of one event to another; there were the chronologies of the rescue workers in New York City, who rushed to their deaths unwittingly as they enacted their practiced rescue missions. Following any of these chains of events entails a narrative, a process of anticipation and reflection, a balancing of what is *normal* against what is unexpected. Each of the survivors, therefore, will tell a different story, all of which have a relationship to the facts of the events, but which have a different chronology. For example, Phil Oye, on his way to work in Tower 2 of the World Trade Center on the morning of September 11, didn't know what was happening around him but used previous events as a template for his immediate experience. He immediately positioned himself within a well-known story, the terrorist bombing of the World Trade Center in 1993. Within the frame of the immediate chronology, he recounts that he saw smoke and he knew people were evacuating: "I thought there was a bomb in the basement like in 1993 . . . [then] I downshift into thinking that [it] was an accident." He exits the building and begins taking photographs. He sees bodies falling from the building, "appearing out of the smoke." He notices that people are "completely calm." His chronology, therefore, is not told from the perspective of the news networks or the terrorists. It is a simple account of walking: he leaves the train he has taken to work, he sees smoke, he takes an escalator upstairs, he exits the building, he circles the building to take pictures, he looks at the WTC, he hears an explosion. At no point does he know that there is a terrorist attack. That knowledge comes later and not only reorders his experience, it positions him as a witness to history, a survivor, someone who can authenticate the horror of the day. Through Oye—and particularly because he recounts his story in present tense—the reader creates a subject space, a place to become the I/eye of the narrative.

Not many of these survivor stories have been published at the writing of this essay. A few have appeared in news magazines, online, or in newspapers, characterized mostly as "eyewitness accounts," a journalistic term indicating that the witness is useful to establishing the facts of the story. This indicates that a period of reflection must ensue before the survivor's story may move into the public sphere as a personal narrative. The significance of the events to the person must be understood and organized into a story. The narrative must have time to take on a culturally significant form, such as a tragedy or a romance. At some point, however, the story will change. Oye and others like him will come to see themselves taking part in an event of significance, actors in a larger drama. At one point in his chronology he notes, "someone says that a tower fell. I attribute this to sheer rumor." Once Oye is familiar with the facts, however, he will dismiss the rumor. Photographs and the official chronologies will certify that both towers of the World Trade Center fell within the hour. His reaction will become a vestigial artifact of trauma, a personal narrative of confusion and distress. It will testify to his inner self but not to the wider events that make up the public history of that day.

Witnessing is both a private and a public act. Initially, the individual is faced with overwhelming and chaotic sensations. Eventually, these sensations are organized in public forms of discourse and, sometimes—but not always—published as oral or written testimony. The language of trauma and memory creates a factual relationship to events through description and chronology but is individuated and articulated to a sympathetic audience through emotional appeal and common narrative forms. Studying personal narratives of trauma, the researcher must enter into a multidiscursive universe of psychology, rhetoric, cultural criticism, and politics, as the narratives themselves shift from representations of occasions of magnitude for the greater public to recounting incidents of personal significance. They move between modes of discourse, from the intimate to the oratorical. Yet, at the heart of each narrative is a voice—a cry—and this is the public and private conscience, the voice of memory.

PART FOUR

The Public and the Private in the Discipline of Composition Studies

13

MIXING IT UP

The Personal in Public Discourse

Bruce Horner

In the last two decades of work in composition studies, the *personal* as a category has come under siege from proponents of post-structuralist, post-Marxist, feminist, and social constructionist theory. This siege has now provoked a backlash in which personal, expressive writing is valorized for its difference from conventional, and especially densely "theoretical," academic writing: scholars engaging in personal writing are now hailed for defying academic disciplinary conventions. Roughly simultaneously, in response to the same theoretical perspectives that have laid siege to the personal, critical ethnographers in and outside composition have concluded that these theories place an ethical responsibility on ethnographers to make public admissions of the involvement of the personal in their work (see Kirsch and Ritchie). Thus, the intrusion of personal writing into a compositionist's scholarly text can currently be taken either as a gesture in defiance of recent critical theory or as a means of complying with the ethical strictures that theory imposes.

In this chapter, I examine how we have arrived at these contradictory positions. I argue that confusion over what constitutes the personal has led to this discrepancy in positions on its use and prevents us from more productive engagement with the personal in public discourse, in both our writing and our teaching. I begin with a brief review of the specific challenges theorists have posed to prior conceptions of the personal and then explore the implications of these challenges for current debate on the rhetoric and ethics of public engagements with the personal in writing. My contention is that those who valorize personal writing for breaking away from academic writing conventions all too often mistake rehearsals of an established public genre of writing for writing that contests dominant social constructions of what is deemed to be personal, and personal in, experience and writing. A commodified notion of personal writing is treated as in itself producing a specific kind of work; the labor of writing, reading, and researching in producing specific use values from that writing is dismissed from consideration. In critical ethnography, this commodified notion of the work of personal writing appears as the fetishizing of specific textual forms, which are treated as in themselves constituting a means by which to conform to ethical strictures. Thus the full material social process of ethnographic work is reduced to a focus on the problematics of textual conventions, with deleterious results.

In my view, it is Marxist-inflected theory that has posed the most serious challenges to dominant conceptions of the *personal* in writing and that has provoked the most serious backlash. Raymond Williams explains the issue of the individual writer for Marxist theory thus:

> To see individuation as a social process is to set limits to the isolation but also perhaps to the autonomy of the individual author. To see form as formative has a similar effect. The familiar question in literary history, "what did this author do to this form?" is often reversed, becoming "what did this form do to this author?" Meanwhile, within these questions, there is the difficult general problem of the nature of the active "subject." (192)

The tendency in Marxist thought that most transforms the question of the individual author is its identification of the individual subject "as a characteristic form of bourgeois thought" (193). Not only is the writer's language defined as social in its forms and conventions, so also are the "contents of [the writer's] consciousness."

It is this last implication of the sociality of writing that, Williams notes, provokes the sharpest reactions. And insofar as it has sometimes led to understanding individual writers as mere "carriers" of determinate social structures, that reaction, that is, the reduction of a writer's consciousness to no more than a particular social or historical category, is fully understandable. Consider the move to categorize writers using the triumvirate of race, class, and gender, say, or the reigning zeitgeist of a given time and place. What is missing in such readings, Williams notes, is any consideration of the "living and reciprocal relationships of the individual and the social" (194).Faced with such reductions, "it is not surprising that many people run back headlong into bourgeois-individualist concepts, forms, and institutions, which they see as their only protection." The social, imagined as monolithic, is deemed not to allow for any possibility of individuation, and so a "social perspective" on the personal is rejected as inadequate and reductive.

In practice, this rejection has led to a renewed valorization of the personal in writing. Identifying academic writing with stylistically dense, abstract, theoretical writing and with what seem to be inappropriate constraints made on writers by the social, represented by the academic institution, compositionists have turned to recognizably nonacademic discursive moves to counter what are seen as the limitations that academic discourse places on what writing may express and accomplish (see, for example, Bridwell-Bowles; Tompkins, "Me"). However, such moves essentially sidestep the sociality of the personal, risking in effect the reinforcement of dominant conceptions of the personal and the social. Williams observes that what modes of domination exclude is often designated as "the personal or the private, or as the natural or even the metaphysical . . . since what the dominant has effectively seized is...the ruling definition of the social" (125). It is this seizure, Williams insists, that has to be resisted. But those writers turning to the personal instead often accept such ruling definitions, turning to what the dominant has deemed "personal" as a refuge from, rather than a contested site of, the social.

Thus, in practice, this turn to the personal has resulted not in new forms of writing but in recapitulations of the generic category of personal writing—that is to say, writing recognizably "personal" because it rehearses those features dominant culture has designated to *be* "personal." And so, as Joseph Harris complains, we often get not a new form of discourse or an intervention in dominant (say, academic) discourse but uncritical adoptions of the "older belletristic" discourse of the personal essay, as cultivated by such canonical figures as Montaigne, Addison, De Quincey, Orwell, E. B. White, and the like (Harris, "Person, Position, Style" 50).

Such uncritical adoptions of this traditional genre are problematic because of the ideological message carried by the genre itself (see Haefner). As Fredric Jameson has warned, because a genre "is essentially a socio-symbolic message . . . [whose form] is imminently and intrinsically an ideology in its own right," this message persists in any reappropriation of the form (141). Those writers who adopt the genre of personal writing under the illusion that they are thereby escaping social discourse—"cultivating some tufts of what grows wild outside," in Peter Elbow's formulation ("Response" 90)—fail to recognize the form's ideological message and so can be said not so much to appropriate the genre but rather to be appropriated by it. If, for example, a genre establishes a "contract" between a writer and his or her specific public (Jameson 106), the genre of personal writing itself comprehends a set of expectations, beliefs, and attitudes about the value and constitution of personal experience, at least the experience of the writer, and a way of approaching that experience, which is profoundly ideological. Writers (and readers) adopting such a contract uncritically reinforce just such expectations, beliefs, and attitudes.

This is not an argument against reappropriating existing genres, the personal essay included. Indeed, from a social perspective, there is no alternative to engaging existing social forms, just as there is no possibility of inventing a purely personal, private language untouched by the social. Rather, it is an argument for confronting, and making strategic use of, the social historicity of any of the genres we adopt in our writing, recognizing both the historical ideological content of any discursive genre, personal writing included, and also the susceptibility of that content to change as it is deployed in different social and cultural contexts. It is in so doing that a particular discursive genre can be reappropriated to new ends.

All this is to redefine the question of the use of the personal in writing as, first, a question of the rhetorical gesture any such use makes, given the specific material social circumstances of that use. Both the rhetorical and ethical significance borne by use of recognizably personal writing will depend considerably on the social location of the speaker, the occasion, the intended purpose, and audience. The particular ethical and rhetorical charge of an instance of personal writing is contingent on both the history of the use of such writing and on the material social circumstances of that instance of use. Hence, calls to valorize, engage in, and teach *personal* writing miss the mark. We need instead to interrogate how a particular writer's engagement in such writing might operate, given the particular circumstances and purposes of that engagement.

Consider, for example, the following situation. A few years ago, as a member of the Iowa Immigrant Rights Project (IRP), I participated in lobbying Iowa state legislators (and others) on behalf of policies affecting the civil rights of recent immigrants to Iowa. This lobbying took the form of conversations with individual legislators, public debate, a newspaper editorial, and letters to the editor. In my lobbying efforts, my claims about immigrants were questioned—their susceptibility to violations of their rights and to prejudice and violence, their commitment to learning English, their alleged criminality, and so on. The Iowa IRP was a loose affiliation of immigrant groups, the local American Friends Service Committee, interested members of various religious and labor organizations, and public interest lawyers. Thus, my membership in the IRP in itself gave me no particular credibility with legislators: it signified at best only my concern—shared by other members of the project—about immigrant rights' issues. The rhetorical difficulty I faced, in my spoken and written discourse, was how to persuade legislators of the validity of my claims.

Any strategy I used involved some sort of personal admission, if we accept that any self-identification other than my affiliation with the IRP constituted an "exposure" of information otherwise private. For example, in discussing English Only legislation and the difficulties of language learning, I might attempt to gain more credibility for my claims by identifying myself as a professor of English, on the assumptions that this would lead my audience to 1) grant me expert status on language learning; and 2) accept my commitment to the English language (a commitment proponents of English Only legislation claim its opponents do not share). Alternatively, in making claims about immigrants' experience of discrimination, I might identify myself as the spouse, stepfather, and in-law of recent immigrants, on the assumption that my claims about the experiences of immigrants would be accepted as reliable by virtue of being close to firsthand.

The rhetorical value of these personal admissions would be contingent on a variety of factors. Most obviously, the rhetorical value of the first admission would depend on the esteem, or lack thereof, with which academics, and particularly English professors, were held. Simply put, would my identification as English professor mark me as expert or egghead? Similarly, admitting to marrying into a family of recent immigrants might work either to validate my claims about the experience of immigrants, and my right to speak for them, or alternatively to call into question my objectivity on the matter and mark me as a *special interest* whose *personal* feelings colored his views of the *public* interest. Public discourse has available a variety of categories into which to place admissions like mine. In fact, in making any of them I am simply offering my listeners a set of possible, and quite public, familiar ways of categorizing me and thus my argument. This highlights the fact that no such thing as *personal* writing exists, if by *personal* we mean writing that does not arise from and invoke some shared, public, socially constructed category: egghead or expert, authentic family man or special pleader. Instead, being *personal* constitutes a rhetorical strategy, successful or not, of donning the mantle of a public category to establish a persuasive ethos.

This is perhaps more readily seen when public figures attempt to *get personal*. For example, when presidential candidate George W. Bush confessed to the world his faith in Jesus Christ as his personal savior, he may have been attesting to a profound experience, but he was not being personal at all. Rather, he was invoking a range of possible publicly available categories into which voters might place him: Bible Belt hick, devout and trustworthy Christian, panderer, moral titan. That it was not an aberration from public discourse is clear from the responses it evoked. While editorialists and pundits disagreed with one another over the political import of Bush's statement, they had no trouble determining the simple meaning of his admission, something they might have experienced if he had offered a statement coming from some realm truly outside the social—if one can imagine any such thing.

But uses of the personal raise not only questions of rhetorical efficacy but also, as the term *ethos* suggests, questions of ethics. If the ability to make rhetorical gestures of personal admission constitutes a kind of cultural capital, then the value of that capital is contingent on one's social capital. The fact that an established figure in literary criticism like Jane Tompkins has gone personal in her academic writing (e.g., "Me and My Shadow") may speak primarily to her social position in the academy—her going personal may function less as a risk taken than a display of that position. We see evidence of this in the conflicted response to Tompkins's essays in which she goes personal ("Me," "Pedagogy"). Olivia Frey expresses the hope that Tompkins's "brave experiment" will pave the way for others (507–08). But Frey also notes that she herself cannot yet go personal because she is, after all, "not Jane Tompkins" (524). Similarly, Terry Myers Zawacki reports: "When I read Tompkins' essay ["Pedagogy of the Distressed"], I can't help thinking about the authority that Tompkins has, because she is 'Jane Tompkins,' to challenge boundaries" (35).

In noting that they themselves are not so free to go personal as Tompkins, Frey and Zawacki raise a second complication for writers contemplating such moves: not only is there nothing ethical about the distribution of capital of whatever kind, the value of that capital is contingent on whether it is recognized by others in positions of dominance. As demonstrated by teachers' responses to students' autobiographical efforts, not all instances of writers "going personal" are accorded the same value. Or, to return to the lobbying example, the options for going personal or not, options that were available to me, were not available to all. Rather, they were contingent on perceptions of my national, racial, and gender identity.

For instance, while my (pale) skin color does not in theory denote my citizenship status (e.g., I might be a citizen of Canada, France, Ireland, the United Kingdom, New Zealand), for the vast majority of Americans, it does. Nor in theory should the particular inflections I might give to my words denote my citizenship. In practice, however, my skin color and vocal inflections are commonly taken (*recognized*) as an indication of my nationality as American. My being male probably furthers this identification, given patriarchal notions of *Americanness.* So, while I might choose to identify myself as a member of a family of recent immigrants, or to leave my family relations unexpressed, that choice was and is not available to many others—for example, those with darker skin tones or those who speak with particular accents. In short, how I choose to represent myself is more than a matter of individual rhetorical strategizing based on surmises about my audience; it is a matter of my material social position as a white male speaking in a particular accent on issues of immigrants' rights in Iowa—a matter not simply of positioning oneself but of contending with how one is positioned materially and socially.

Questions of how to confront the power relations of social material positioning have been addressed most prominently in the work of critical and feminist pedagogy and critical ethnography. In this work, the personal is understood not as a way of writing emerging from and answerable to a realm outside the social but as a site where the social, understood as heterogeneous, is negotiated. This recognition of the sociality of the personal raises questions of epistemology, rhetorical efficacy, and ethics. First, to put it crudely, if knowledge, personal and otherwise, is socially constructed and continually under construction, as it were, then claims to the objectivity of one's knowledge are untenable and, therefore, rhetorically inefficacious. Second, the operation of power relations between speaker and listener, and between researcher and informant, has to be recognized in the production of any representation of their interactions. My representation of another's experience is not only epistemologically suspect but politically suspect as well: by what authority, it may be asked, do I speak for, and in the name of, others—such as recent immigrants? Third, just as my authority for speaking in the name of others is suspect, so I need to be wary of the likely political, material, and social effects of my representations of others on them. I cannot disavow responsibility for such effects by claiming that I am simply speaking the objective truth or have the best intentions for those in the name of and for whom I claim to speak.

It is difficult to argue against the strictures these concerns place on ethnographers. And the history of anthropology provides ample testimony of the dire effects of work uninformed by these concerns. Nonetheless, those attempting to follow these strictures in their writing now confront new ethical dilemmas. For critical ethnographers who intend their work not simply to increase the general stock of knowledge but to improve the material social conditions of those living at the field site, the more closely they attempt to follow these strictures in their writing, the more ineffectual that writing appears to be in achieving such ends. In "Beyond the Personal," Gesa Kirsch and Joy Ritchie have argued that ethnographers need not only to "encode in [their] research narratives the provisional nature of knowledge that [their] work generates and the moral dilemmas inherent in research" but also to "reconsider our privileging of certain, coherent, and univocal writing and include multiple voices and diverse interpretations in our research narratives, highlighting the ideologies that govern our thinking as well as those that may contradict our own" (24). Heeding such calls, ethnographers have produced a wealth of texts presenting multivocal, tentative, personal perspectives. Unfortunately, as Kirsch remarks in a subsequent essay, these textual practices themselves

> can disguise writers' continuing authorial control, they can fail to provide the theoretical framework and cultural context necessary for understanding the multiple voices merging in a single text, they make new and difficult demands on readers, they require tolerance for ambiguity and contradictory claims, and they easily become elitist and exclusionary. (193–94)

Too often, Kirsch warns, the politically emancipatory aims of the writers can be contradicted by the exclusionary effects of their writing.

Ralph Cintron echoes this warning, observing of educational ethnographies that the "pragmatic needs of education [may] . . . inhibit ethnographic experimentation" (401). For Cintron, only those writers who "need not answer to institutions that are significantly controlled by 'bottom-line' economics," who instead "have the luxury to experiment," can legitimately engage in such experimentation. Thus, just as critics indulging in recognizably "personal" writing can be said to be displaying the privileged position that enables them to afford to do so, so for Cintron only those ethnographers in the privileged position of being free of responsibility to "bottom-line economics" or material consequences on others from their writing can afford to write other than traditional, impersonal ethnographies. Indeed, we may understand their experiments, like authors' engagements in the "personal," primarily as displays of that privilege.

However, rather than assuming display of privilege as the motivating impulse for such textual experiments, I would argue that they arise instead from significantly mistaking where the work of ethnography, and the emancipation it is meant to effect, is located. If work comes to be located primarily in the text, then writers will focus attention on applying the strictures to the formal features of the written commodity. It is thus that a writer can come to substitute his or her own emancipation from writing conventions for the emancipation of those living at the research site, and thus that complexities of textual notation can come to stand in for the complexities of negotiating the experience, politics, and ethics of face-to-face encounters between the ethnographer and informants. To return to the example of my lobbying, it would be as if my concern to accurately represent the ethical complexities of the issues surrounding immigration, my own investment in such issues, and the problematic of my speaking on behalf of others were to override my efforts at persuading tired and impatient legislators to adopt a particular stance on pending legislation, so that I produced discourse fraught with disclaimers of my objectivity, qualifications to my positions, attempts at the presentation of multiple perspectives and voices, and the like. After all, in my experience with the IRP, members constantly confronted such issues in the process of researching and developing position statements, organizing events, forming coalitions, and reviewing crises both unexpected and ongoing. But while I would agree that questioning one's own positionality, interests, and the politics and problematics of representation is indeed crucial work for those involved in such projects, that is not to say that a text emerging from that work should attempt to capture those dynamics in its notational strategies, any more than a text needs to incorporate all the alternative drafts produced in the process of its composition. While such a text might be useful to the writer or those studying the writing process (think of scholarly editions of literary texts), it would carry significantly less use value as a lobbying tool. In short, much of what theorists like Kirsch and Ritchie quite rightly call for in the work of ethnography could (and does) take place in the work that goes on at the research site, which can then inform, rather than find formal textual equivalents in, some of the published writing that emanates from and reports on that research. But there exists no necessary equivalence between a textual form and the ethics of the interactions on which the text itself reports.

This confusion between a textual form and the ethics of the work, part of which includes textual production, mirrors compositionists' confusion in their recent valorizations of personal writing. In both cases, a textual form, or set of forms, is imagined in itself to produce specific effects, good or bad, rather than being seen as notations whose ethical value depends on the specific practices, and conditions (including histories) of practices, with them. This confusion instances commodity fetishism, in which "the products of the human brain appear as autonomous figures endowed with a life of their own, which enter into relations both with each other and with the human race" (Marx 164–65). The value of the form is identified not with the social relations of its production (including reception) but with the form itself. Consequently, it is the exchange value of the form, rather than its use value in achieving particular ends in specific circumstances, arising from particular kinds of labor with it, that is recognized.

We can see this treatment of writing as commodity in the kinds of valorization given to writing highlighting the personal location of the writer. Critics' praise of such writing rarely addresses the specific use it has had. As Harris observes, praise for Jane Tompkins's personal essay "Pedagogy of the Distressed" was directed at Tompkins herself for taking such a risk—not, significantly, for any insights it offered. (In fact, as Harris observes, Tompkins's essay simply "recycl[ed] many of the insights of writing teachers from Britton to Bruffee to Elbow without citation" [Harris, *Person, Position, Style* 47–48]). And as David Shumway observes in a rejoinder to Frey, Tompkins's essay "Me and My Shadow" was successful first and foremost at achieving distinction for the writer, for being "noticed" ("Solidarity" 107–09; "Comment" 833).

On those occasions when some use for the personal in writing is identified, its use for the writer is often conflated with its general use for all. In other words, the writing is again treated as a textual commodity: its effects are imagined to inhere in the text and, like any commercial product, to be guaranteed for any and all consumers. Such an approach ignores the ways in which the use value of writing varies by the writer, the occasion of its production, the reader and the practices of reading and conditions of reading it—that is, by the labor and social conditions of production. Writing, personal or otherwise, is not in itself useful but rather can be used for particular, different purposes by particular readers following specific practices, which themselves merit interrogation. For example, it seems quite likely that, as Jane Hindman argues in a recent essay defending personal writing, a "glimpse into one's life [can] provide a way to rethink professional work," and, as she quotes Victor Villanueva, Jr. observing, autobiography can be used "as a way of knowing our predispositions to see things certain ways" (Villanueva, "The Personal" 51; qtd. in Hindman 37). These sound like eminently laudable goals for a writer to pursue for herself, at least some of the time. For a particular writer to use the activity of writing as a way to rethink his professional work and come to know his predispositions might be just the thing for that writer to pursue in his private journal, written to himself, should he have the time and means and need to do so. But the writing produced might well be useless in helping other readers rethink their professional work, or come to know their predispositions, or indeed accomplish any number of other tasks. The use value of the writing, in other words, is particular not to the text but to the user, occasion of using, and mode and condition of use.

If the value of personal writing is itself contingent in these ways, then its place in writing pedagogy needs to be rethought. Recent arguments for the inclusion of personal writing contend that personal writing offers a way to enable students to break free from the confines of academic discourse (Annas; Bridwell-Bowles 350; Torgovnick 27; see Haefner 127–28). The aim here is to make possible the emergence of forms of thought not expressible within such confines. But here again, the labor of producing writing, of writing as an activity, is often elided, and features of the commodified form of the personal essay are often treated as in themselves giving students this freedom. It makes good—if by now common—pedagogic sense to warn students against paying too much attention to conventions of form at certain stages of their writing and to encourage them to find ways to link their writing to their personal lives. However, doing this is not the same as advising them to participate in a particular genre—that is, to produce the product commonly recognized as *personal writing*. For writing that may exhibit few or no traces of personal writing in its forms may nonetheless stem productively from a writer's personal engagement in the writing. Harris has observed that while Harry Braverman's *Labor and Monopoly Capital* bears no features of that genre of writing recognized as "personal," it is nonetheless personal in the sense that Braverman shows "passionate commitment to his subject through the range of his reading and the clarity and care of his argument" ("Person, Position, Style" 49). In the introduction to his book, Braverman admits that "[l]ike all craftsmen, even the most inarticulate, I always resented [being robbed of a craft heritage and given little or nothing to take its place], and as I reread these pages, I find in them a sense not only of social outrage . . . but also perhaps of personal affront" (6; qtd. in Harris, *Person, Position, Style* 49). Thus, for Braverman, there is a personal resonance in making his argument in *Labor and Monopoly Capital* against the degradation, through deskilling, of work and workers.

Yet, Pamela Annas, in "Style as Politics," compares Braverman's style of writing unfavorably to writing that is more recognizably personal in style. Annas encourages her students to produce writing in which they base their arguments "at least as much on lived personal experience as on more conventional sources of information" (369, qtd. in Harris, *Person, Position, Style* 48). But she fails to recognize Braverman's writing as such, even though from his introduction it too appears quite clearly to be based "at least as much on lived personal experience" as other writing Annas singles out for praise that is more recognizably personal in the textual forms it takes (e.g., Virginia Woolf's *A Room of One's Own* and Robin Lakoff's *Language and Women's Place*). What distinguishes Braverman's book is not its absence of foundation in personal experience but the rhetoric Braverman employs in his writing. In other words, Annas identifies the personal only in writing with a set of recognizable textual features. She is thus blind to the possibility that writing that follows conventions of impersonality might be as profoundly personal as—perhaps in some instances more so than—conventionally, and thus recognizably, personal writing.

This is not to condemn writing that draws on conventions of personal writing but to insist that any conventions be interrogated for the uses to which they are put, for whom, by whom, and how. In his contribution to a recent *College English* symposium, "The Politics of the Personal," Villanueva, regularly cited for his autobiographical *Bootstraps,* ends up warning against writing that constitutes effectively "the reverse of the wolf in sheep's clothing . . . expressionism with a social and political rationale" (52). While he insists that "[t]here must be room for elements of autobiography" in our writing, he calls for "the autobiographical *as critique,*" "not as confession and errant self-indulgence, not as the measure on which to assess theory, not as a replacement for rigor" (51; my emphasis).

The question of whether to allow for the personal and private in writing is, in short, a misguided question. What matters is not whether writers employ the conventions of personal writing in their writing, but the ends to which they employ them and the circumstances, and reading practices, that might allow for such ends to be achieved. Do we want, or need, writing that rehearses the conventions of personal writing to reinscribe the ideology of individualism? Can we deploy personal writing to call into question conventional understandings of what the *personal* means, to mix it up, as it were, in our writing? Under what circumstances might such mixing end up valorizing, again, conventional understandings of the *personal?* By what reading practices might such conventional understandings be undermined? Insofar as all writing is, in some sense, personal; insofar as all writing is also, in a profound sense, public; and insofar as the personal and the public in writing are not commodities but effects, it makes no sense to ask whether we, or our students, should produce, or be allowed to produce, either. Instead, we can ask of any writing and reading practice how conventions associated with either the *personal* or the *public,* conventionally understood, are deployed, and how we ourselves in our reading and writing might mix up, to contest, the conventional understandings of both.

14

CULTURAL AUTOBIOGRAPHICS

Complicating the "Personal Turns" in Rhetoric and Composition Studies

Krista Ratcliffe

For the past few summers, I have taught a course entitled Rhetorics of Women's Multicultural Autobiographies in which students and I read American women autobiographers (Maya Angelou, Dorothy Day, Diane Glancy) and autobiography theorists (Joanne Braxton, Leigh Gilmore, Sidonie Smith). Although the stated purpose of the course is to question definitions of *autobiography* as well as to critique its purposes, tactics, and effects, a side benefit for me is that teaching autobiography theory has helped me to rethink the *personal turns* in rhetoric and composition studies.

DIGRESSION 1: *I know it's more accepted these days to say "composition studies," but I recently realized that on this matter, I am a "conservative" in that I refuse to relinquish either the founding role of rhetoric in our field or the rhetorical dimension of all the work we do, both scholarly and pedagogically.*

The phrase *personal turns* signifies moves within rhetoric and composition studies to employ personal stories—often autobiographical—within scholarship and pedagogy. Two such turns have occurred. Like the bellbottom pants students now sport, the first personal turn (expressivism) had a previous life in the late 1960s and early 1970s. It emerged in reaction to revived classical schools of rhetoric, primarily Aristotelian, which posit writing as an invention process that can proceed rationally and systematically on any topic, though topics were usually academic or public, not personal. Expressivism generated a debate about *whether* to use personal topics in writing pedagogy and couched the debate in terms of invention (classical heuristics vs. expressive freewriting) and genre (academic essay vs. personal narrative). In the mid-1990s, a second personal turn emerged in reaction to heavily theorized post-structuralist and feminist/cultural studies schools of rhetoric, which posit writing as multiple signifying processes functioning within linguistic and cultural systems and which invite writers to analyze how they use language and how language uses them. This second turn generated a debate about *how* to use personal writing in scholarship and pedagogy and couched this debate in terms of function; for example, "Should a story stand alone (à la Wendy Bishop, Peter Elbow, and Joe Trimmer) or be employed as cultural critique (à la Susan Jarratt, Jackie Royster, Victor Villanueva, and Lynn Worsham)?"

In this chapter, I argue that these two personal turns, though related, generate debates with different histories, definitions, and stakes. I conclude by imagining how autobiography theory, particularly a concept of cultural autobiographics, may productively complicate our field's thinking about "personal turns."

MAPPING A HISTORY OF THE PERSONAL TURNS

To map a history, let's circle back to 1963, when Albert R. Kitzhaber's report on the Dartmouth study of student writing was first published and when the number-one TV show in the United States was *The Beverly Hillbillies.* While Jed and all his kin were heading west toward the cement pond, Kitzhaber, Edward Corbett, and James Golden were circling back through Western history to classical Greece, later joined in their journey by Winifred Horner.

DIGRESSION 2: *My favorite Win Horner story is that she flunked first-year English. Well, actually, she chose not to complete a writing correspondence course that she had signed up for while living on a farm and rearing her children, letting them run around the living room while she climbed into their playpen with her typewriter.*

When Edward Corbett and others argued that English departments should revive the study of classical rhetoric, with a healthy dose of eighteenth-century theory thrown in for good measure, what they meant was that writing teachers should teach Aristotelian invention (topoi, enthymemes, and appeals) along with elements of Hugh Blair's style. Motivated by the task of training TAs to teach composition to an increasingly large and diverse student body, these scholar-administrators argued that classical rhetoric provided foundational principles for teaching writing. Their collective action laid a cornerstone of our discipline, rhetoric and composition studies.

In reaction to this emphasis on classical rhetoric, the first personal turn emerged. Consider, for a moment, the late 1960s and early 1970s. People were rejecting any expert over thirty and any method that didn't enable students to turn on and tune in to the times; simultaneously, people were embracing a journey into the self. In 1973, the first personal turn was taken by Peter Elbow, who offered students teacherless classrooms with freewriting and peer review via his *Writing without Teachers.* Granted, Elbow has argued that freewriting is not self-centered but rather an "invitation [for students] to take a ride on language itself, and . . . to 'get out of the self': to relinquish volition and planning and see what words and phrases come out of the head when you just kick it and give language and culture a start" ("Response" 506). While I recognize this potential, in my experience as a college student in the late 1970s and as a beginning teacher in the early 1980s, freewriting was often employed in ways that asked students to generate ideas from the inside out—that is, to go inside themselves to "find themselves" and to discover what they didn't know they knew; it was rarely employed to expose cultural discourses that inform their identities. As such, this "finding oneself" form of invention was a far cry from Aristotelian invention.

To clothe "finding oneself" in academic dress, cognitive theorists arose in the 1970s and early 1980s, hoping to map the inner journey of successful student writers so that teachers could use such maps to help not so good student writers learn to navigate *the* writing process.

DIGRESSION 3: *In the twilight of cognitive theory, I was hooked up to a brain machine, thanks to Roxanne Mountford, to test my brain for left-side, right-side activities. According to the guy operating the machine and the pictures he gave me afterwards, my brain negated this spherical schemata. When I performed the tasks designed to test one side of my brain or the other, both sides lit up. I couldn't decide if that meant that I was really smart . . . or (more likely) that I just needed a whole lot more brainpower than most people to perform the mundane tasks the operator gave me, my favorite being to think of all the words I could that begin with "P." For the record, Roxanne abandoned this research.*

Again, because rhetoric and composition studies does not exist in a vacuum, the same cultural impulse that celebrated natural food and natural childbirth and encouraged Aretha to belt out "You Make Me Feel Like a Natural Woman" may have encouraged Janet Emig, Linda

Flower, and John Hayes and, later, Mountford to investigate "what comes naturally" to good writers. But alas, mapping *the* writing process proved impossible because, while there may be general patterns of brain activity, there are also patterns dependent not simply upon nature but upon a person's particular experiences within culture.

Once our field found itself contemplating people's experiences within culture, we were in the mid-1980s, in the heyday of social constructionism, which challenged expressivism. Instead of foregrounding the personal, different factions of social constructionism foregrounded the textual and the cultural, respectively. The first faction, which promoted the textual, was heavily influenced by poststructuralism. Followers of Jacques Derrida argued that deconstructive textuality was the only game in town. Followers of Roland Barthes declared the author dead, the self a lexical subject, and personal thoughts merely discursive citations of all the discourses surrounding and embodying us. Followers of Michel Foucault declared the author simply a function. What's a writing teacher to do? Well, Greg Ulmer started holding textshops instead of workshops, and Victor Vitanza honed his call for a third sophistic. At the same time, a second faction of social constructionists, such as David Bartholomae, Pat Bizzell, Jim Berlin, and Joe Harris were also influenced by post-structuralist thought but mainly as it intersected with cultural theory. Uncomfortable with the ideas that language is the only game in town and that life is only a linguistic game, they argued that violence in a written text is not the same as violence in the streets. Though both a book and the street may be read as texts, they may not be reduced to identical textuality. Hence the rise of the cultural. According to Berlin, that rise engendered a merger of rhetoric, post-structuralism, and cultural studies (*Poststructuralism* 16). This merger was designed to impress two ideas upon teachers and students: 1) the cultural discourses into which we're born possess an agency to influence our thinking via socialization; and 2) we possess a personal agency (however limited) with which to articulate cultural discourses and "talk back" to them (Trimbur, "Agency").

DIGRESSION 4: *Of course, I can't resist adding here the now oft-repeated claim: many feminist and ethnicity scholars had been saying these things all along, wondering why the author had been declared dead just when women and nondominant ethnic groups were gaining entry into the academy in greater numbers.*

Although this second faction researched the tensions between discursive/cultural agency and personal agency in many different cultural sites (such as ethnic groups, religious institutions, and popular media), Bartholomae and Bizzell were interested in university culture, especially student writing—thus, their emphasis on theorizing and teaching "academic discourse" (Bartholomae, *Inventing* 134; Bizzell, *Foundationalism* 53; Harris, *A Teaching Subject* 98–107).

The early 1990s saw a debate between Bartholomae and Elbow on the merits of academic writing vs. personal writing in the composition classroom. Bartholomae defined *academic discourse* as critical writing "where students (with instruction—more precisely, with lessons in critical reading) can learn to feel and see their position inside a text they did not invent and can never, at least completely, control" ("Writing" 482); Elbow defined *personal writing* as separate from academic writing, as writing that focuses on students' ideas and enables students to say, "I feel like I *am* a writer" ("Being" 489). This debate demonstrated that, although social constructionism had at that moment gained disciplinary ascendancy over expressivism, expressivism was far from dead.

On the heels of this debate, a second personal turn emerged in our field in the mid-1990s, bringing together (if you'll pardon my parlance) strange bedfellows: the far from dead expressivists and the feminist/cultural folks who never really believed that the author was dead. Expressivist threads were picked up by Wendy Bishop in her article "Places to Stand: The Reflective Writer-Teacher-Writer in Composition" and by Joe Trimmer in his collection *Narration as Knowledge*, both of whom defend the role of "story" as scholarship and pedagogy. Simultaneously, the feminist/cultural studies folks were exposing, in both scholarly and student writing, that the personal is always implicated in cultural critique and that the cultural is always implicated in personal writing. In "When the First Voice You Hear Is Not Your Own," Royster argues for an emphasis on—indeed a respect for—the "subject positions" of particular readers and writers (29). Jarratt and Worsham's collection, *Feminism and Composition Studies: In Other Words,* echoes Royster, and to some extent Julia Kristeva: that is, when historical women and the category Woman are inserted into the history of composition studies, also inserted is an invitation to rethink not just our field but our own subjectivities, our politics, our texts, and our pedagogies. Given these strange bedfellows, the second personal turn engendered a debate not about *whether* to use personal writing in scholarship and pedagogy but about *how.* In other words, the second personal turn engendered a debate about politics.

DEFINING THE DEBATES AND TERMS OF THE SECOND PERSONAL TURN

Within the second personal turn, expressivists and feminist/cultural studies folks both advocate the personal but in different ways. These differences are evidenced in the CCCC's programs of 1998 and 2000. With the 1998 theme "Ideas, Historias, y Cuentos," Victor Villanueva located himself more in the cultural studies camp by offering conferencegoers an opportunity to link ideas, history, and personal stories; with the 2000 theme "Educating the Imagination and Reimagining Education," Wendy Bishop located herself more in the expressivist camp by offering conference-goers an opportunity to reaffirm the creative imagination's place in our field, and if you examine the program, you'll see lots of panels on stories, very few on the history of rhetoric. Now I don't offer these examples to celebrate Villanueva and excoriate Bishop; as Pat Bizzell once mentioned in an e-mail message, it's probably a good idea to have the conference rotate its emphasis. I do, however, offer these examples to demonstrate that the debate between expressivists and feminist/cultural studies folks is alive and kicking.

DIGRESSION 5: *My naming two sides of this debate "expressivist" and "feminist/cultural studies folks" is admittedly both accurate and troublesome. The labels work to define how the debate functions, but they also elide certain issues, or more importantly, certain subject positions: e.g., some expressivists are feminists; moreover, some feminists and cultural studies scholars disagree about the role of gender in cultural critique.*

The debate between expressivists and feminist/cultural studies folks may be better understood, however, by examining the terms that inform it. For although the differing emphases of the two schools may be clear, as Jane Hindman points out in a 2001 *College English* symposium on personal writing, "[m]uch less clear . . . is just what we mean when we use the terms 'the personal' and 'personal writing'" (34–35). In the wake of critical theory's upheaval of all our sacred *terms* (e.g., *author, reading, writing, reader*), the second personal turn must contend with terms that are more contested, less self-evident.

Yet the expressivist ideology of the second personal turn is haunted by the first turn's fairly self-evident terms: *personal, writer, writing,* and *story. Personal* represents experiences of writers; *writer* signifies people who are individual agents; *writing* refers to processes of discovering, communicating, and narrating; and *story* represents a self-contained narrative. Thus, writers write stories about their personal lives. Given these terms, the hermeneutic circle closes, apparently complete. As Christine Farris has argued, this ideology was foregrounded in a 1999 call for papers for a special edition of *Writing on the Edge*, which Elbow guest-edited, a special edition entitled "True Stories" ("Feminist" 10–11). Although that title resonates with echoes of the Hollywood glamour magazines that populated the "beauty shops" of my childhood, Elbow has something quite different in mind. He invites readers to submit the following: "Any stories related to writing, teaching writing, or teaching and learning are welcome, but *please* let the story work on its own; don't include a moral or point or piece of wisdom. We are looking for student stories, teacher stories, convention stories, dream stories, transcribed oral stories, writing program stories, classroom stories, writing stories, stories from the past, stories from the present, stories of any form, shape, or possibility" (*CCC* Online; my emphasis). Note the "please." Elbow is imploring us to curtail our impulse for academic critique and to foreground the story, the implication being a call for an *ars narratia*, the idea that a story should not critique but be.

DIGRESSION 6: *When I spoke on this topic at the 2000 Summer Seminar in Rhetoric and Composition Studies at Millikin University, a student showed me to my dorm room and told me in an awed, hushed tone, "This was Peter Elbow's room. He just left this morning." In Elbow's honor (and I do truly respect his role in opening a space for the personal in our field), I'll refrain from making a point about this story.*

Feminist/cultural studies ideology of the second turn is more clearly haunted by critical theory's upheaval of all our sacred terms. The term *personal* signifies people's experiences and opinions, which are always implicated within cultural systems; *writer* signifies culturally located subjects who are socialized by cultural discourses and who also possess a certain agency for talking back to these discourses; *writing* signifies processes of recognizing this discursive socialization and of either reinforcing or resisting it; and *story* refers to a narrative that is at once both personal and cultural, both representational and representationally suspect. This ideology promotes writers telling stories as a means of identifying and critiquing not just their own always changing cultural locations but also the attitudes and actions that emerge from these cultural locations—the idea being that an awareness of intersecting discourses of race, gender, class, age, nationality, region, and so forth makes a person more able to understand and negotiate with other people, who also have their own particular always changing cultural locations. In "As We Were Saying," Jarratt articulates this stance: "The difference between self-reflective feminist narratives and expressivist paradigms is theoretical, political, and rhetorical: the difference between the collective 'we' of my title and the unbracketed first person evoked by some advocates of personal writing in the composition class" (6). Note Jarratt's "we." With its use, she insists on a writer's culturally, and hence chorally, implicated subjectivity even when that writer says "I." And it is just this cultural implication, she claims, that the expressivist "I" ignores by remaining naively unmarked.

Although the undergraduates in my autobiography class are unaware of this debate, they often rehearse it. In the summer of 2000 while reading Nikki Giovanni's *Sacred Cows . . . and Other Edibles*, several white students commented that they didn't realize Giovanni was black until she told them. I asked if they thought she was white. No, they replied, they just didn't think about race/ethnicity at all; further, they replied, Giovanni's being African American didn't matter. Their replies may be read in a couple ways: 1) they are not prejudiced and are happy to read writers of any ancestry; and/or 2) they believe that race and ethnicity should not factor into writing and reading. So we talked for a moment about cultural markers (such as race, motherhood, gender, and age) in the texts that we had been reading. We talked about why some writers have the privilege to ignore these markers and why others don't. We talked about Giovanni's decision to explicitly include them in her text so that readers cannot read her as unmarked. In their initial replies, the students were echoing the expressivist stance: what's important is the story, not the cultural location of the writer. Giovanni herself, however, was echoing the other side of the debate: what's important is not just the story but also how it is *visibly* informed by the author's and readers' subject positions.

DIGRESSION 7: *I wonder how the students would have told this story? What kind of character would I be?*

At this point in this chapter, it would be easy, as I noted earlier, simply to align myself with Royster, Jarratt, Worsham, and Villanueva and feel smugly self-righteous about my choice. But to my mind, the road to self-righteousness (especially my own) is always suspect. So that idea, coupled with my hunch that this debate may have something more to tell us than the simple binary that meets the eye, leads me to yet another issue: the stakes of getting personal.

ASSESSING THE STAKES OF GETTING PERSONAL

Although I've clearly located myself within the feminist/cultural studies camp, I know some really good scholars and teachers who are expressivists (and yes, I know how that sentence sounds, but it's true). Moreover, I respect how these teachers use their (dare I say) values and beliefs about language and writing to excite students into wanting to write. So whether theorized from the sites of expressivism or feminist/cultural studies, our field's personal turn in many ways heartens me. But the story does not end there because I am also troubled. I'm troubled not because I want to convert the expressivists. I don't (except on days when I'm really cranky). I'm troubled because I see problems that haunt both camps, these being the stakes of getting personal. Although the stakes of *how* personal writing is employed in rhetoric and composition studies raise myriad questions, here I address only three: 1) How does the personal count in scholarship? 2) How does it count in pedagogy? and 3) How does it count in cross-cultural communication?

First, in terms of scholarship, one stake concerns the role of theory. Although expressivists and feminist/cultural studies folks make similar textual moves in their scholarship, they position themselves differently in terms of theory. In the scholarship where Bartholomae engages Elbow and Elbow engages Bartholomae, where Jarratt engages expressivists and Bishop engages social constructionists, they all set up a thesis, establish reasons that may be enumerated and relegated into logical categories, and weave personal stories into the piece as evidence. But Bartholomae and Jarratt embrace theory; Elbow and Bishop seem . . . well . . . a little more suspicious of it. In "Places to Stand," Bishop confronts this issue head-on when she says: "[I]t seems so uncanny for me today to be hearing . . . that expressivists don't do other things ('things' are often represented by the word 'theory') because they 'can't,' not because they choose not to" (11). This "choosing not to" idea was reinforced to me by Joe Trimmer, to whom I owe a great debt for encouraging me to enter this field at a time when I wasn't sure I was smart enough for Ph.D. studies. Years later, after attending one of my CCCC's talks, he sent me a piece he had written along with a note that said something like: Here's my foray into multicultural autobiography, but notice, no theory jargon. What I get from reading Elbow, Bishop, and Trimmer is that they are all more than a little fed up with academic jargon in scholars' and students' writings—and in some cases, rightly so. Their eyes and ears desire a cleaner prose; their writerly sensibilities demand a broader audience reminiscent of the public intellectuals of old. In some ways, I'm sympathetic to those ideas. Theoretical writings are sometimes poorly written. But so are stories. Conversely, both theoretical articles and stories can be done well. The question for me about the role of theory in rhetoric and composition studies is not so much a question of writing quality as one of disciplinary function: what does theory make (im)possible? For me, as a scholar, theory productively complicates my thinking, my writing, my teaching, and my daily living; it offers me a forum for framing my own ideas; and it offers me a humility in recognizing that *my* ideas, experiences, and stories are rhetorically linked to a community of thinkers beyond myself.

Another scholarly stake of getting personal concerns negotiating the question: what counts as disciplinary knowledge? When reviewers of book manuscripts and tenure cases assess scholarship in terms of how well it extends disciplinary knowledge, what are they to do with stories that stand alone? Can story count as theory? You bet. Even Judith Butler agrees. But can it stand alone? That is the question, and it invokes a tension that is felt by expressivists and feminist/cultural studies folks even though personal writing is widely employed today. Otherwise, why would Bishop feel compelled in "Places to Stand" to assure readers that she wants to hear their stories? "Did you not know I wanted to know about it? I do" (29). And why would Worsham, citing Toni Morrison's Nobel lecture, assure readers that "[n]arrative is radical . . . creating us at the very moment it is being created" (337)? The conventions of scholarly readership (e.g., for reviewing book manuscripts and tenure cases) are such that personal writing cannot simply stand alone but must further disciplinary knowledge; in other words, scholars (especially beginning ones) must navigate existing institutional structures that demand they distinguish a *Harper's* creative nonfiction essay from a *CCC*'s scholarly article. Granted, a third option does exist. Villanueva names this option "critical autobiography" and defines it, via Antonio Gramsci, as a "mixed-genre," a hybrid of personal story and intellectual critique (Symposium Collective 51). But as Chris Farris argues, negotiating this textual terrain is tricky. What if one reads it from within traditional scholarly criteria? What if one develops new criteria (telephone conversation) for reading it? These are not impossible questions, but they are important ones that need to be more fully disseminated and discussed so as to clarify for scholarly writers and readers the stakes of getting personal. Second, in terms of pedagogy, the stakes of getting personal include how well teachers and students perform in the classroom. Again, similarities exist between expressivists and feminist/cultural studies folks. We all want students to leave a writing course with a increased appreciation for writing, with an increased respect for the power of language, with an increased ability to engage in writing as intellectual and communicative acts. And we may all use freewriting and peer groups, circled chairs and portfolios.

One pedagogical stake lies, again, in teachers' orientation toward theory. Teachers' theoretical assumptions (whether articulated or not) drive their use of pedagogical tactics. For instance, freewriting may be used by an expressivist to dig into the self; it may also be used by a cultural studies person to expose cultural discourses that embody us. Circled chairs may be used by a feminist to promote a more equal forum; they may also be used by a tyrannical teacher to better control students. I could go on, but I won't. My point (and personal pet peeve) is that pedagogical tactics are not inherently expressivist or feminist or anything else. Just as Aristotle argues that rhetoric becomes good or bad in the hands of a moral or immoral rhetorician, pedagogical tactics gain meaning from how they are employed. Granted, rhetorical structures and pedagogical tactics have inherent limitations and possibilities. But that is precisely why teachers of writing need to clarify their theoretical positions and then clearly articulate these positions for students and for themselves. Otherwise, freewriting in the hands of a cultural studies teacher might still be perceived by a student as a means of purely private investigation.

Another pedagogical stake lies in the question of course content. Horner rehearsed this question in her oft-cited *Bridging the Gap*, a 1983 collection in which everyone from J. Hillis Miller to Wayne Booth weighed in on whether readings should be used to teach writing. (Horner said no; Miller and Booth said yes). Bartholomae makes critical reading and writing about texts, such as Richard Rodriguez's *Hunger from Memory* and Plato's *Phaedrus,* a focus of his composition course ("Wandering" 97); although Elbow agrees that students should read texts, he advocates spending less class time on reading and more having students write by "*pretend[ing]* that no authorities have ever written about their subject before" ("Being" 491, 496). For a teacher, this choice has institutional and disciplinary implications. For example, listen to the following tirade against personal writing by Richard Marius, a Harvard professor who wrote the "Composition Studies" chapter in Stephen Greenblatt and Giles Gunn's *Redrawing the Boundaries*: "Get rid of autobiographical writing in the classroom. . . . Autobiographical writing demeans our profession. While our colleagues in history, literature, and other liberal arts are asking for writing about the world out there, we often look like a crowd of amateur therapists delivering dime store psychology to adolescents. Our discipline then becomes trivial in the eyes of the larger faculty" (475–76). My point is not that one should be intimidated by Marius's admonition; actually, his dismissive tone about personal writing makes me want to pledge allegiance to expressivism. My point is that this bias is still "out there," affecting things like hiring, tenure, promotion, pay raises, and personal status within one's department. Part-time and untenured pedagogues know this better than anyone else.

Third, in terms of cross-cultural communication, a stake in getting personal concerns how well U.S. cultures develop tactics for negotiating commonalities and differences. Although this issue is so complex as to make me throw up my hands before I begin, I choose to focus on one tactic: the trump card, particularly its reception. A trump card is a personal story linked to a cultural location; it is used as a shortcut to a conclusion, functioning enthymemically via traditional common sense. In rhetorical exchanges, a trump card can take any claim on any topic. The trump card wins the argument—unless, of course, it is overtrumped by a more powerful trump card. And there's a whole deck of them—both traditional and revisionary. Traditional trump cards may be classified according to relational roles, such as the parent card, the teacher card, the boss card. For example, when I tell my six-year-old daughter to pick up her toys "because I say so," I'm hoping she'll be sufficiently intimidated by the parent card to do as I ask. As this example indicates, such trump cards work only because there is an accompanying subordinate position to be trumped (child, student, employee). Traditional trump cards may also be classified according to cultural markings such as race, gender, class, age, and nationality. For example, when white students say that Giovanni's race does not matter, they are speaking from a position of privilege. Common sense tells us that if a traditional card is played and we occupy a subordinate position, then we had better listen and act accordingly . . . or resist and be aware of the consequences. Obviously, traditional trump cards still resonate within the United States: parents still say pick up your room because I say so, and privileged whites still say race does not matter. Yet, these traditional trump cards may be stood on their heads when proved unjust, for example, when adolescent or adult children challenge the parent card or when civil rights movements challenge the traditional race privilege card. Interestingly, though, traditional trump cards are often received not as trump cards but as norms; it is mainly revisionary actions, such as children arguing for rights or nonwhites arguing that race does matter, that suffer the label "trump card." And this phenomenon leads me to questions of reception.

In terms of trump card reception, sometimes a trump card is simply a trump card. It happens. People of every cultural location use them to achieve their own ends. But sometimes what is *received* as a "trump card" is not *intended* to be one. Sometimes what is received as a trump card is actually intended as a necessary corollary to the topic under discussion. What is at stake in getting personal is that people in authority often choose to interpret another's story as a trump card. The O. J. Simpson trial is a perfect example. When Johnny Cochran and his defense team introduced LAPD attitudes toward African Americans into the defense, the media accused him of playing the race card. But, as Cochran and his team showed, racist attitudes did exist among LAPD officers; consequently, Cochran and his team deemed questions of race a necessary corollary to their defense of the murder charge. But the (dominant white) media's and John Q. Public's reception of this corollary as "the race card" prevented productive discussion of LAPD corruption. Stasis theory helps explain the problem. The media and public obsessed on the stasis of conjecture (i.e., is race an issue?); actually, the majority obsessed on arguing that race was not an issue and concluded that Cochran was simply attempting to deflect discussion of the real issue, murder. A more productive option for discussion might have been to pursue the stasis of quality (i.e., given that race is always already a factor in daily U.S. life, to what degree did racist attitudes inform white officers' handling of the evidence and to what degree should such attitudes influence the verdict?). From this point of stasis, there would have been heated discussions but perhaps not such racially divisive ones.

When people choose to interpret an/other person's personal story as a trump card (and, remember, it is always a choice), they often enact one of three dysfunctional receptions: 1) they remain silent; 2) they talk back to the "other" person but remain overly suspicious; or 3) they speak in ways that essentialize gender and other cultural categories by saying, for example, "oh, that's just how *they* are"—as if all the *they*s are exactly alike.

DIGRESSION 8: *It probably hasn't escaped your notice that calling someone an expressivist or social constructionist may also function as a trump card.*

The danger with trump cards is that when they are used or, worse, when necessary corollaries are received as trump cards, three negative consequences ensue: 1) cultural categories (such as gender, ethnicity, age, nationality) are reified; 2) the potential of both the personal and cultural are downplayed and sometimes downright denied; and 3) possibilities for cross-cultural dialogues are shut down. In sum, the status quo reigns.

So our discipline's stakes in how to use personal writing are greater than just a question of differences in theory and pedagogy. The stakes are also in how well we help facilitate cross-cultural communication. Perhaps in further interrogating the trump card and other cross-cultural tactics, expressivists and social constructionists may find adjoining ground.

RE/THEORIZING THE PERSONAL—OR, HOW AUTOBIOGRAPHY THEORY MIGHT INFORM OUR CURRENT PERSONAL TURN

Like rhetoric and composition studies, autobiography studies gained respectability within the academy only within the last thirty years, with founding texts being James Olney's 1972 *Metaphors of Self: The Meaning of Autobiography* and his 1980 *Autobiography: Essays Theoretical and Critical.* When the field's early focus stayed on great men, the field of women's autobiography emerged, and when that field's early focus stayed on white women, an emphasis on women's multicultural autobiography emerged. During this evolution, old definitions of autobiography were exploded. The old definitions posit autobiography, historically, as a literary genre—a genre defined as the "full factual account of the author's public self, . . . [in] a linear, chronological exposition of events, . . . within a single work" (Morgan 5), a genre that operates as a not so thinly veiled hero's tale, a genre that purports to be didactic or confessional or some combination of the two. Literary scholars have often dismissed this genre, ranking autobiography as inferior to other genres (such as poetry and drama), fearing that if personal experience entered the literary realm, then somehow the aesthetic might be polluted by the didactic/confessional. Feminist literary scholars have often dismissed not the genre but the traditional definition, questioning the gendered assumptions behind phrases such as "full factual account," "author's public self," and "linear, chronological order exposition." Rhetoric and composition scholars have often dismissed this definition, too, questioning its positivistic overtones. To help rhetoric and composition studies incorporate more productive ideas about autobiography, which in turn may help our field complicate notions of the personal, I offer a concept of cultural autobiographics, a concept indebted to many rhetoric and composition and autobiography theorists. Cultural autobiographics posits autobiography, or personal writing, as both genre and rhetorical tactic; it interweaves the personal with the textual and the cultural, and it exposes the material dimensions of language and written texts.

When positing personal writing as a genre, cultural autobiographics presumes not a stand-alone story but Villanueva's "critical autobiography," a "mixed-genre" or hybrid of personal story and intellectual critique (Symposium Collective 51). When positing personal writing as a rhetorical strategy that permeates all genres, cultural autobiographics complements Villanueva's ideas with Leigh Gilmore's. Gilmore coins the term *autobiographics* and defines its "elements" as

> those elements of self-representation which are not bound by a philosophical definition of self derived from Augustine, not content with the literary history of autobiography, those elements that instead mark a location in a text where self-invention, self-discovery, and self-representation emerge within the technologies of autobiography—namely, those legalistic, literary, social, and ecclesiastical discourses of truth and identity through which the subject of autobiography is produced. . . . Autobiographics, as a description of self-representation and as a reading practice, is concerned with interruptions and eruptions, with resistance and contradictions as strategies of self-representation . . . [and] is the site of multiple solicitations, multiple markings of "identity," multiple figurations of agency. . . . The *I*, then, does not disappear into an identity-less textual universe. Rather, the autobiographicality of the *I* in a variety of discourses is emphasized as a point of resistance in self-representation. (42)

In conceptualizing autobiographics, Gilmore asks us to imagine the "presence" of autobiography in all texts; thus, she shifts the question from whether the autobiographical exists in a text to questions of degree and manner.

To demonstrate how the personal, the textual, and the cultural intersect, cultural autobiographics hearkens back to Janice Morgan, who (echoing Olney) reminds us that the term *autobiography* contains etymological echoes of all three categories. That is, *autobiography* contains *auto* (signifying self), *bio* (signifying life), and *graphy* (signifying writing/textuality). According to Morgan, depending on which etymology is emphasized, we get three different views of autobiography. Focusing on *bio* gives us a premodern emphasis on the life of a person in relation to existing cultural structures; for example, one was born either a serf or a king with little or no options for change. Focusing on *auto* gives us a modern emphasis on the life of a person as an autonomous self, as with Ben Franklin's argument that a person's hard work promotes success. And focusing on *graphy* gives us a postmodern emphasis on the life of a person as lexicon of textuality *à l'écriture feminine* (Morgan 5). Although I agree with Morgan (and Olney) that playing with etymologies is fruitful, I want to argue that instead of relegating these three emphases to differing philosophical systems, we might try merging them into one: materialist feminism. Within this framework, autobiography may be imagined as cultural autobiographics—i.e., as a space where the personal (*auto*), the cultural (*bio*), and the textual (*graphy*) intersect as competing agents.

DIGRESSION 9*: Because Leigh Gilmore's* autobiographics *signifies cultural discourses and because Janice Morgan's* bio *signifies culture, my use of the "cultural" marker preceding "autobiographics" may seem redundant, but given the pervasiveness of individualism in U.S. culture, I've found it a useful emphasis with students.*

Within this materialist emphasis of cultural autobiographics, personal writing emerges as a textual map of the personal and the cultural. Such textual maps function as a metonym for culture, not as a metaphor for it, in that an individual's text is associated with a culture, not representative of its entirety. And such textual maps have material effects on people's lives, other texts, and cultures. Conceiving personal writing as cultural autobiographics enables students and scholars/teachers to write the personal as described by Victor Villanueva in the *College English*

Symposium Collective (51), to read the personal as described by Min Zhan Lu in the same symposium (52–55), and to listen to the personal as described by Joanne Braxton in *Black Women Writing Autobiography* (5). Writing, reading, and listening to personal writing—whether women's multicultural autobiographies *or any other text*—enables students and scholars/teachers to map intersections of various cultural categories, such as gender and whiteness, as they merge in particular ways in particular people's lives and texts. Conceiving personal writing as cultural autobiographics also enables students and scholars/teachers to foreground the representational gaps in time and place inherent in all personal writing. In sum, practicing cultural autobiographics as writers, readers, and listeners necessarily engages students and scholars/teachers in conversations about the ethics of writing, reading, and listening.

DIGRESSION 10: *I admire the following quote by Victor Villanueva: "There must be room for elements of autobiography, not as confession and errant self-indulgence, not as the measure on which to assess theory, not as a replacement for rigor, but as a way of knowing our predispositions to see things certain ways, of understanding what it is that guides our intuitions in certain ways. This is autobiography as critique" (Symposium Collective 51).*

This is what Adrienne Rich calls recognizing our own "politics of location" (212).

FINAL DIGRESSION: A STORY OF MY STORIES—OR, THE PERSONAL AS SYNECDOCHE

My ten numbered digressions interrupt the text proper, yet they serve the text, too, demonstrating different functions of stories and storytelling. Digression 1 (which attempts to recover the name rhetoric and composition studies) locates my current disciplinary standpoint but only hints at its cause, i.e., my training with Ed Corbett. Digression 2 (which tells Win Horner's story) exemplifies my commitment to foregrounding the lives of women. Digression 3 (which recounts my brain machine experience) historicizes me within a particular (cognitive) moment of our field, but it uses Roxanne Mountford as a character and backgrounds her story within our field, a success story that extends far beyond this anecdote. Digression 4 (which questions the timing of the death of the author) preaches. Digression 5 (which questions the terms

I employ) acknowledges the slipperiness of terms and the violence inherent in all definitions. Digression 6 (which relays my Peter Elbow story) attempts to have fun, not make fun; but I'm not sure that it works, and I'm not sure that it's scholarship. Digression 7 (which narrates a classroom moment) acknowledges that a narrator's point of view determines the story and that we are all the "heroes" of our own stories. Digression 8 (which admits that my terms may be used as trump cards) turns my critique on myself—but not too seriously. Digression 9 (which lays Leigh Gilmore, Janice Morgan, and my students alongside one another) attempts to define and defend my use of cultural autobiographics within scholarly conversations and within pedagogical practices. And digression 10 (which highlights a quote I admire) only hints that I collect quotes to help me think things through, but you might not know that from my text; it might just look as if I threw in Villanueva's quotation in a rather sloppy fashion, leaving it hanging in ways we encourage our undergraduate writers not to do.

Because these digressions are texts, they are representations of people, places, and ideas. At best they function as synecdoches; at worst they function as misrepresentations, appropriations, or silenced voices. As the writer, I control some part of how these representations are received; as readers, you control more; and our common discourse . . . well, it controls even more. So in contemplating *how* to use the personal in scholarship and pedagogy in this our second personal turn, rhetoric and composition studies needs to theorize further both the synecdochic methods of representation and the ethics of such representations in the personal writing that haunts our scholarship and our pedagogy. That's what I believe . . . but *I* am also echoing what Chris Farris said on the phone last evening. That's the problem—and the beauty—of personal writing: it is written, as we all are, by the people and the discourses we encounter. We all know that. But given that we live within an academic discourse community where who-says-what counts, and where, presumably, people count too, we must proceed with care—in all senses of the word.

15

GOING PUBLIC

Locating Public/Private Discourse

Sidney I. Dobrin

It is surprising, in many ways, that this deep into the postmodern era we still make distinctions between public and private discourse(s) (or any discourses, for that matter). It seems that one of the primary characteristics of postmodernity is the debunking of narratives that cubbyhole phenomena in convenient, codifiable locations. Yet, our conversations regarding public and/or private discourses frequently maintain a binary opposition between the two. As Andrea Stover has noted: "The public and private frequently collide in my classroom, and I worry about it" (5). *Collision.* The term suggests both fundamental distinction between the colliding items and conflict between the two. Collision, not convergence. Conflict, not coherence. And worry.

Simply put, what I want to do here is to take this binary, this potential for collision, to task and argue that the distinction between public and private discourses is both false and limiting in our understanding of communication. In order to do so, I propose an ecological model for understanding discourse and turn to the work of postprocess writing theorists to explore the ways in which all discourse, be it defined as either public or private, emanates from the same location and serves, in fact, the same function, construction, and production. In turn, I will consider that individual communicators rely on a host of prior discursive moments to develop passing theories for engaging particular communicative moments and at no time separate those prior theories into realms of public or private but instead rely on all prior theories to enter into any communicative scenario. Hence, the distinction between public and private dissolve as each communicative moment is at once dependant upon and moderated by both "private" and "public" prior theories, and neither can be codified as anything more than a unique, individual moment of discursive production/interpretation. Ultimately, what I argue is that the binary distinction of private and public is counterproductive in that it encourages discursive collision rather than a more holistic, ecological vision of the function of discourse and discourages particular discursive maneuvers in certain discursive scenarios, hence limiting discursive possibilities and potentially silencing users of discourse (the private denied access in the public). That is, I opt for an ecological, postprocess vision of discourse that sees all discursive moments as unique events that encompass all that is public and private at once. In other words, public discourse is as much private discourse as private discourse is public. And separating the two leads toward a disempowering discursive collision.

PUBLIC/PRIVATE DISCOURSE

In the introduction to the collection *Post-Process Theory: Beyond the Writing-Process Paradigm,* Thomas Kent begins to explain that those who subscribe to postprocess writing theories generally endorse "the fundamental idea that no codifiable or generalizable writing process exists or could exist" (1). He goes on to explain that "most post-process theorists hold three assumptions about the act of writing: 1) writing is public; 2) writing is interpretive; and 3) writing is situated." I would like to begin by extending Kent's notion of postprocess *writing* theory to an understanding of a postprocess *discourse* theory. Of course, the idea of postprocess writing theories directly reflects a reaction to the idea that the production of writing can be marked in an identifiable process, an idea that is distinctly a theory of composition studies. To theorize beyond the entrenched notion that student writers—in fact, all writers—engage in a recursive process of composing is to propose a rather disciplinary-specific theory. What I do not want to suggest here is that "discourse" is produced in a process similar to the ways in which we for so long assumed "writing" to be produced. We cannot theorize discourse in the exact same ways we theorize writing. In fact, I do not believe that I have ever encountered such a thing as process discourse theory or a discourse process paradigm. Discourse, that is, is more problematic, less tangible, even less codifiable (in the traditional view) than is writing.

Discourse, if it is possible to talk about such a thing, if such a thing exists, is nontotalizeable. Yet, we need some vocabulary for talking about and for theorizing an idea of discourse, and what we learn from postprocess writing theories can help lead to a theory of discourse which, while originating in postprocess composition studies, should rightfully be called something other than *postprocess discourse theory* as there is no process discourse theory from which to be post. In fact, to name some verbal exchange *postprocess* or *paralogic* discourse is both redundant and poor modification. Writing is a technology; it is a secondary representation of discourse, a sort of a metaphysical technology, one that perpetually contributes to and is bound by discourse but exists as a representative technology of discourse. That is, writing is not discourse per se, but rather a technological representation of discourse. Hence, the term *written discourse* is also problematic, and it should probably be recast as *written (representation of) discourse.* Discourse, too, is a technology, but discourse is discourse, neither postprocess nor paralogic, unlike writing, which can be both. Discourse is at all times only and totally discourse. So, what I offer here is neither postprocess discourse theory nor paralogic discourse theory but an understanding of discourse that draws from an understanding of postprocess writing theory and paralogic rhetoric.

To understand the postprocess model, it is important to note that postprocess thinking initiated both a shift from thinking about writing as an activity that begins "inside" a writer and a shift from scholarship that focused on individual writers (those theories often labeled historically as cognitivist or expressivist) to scholarship that acknowledges how external forces—ideology, culture, society, race, gender, environment, etc.—affect and are affected by writers (those theories often historically labeled social constructionist). Indeed, most scholarship about writing now acknowledges that writing takes place in relation not only to individual writers but also to the worlds in which they live and function. For Kent, this move in theoretical focus from individual writers to communication contexts was a move from what he has called "internalism" to "externalism" (*Paralogic*). (For an excellent critique of Kent's internalism/externalism discussion, see Davis.) As Gail Hawisher et al. explain: "During the period of 1983–1985, composition studies absorbed the changes brought about by the new emphasis upon process and began to chart the course it would follow postprocess, looking beyond the individual writer toward the larger systems of which the writer was a part" (65). It is from these locations that I begin to consider discourse.

Gleaning, then, from this glossing of the postprocess composition model, I want to propose a "postprocess" understanding of discourse (though, again, this is a poor label). In order to do so, I offer a paraphrase of Kent: central to understanding discourse is the fundamental idea that no identifiable, codifiable, or generalizable discourse exists or could exist. There are three assumptions about discourse that are crucial: 1) discourse is public; 2) discourse is interpretive; and 3) discourse is situated. From here we can begin.

I take my central claim that there can be no identifiable, codifiable, or generalizable discourse from Kent's work in the postprocess theory of paralogic rhetoric. To summarize and offer an overly simplified explanation of paralogic rhetoric, as I have before in my essay "Paralogic Hermeneutic Theories: Power and the Possibility for Liberating Pedagogies," these theories state that each moment of communicative interaction is singularly unique and that the ways in which we interpret our communicative moments are not codifiable or verifiable in any logical manner (for a detailed explanation of paralogic rhetorical theories, see also Kent, *Paralogic* or Dobrin, *Constructing*). Ultimately, what paralogic rhetorical theories identify, then, is that discourse does not operate in any logicosystemic manner and never remains stable long enough for one to develop concrete understandings of the communicative interaction it encompasses. In other words, there are no codifiable processes by which we can characterize, identify, solidify, and grasp discourse. Communicative interaction, then, relies on strategies of what Kent labels "hermeneutic guessing," wherein participants develop strategies based on previous experience to interpret discourse for that moment of communication. Kent draws his notion of hermeneutic guessing from Donald Davidson's theory of triangulation:

> Each of two people finds certain behavior of the other salient, and each finds the observed behavior of the other to be correlated with events and objects he finds salient in the world. This much can take place without developed thought, but it is the necessary basis for thought and language learning. For until the triangle is completed connecting two creatures and each creature with common objects in the world there can be no answer to the question whether a creature, in discriminating between stimuli, is discriminating between stimuli at the sensory surfaces or somewhere further out, or further in. It takes two to triangulate. For each of us there are three sorts of knowledge corresponding to the three apices of the triangle: knowledge of our own minds, knowledge of other minds, and knowledge of the shared world. Contrary to traditional empiricism, the first of those is the least important,

for if we have it we must have the others, so the idea that knowledge could take it as foundation is absurd. (qtd. in "Externalism" 65–66)

"We come to know and understand objects in the world and each other," Anis Bawarshi explains of triangulation, "only when our interpretations match others' interpretations" (73). Theories of paralogic rhetoric make the similar claim that an individual comes to know an object through interpretive moves with other interpreters. In other words, knowledge is social and discursively constructed, but can only be discussed as such as a means of convenience, as the very discourse through which knowledge is made socially (publicly) can never be codified, confirmed, identified, or totalized.

Kent explains, via Davidson, that triangulation is dependent upon two theories: passing theory and prior theory. Prior theories are the interpretive strategies one brings to a particular communicative scenario—the hermeneutic guessing skills one has developed prior to a particular situation. Passing theories are the strategies one employs *during* the particular instance of communication. Each communicative act, then, becomes an interpretive moment unique unto itself in which a participant relies on particular prior theories to develop a passing theory in order to achieve successful communication with another. The skills we develop through prior theories, then, determine how effective our passing theories might be situation to situation.

To further examine the issue of discourse, then, what can be understood, too, is that discourse, the very medium through which we come to develop prior and passing theories, is also known only through our communicative interactions and interpretations with others. That is to say, discourse is a product of triangulation, a socially mapped construction, a phenomenon that cannot be codified but that must be assumed to be product and purveyor of social interaction. One does not come to discourse, come to know discourse, without social interaction. Hence, discourse itself is socially constructed, socially construed. Functioning, then, as the medium through which we come to know both discourse itself and the world, discourse is itself discursively constructed and is thus necessarily public. The idea of private discourse has become a term used as a sort of self-validation of the authentic, a resistance to this very idea that all discourse—in fact, all existence—is public. It provides the inaccurate idea of being able to escape the public while maintaining a hold on an identifiable, confirmable self that is separate from public discourse, from social interaction, and somehow identifiable as such. If we are to accept Kent and Davidson's notion of triangulation as an explanation of the act of communication, then private discourse cannot exist free of the public; it is, in fact, itself public.

Turning back to my paraphrase of Kent, discourse, then, is public at all times. Private discourse may be identified as a discourse known and used only by one's self, but the fact of the matter is that before a discourse can be made private (the privatization of discourse?), it must first be experienced publicly. Certainly, then, we can say that there is a distinction between public and private discourse, but only as a matter of convenience and codification. That discourse which we conveniently call private is in no way different from that discourse we call public. However, we must recognize that because of the ways in which we come to know discourse, come to know through discourse, discourse does not begin private and then earn a label or stature of public discourse as it is made public. Rather, discourse begins public and is labeled private as is needed. This is an important distinction to make, for it allows us to recognize that any discourse, whether we call it private, public, home, hybrid, or alternative, is always already public. There can be no other kind of discourse, for discourse by its very nature, its very construction, is a public, social, triangulative, interpretive entity. Identifying something as discourse identifies it as a product of, mediator of, and a purveyor of the public. While individuals' discourses affect all discourse, discourse itself is that which makes individuals' discourses.

If we accept the maxim "all discourse is public," then we must also identify that all discourse is interpretive. Returning to Kent's explanation that each communicative scenario is unique and dependent upon individual interpretive moments, it becomes clear that discourse itself is dependent upon those very interpretive moments. In order for discourse to exist, each moment of triangulation requires a moment of interpretation. Each moment of interpretation requires a growing resource of prior theories to engage and successfully interpret each new communicative moment in order to develop a passing theory for that scenario. Now, it might seem reasonable to assume, then, that each communicative scenario requires the individual to develop an internalized or private theory for engaging each new communicative scenario, that, in fact, discourse originates internally, in the private self, before being made public. However, such an assumption neglects that all prior theories originated in public, shared discourse before ever becoming prior theories. That is, in the chronology of prior theories, our first prior theories and all subsequent prior theories were developed through public interaction. No prior theory, no discursive experience, no internal conversation initiated prior to public conversation exists prior to triangulation, prior to interpretation. Hence, in order to engage something conveniently called "private" discourse, one must first have public discourse and must have interpreted moments of that public discourse in order to develop even a label of "private." Private discourse is nothing more than a manifestation of public discourse internalized. All discourse, then, is reliant upon individuals' experiences of interpreting discourse and making use of that discourse in order to develop prior theories of communicative interaction. Private discourse is merely symptomatic of public discourse.

Writing is, as I have said, a technology, and, as Kent identifies, it is necessarily place-based. Discourse, too, is a sort of technology and it is always place-based. Discourse is situated. Discourse always comes from someplace; discourse, to paraphrase Kent, is never nowhere. I have argued in my essay "Writing Takes Place" that writing is an ecological pursuit, that "in order to be successful, it must situate itself in context; it must grow from location (contextual, historical, ideological)" (18). I go on to explain: "Writing does not begin in the self; rather, writers begin writing by situating themselves, by putting themselves in a place, by locating within a space. Writing begins with *topoi*, quite literally with place" (18–19). Here, I want to argue likewise that discourse is place-based, is situated. Discourse, that is, is at all times local. Discourse exists in context. By this I mean more than a physical location, I mean to suggest that discourse is place-based in terms of historical location, ideological location, physical location, political location, imagined location, and so on. Discourse is a place-based technology, a thing that is altered to the needs of a particular context, made by that context, and ultimately the very thing that makes that context. That is to say, discourse constructs the places that construct it. The relationship between discourse and place is reciprocal, uncodifiable. Discourse makes place as much as place makes discourse. In our book, *Natural Discourse: Toward Ecocomposition*, Christian Weisser and I argue that this very idea of discourse constructing place, or *environment* as we term it, and place constructing discourse is the cornerstone of understanding ecocomposition, to seeing the relationships among places, environments, and discourse. What we argue is that discourse is dependent upon the environments from which it grows, and those very environments are dependent upon, created by, those same discourses. Separating discourse from place is impossible; they are inextricably bound. Of course, making such a statement allows, then, for work to be done that sees the links between other discursive constructions—history, gender, race, culture, ideology, nature, and so on—and place. That is, the proposal that discourse is placed-based allows for the development of an ecological view of discourse.

ECOLOGICAL PUBLIC/PRIVATE

Before proposing an ecological model of discourse, I want to briefly examine what I mean by *ecological*. Unfortunately, the concept of ecology—and the oft-used prefix *eco*—has been popularly adopted to resound with the idea of environmentalism and with a particular political position. While I approve of such a position, I do want to emphasize that this is not the political position I take when I refer to an ecological model of discourse. Rather, I mean to allude to the science(s) of ecology, those inquiries that seek to examine relationships among organisms and their environments. That is, when I say that I want to propose an ecological model of discourse, I am suggesting a relational understanding of discourse, an environmental and place-based understanding of discourse.

In her 1986 article "The Ecology of Writing," Marilyn Cooper contributes to the initiation of the postprocess endeavor when she proposes an ecological model of writing "whose fundamental tenet is that writing is an activity through which a person is continuously engaged with a variety of socially constituted systems" (367). In other words, Cooper suggests that writing be examined not as an individual process but as a functioning and reliant part of the systems in which that writing is situated. While Cooper, like Kent and other postprocess theorists, addresses writing in particular, what she teaches us can help us to develop an ecological model of discourse as well. She writes:

> All the characteristics of any individual writer or piece of writing both determine and are determined by the characteristics of all other writers and writing systems. An important characteristic of ecological systems is that they are inherently dynamic; though their structures and contents can be specified at a given moment, in real time they are constantly changing, limited only by parameters that they themselves subject to change over longer spans of time. (368)

To once again paraphrase (and alter a bit) our view of writing so that it encompasses discourse, we see that all the characteristics of discourse are determined by the characteristics of all users of discourse and all other discourses. Discourse is inherently dynamic. Its structure cannot be specified, codified, totalized, or identified at any given moment as it is constantly changing, limited only by parameters that discourse itself is subject to change. Discourse, then, can be seen as ecological: a system (albeit, as I have explained it, and to borrow again from Kent, discourse is beyond system, as system suggests having identifiable characteristics) that is dependent upon the relationships of discourse users to each other in order for discourse to survive, reproduce, evolve.

What is critical about Cooper's ecological model is that it introduces the notion that writers interact with systems that affect their writing. As Erika Lindemann explains when writing about Cooper's article and about writing as system: "The ecological model usefully complicates the learning and teaching of writing because it reminds us of the social context in which all writers work" (296). Writers—or more to the point of this discussion, users of discourse—in essence are dependent upon their surroundings—surroundings that are dynamic, difficult to define, and susceptible to the forces imposed by other users of discourse. As Cooper notes, ecological models are not simply new ways of saying "contextual" (367). Context suggests that potential effects of *all* local systems can be identified through heuristics in order to provide writers with accurate and complete information prior to writing. Cooper points out: "In place of the static and limited categories of contextual models, the ecological model postulates dynamic interlocking systems that structure the social activity of writing. . . . The systems are not given, not limitations on writers; instead they are made and remade by writers in the act of writing" (368). Again, in a larger, more encompassing view, discourse is not systemic, yet it is ecological in that its users are dependent upon, inextricably linked with, and a product of those very discourses. Hence, an ecological model of discourse removes the need for a binary distinction between private and public discourse in favor of a dynamic interlocking view of discourse, one in which private and public discourse function in relation, connection, and dependence upon one another.

Cooper explains that "the metaphor for writing suggested by the ecological model is that of a web, in which anything that affects one strand of the web vibrates throughout the whole" (370). She posits:

> Two determinants of the nature of a writer's interactions with others are intimacy, a measure of closeness based on any similarity seen to be relevant—kinship, religion, occupation, and power, a measure of the degree to which a writer can control the action of others. . . . Writers may play a number of different roles in relation to one another: editor, co-writer, or addressee, for instance. Writers signal how they view their relationship with other writers through conventional forms and strategies, but they can also change their relationships—or even initiate or terminate relationships—through the use of these conventions if others accept the new relationship that is implied. (369–370)

Cooper also claims: "In contrast, then, to the solitary author projected by the cognitive model, the ideal image the ecological model projects is of an infinitely extended group of people who interact through writing, who are connected by the various systems that constitute the activity of writing" (372). To extend Cooper's statement to include not just writing but all discourse, we must see the web of discourse as a much more all-encompassing and dynamic web, one that is perpetually shifting, always vibrating, and constantly reforming itself in terms that cannot be defined long enough to grasp the identity, shape, or characteristics of that web. That is, from moment to moment, the web of discourse maintains operational integrity through its relationships with users of discourse, the place in which those users of discourse use discourse, and its own shifting (lack of) form. In other words, when Cooper proposed a model of system and a metaphor of web, she began to see the relational value of writing but did not see the limits placed on writing or discourse by identifying either as a system, as a measurable structure. To envision discourse as more than a web like that of a spider and instead see it as something more dynamic and more elusive is to begin to develop an ecological model of discourse. This means creating a more holistic vision of discourse and seeing users of that discourse to be more active participants in it. An ecological model of discourse allows, in fact, the binary of private/public to fracture in favor of a more holistic concept of discourse as a perpetually public, perpetually discursive entity. It disallows the false authentication of self through private discourse in favor of authenticating a public self through discursive relationships, and finally, it allows for that public (the only) self to be an active contributor to, participant in, manufacturer of, and product of discourse.

Simply put, an ecological view of discourse suggests relationships. It places all participants in and of discourse in relation to one another; it situates all users of discourse in and of a public discourse. It does not suggest that all users of discourse are the same, communicate the same, or use the same discourse. In fact, it does not suggest that discourse itself is ever the same. It identifies the perpetually shifting and dynamic nature of discourse as the environmental force that maintains all discursive relationships. Discourse itself is engaged in an ongoing, fluctuating relationship with all users of discourse. It (if there is even an appropriate pronoun through which to represent discourse) is affected by and affects all that stand in relation to it. Even those discourses we choose to label as private, hybrid, alternative, personal, and so on function in relation to discourse as a whole. That is to say, the labels we place for convenience, to distinguish what we interpret as different discourse, do not actually separate those fractions of discourse from the more encompassing concept of discourse. Again, to simplify, all discourse is public, all discourse is interpretive, all discourse is place-based, all discourse affects and is affected by its users, all users of discourse affect and are affected by discourse.

COLLISION

At the beginning of this short ramble, I noted that perpetuating the public/private binary gives rise to conflict, to the kinds of collision that Stover identifies as occurring in her classroom. It is particularly this sort of collision, this location for conflict, that I wish to avoid through a reconceptualization of discourse as an all-inclusively public, ecological entity. What I posit is that by disavowing the self-authentication through private discourse, through discourses that we identify as somehow representative of our own or our students' own true self, the risk of exposing particular discourses in larger discursive moments is reduced. Any time an individual enters into a communicative scenario, that individual makes certain choices as to what to bring to that scenario, what prior theories to make use of: choices, simply, of what to say and what not to say, choices of what and how to interpret. In any communicative instance, users of discourse make decisions as to what they wish to reveal, what they wish to expose within the discourse. Once a communicator has made particular interpretations available to others, that user risks vulnerability through exposure. Part of this vulnerability comes from the long-professed idea that revealing the personal places the discourse user at greater risk of vulnerability because that which is exposed represents the authentic self, represents private discourse. By rethinking the emphasis we place on the risk of exposing the private as representation of self and instead seeing exposure as a participatory, public discourse, we stand to lessen the vulnerability of the discourse user. Let me offer a quick example.

On the morning of September 11, 2001, I watched the horrific events unfold on television as most of America did. At some point, I logged onto my computer to check CNN online. When my e-mail popped up, there were, as there always are, a series of e-mails from the WPA Listserve. At 08:46 (Mountain Time, I believe) Bonnie Kyburz posted the first message to the list with the subject line "Terrorism (?)" Prior to this message, all messages had been about general WPA-type issues. The messages following Kyburz's initial post began a thread discussing the 9-11 events, first relaying news of the events to those in their offices away from televisions or radios (I never thought of my office as particularly shut off from the world). The thread also bears marks of a community looking for comfort, extending wishes of safety to one another, of information. A few posts go on about business as usual, answering questions of writing majors and writing requirements. At 9:34 (Pacific Time), Gordon Thomas of the University of Idaho posted the following request: "I'd like to hear how people are responding to these plane crashes in their Writing Programs." He asks in regard to teaching about the event: "Does asking students to write or even discuss these events unduly inflame their emotions and make later teaching more difficult?" The conversation then turned to what composition instructors should ask their students to write, to how writing could be seen as a therapeutic response to the horrible events. Deb Core, for instance, at 12:49 (Eastern Time, I think) wrote: "Seems to me that letting them talk is more appropriate at this point than asking them to write, to the extent that writing is private and students need the communal at this point." The public/private binary became central within hours of the event. And writing teachers began to decide what "students need." At 10:41 (Pacific Time) Gordon Thomas posted a writing assignment, part of which included these directions:

> Writing Exercise Concerning the Events of September 11, 2001, for classes meeting on September 12–14:
>
> Start by just having a general discussion for a few moments about the events of Tuesday, September 11, 2001. Try to get the students to contextualize

the event historically (many news commentators are now saying that the only thing that this compares to is the attack on Pearl Harbor and the Oklahoma City bombing, these comparisons may be controversial, but they are already being made).

Be prepared for the possibility of some students expressing great anger or fear (or both). It is quite possible that some students may say things that they don't really mean. Do your best not to inflame such feelings, and keep in mind that it does help some people to talk about this at the time. The best attitude for you to take is to be nonjudgmental about their responses unless someone says something that is overtly hostile to international students, Moslem students in particular. . . .

After this short oral discussion, ask them to take out paper and write freely in answer to the following questions.

> Now that some time has passed since your first heard the news, write down some of the pieces of information that you have learned since the initial news. Just list the information, not how you feel about it (yet).
>
> Describe how your initial response changed as you learned more about what had happened.
>
> What is the primary feeling that you have concerning these events? Why do you feel that way?
>
> What do you think the response of the U.S. government will be to these events? How do you feel about that potential response?

When the students have finished writing, ask them to put their writing away and keep it until later in the semester. Explain that you won't be collecting or reading their work. Tell them that they may want to save this writing as a personal record of what has happened.

Let me offer an explication of this questionable and inappropriate assignment: something horrible has happened in the world, and we as writing teachers should have our students expose themselves before us. In other words, as writing teachers, it is our duty to ask our students to perform the private in a public forum on demand. I can think of no other example of a larger instance of collision or of providing the place for collision to happen. (Please note my apology for the seemingly insensitive metaphor of collision here in relation to the events of 9-11.) I also fail to see how this assignment teaches writing, but that's another matter. I understand that carrying out Andrea Stover's metaphor here is a bit uncomfortable, but as I explain to my students, my primary objective as a teacher, writer, scholar is to make folks uncomfortable. We tend to pay attention to things that are uncomfortable; we try to adjust them. Uncomfortable clothes for instance, get altered; uncomfortable discourses don't seem natural, like they belong somehow.

The WPA discussion and the writing assignments proposed in this discussion seek to validate the student's authentic self by asking (in fact, demanding) that the student express feelings, the private, in a public forum under the guise of therapy, under the guise of helping the student. I would like to point out as well that such therapeutic assignments often stem from instructors' needs for a therapeutic response to a situation inflicted upon students. Yes, the September 11 disaster was hideous, and many students and teachers wanted/needed to discuss it and should be able to, but not under the aegis of writing assignments, not at the command of a writing instructor.

Don't hear, however, that I am arguing against the expression of feelings, against the rights of students or any other users of discourses, to self-expression (for more on the role of emotions see Dobrin and Weisser). I am in favor of and even encourage such things. However, to suggest that, first, the feelings of students are somehow private expressions of themselves, and, second, that teachers of writing have a right to demand those discourses be made public is abhorrent. However, when we encourage students to see how their reactions and their feelings are part of a more encompassing discourse that is affected by its relational aspects, students are in a better position to act in that discourse rather than be exposed in that discourse, made vulnerable in that discourse. Asking students to perform the private publicly is counterproductive. Asking students to make decisions about their public discourse participation seems more empowering, more discursively responsible. I find it difficult, in fact, to find a reason to want to maintain a concept of private discourse, of an authenticated self; doing so merely provides an opportunity to allow expressionism to raise its dying head and maintain a foothold in the conversations of discourse studies.

Let me conclude, then, with a final maxim: discourse is always already. Period. In order for discourse to be, it must be public, it must be interpretive, it must be place-based. Hence, any discourse exists only in relation to discourse and to users of discourse. Discourse is itself affected by and affects its users, constructs and is constructed by its users. Any discourse, no matter what we chose to label it for the sake of convenience—not the sake of actual identification or codification—is, then, always already public.

16

PUBLIC WRITING AND RHETORIC

A New Place for Composition

Christian R. Weisser

Public spheres are not only arenas for the formation of discursive opinion; in addition, they are arenas for the formation and enactment of social identities. This means that participation is not simply a matter of being able to state propositional contents that are neutral with respect to form of expression. Rather . . . participation means being able to speak in one's own voice, and thereby simultaneously to construct and express one's own cultural identity through idiom and style.

Nancy Fraser, "Rethinking the Public Sphere"

Due to a number of internal and external forces, the field of composition has begun to embrace courses, pedagogies, and theories that engage in discourse with and about the public—and rightly so. (For a fuller explication of the recent move in rhetoric and composition toward public writing, see Weisser; Dobrin and Weisser.) A focus on public writing—which might loosely be defined as written discourse that attempts to engage an audience of local, regional, or national groups or individuals in order to bring about progressive societal change—offers much more than the relatively "arhetorical" approaches to writing instruction that ask students to write to no one for no particular purpose. (For practical purposes, I offer this definition, which is limiting yet necessary for the task at hand. The distinction between "public" and "private" that seems implicit here is itself problematic and worthy of more attention than space permits.) Instead, courses focusing on public writing have the potential to give student writing real significance; they allow students to produce meaningful discourse that has the potential to change their lives and the lives of others. In this respect, students see public writing as more "real" than, for example, an essay about what they did last summer or an analysis of a particular piece of literature. Public writing can help students to see the value of adopting a particular rhetorical stance, since public writing is often directed toward a particular audience that might be influenced by a student's writing. Students often come away from a course or assignment that focuses on public writing with a better understanding of the importance of shaping the style, form, and tone of their written work in ways that might be most persuasive and convincing. In addition, public writing more easily allows students to see that language is a powerful tool for swaying opinions and actions. When a student's writing generates further public discussion or leads to some political or social change, he or she comes to see how discourse is deeply implicated in the structures of power in a society. It is easy to understand, then, why Gary A. Olson suggests that "public writing is clearly emerging as a powerful expression of some of the field's most cherished values" (ix).

This is not to say, though, that public-writing assignments are a panacea for national or even local ills. Helping students find avenues and situations for public discourse demands an enormous amount of time, and even when they are found, public discursive spheres are often difficult to enter. Public forums usually work on a different schedule than that of a university course, and grading students for their "participation" in such forums creates new problems for both student and instructor. Even when students successfully enter and participate in public discourse, there is no guarantee that their opinions will be listened to and acted upon. In fact, the odds are against them.

So, many writing instructors see the value of courses and assignments that focus on public writing and rhetoric, but they just as wisely anticipate the pedagogical difficulties and risks associated with them. As a result, some advocates of public writing rely upon established, conventional pedagogical assignments for addressing the public, such as letters to the editor of the local newspaper on a current topic. The occasional student letter that is published in the local newspaper is very often a rewarding experience for that student and may encourage him or her to write and speak in other public forums and situations. Now and then, these letters compel others to write in response, and once in a while (though rarely), student letters elicit response and discussion in other public forums. However, while these assignments have some potential merit, they are more often than not an exercise in frustration and discouragement for most student authors. Letters to the editor are usually one-way assignments; students put effort into writing them but get little response. As a result, these types of assignments are often counterproductive. Perhaps more significantly, such exercises do little to cultivate the students' facility with public writing. In many instances, the students' letters are very often generated just to fulfill the assignment. I don't wish to imply that the newspaper editorial column should be overlooked as an appropriate forum for student-generated discourse. Occasionally, students may come across a public issue that they are genuinely interested in, but more often than not, the issues students write about in their letters have little bearing on their lives outside of the classroom. Unfortunately, students often come to feel that participating in public discourse, if letters to the editor are indeed public discourse, has little effect on what happens in their world. They surmise that the public sphere is a realm where nothing actually gets accomplished—at least not by them.

If we wish to create assignments, courses, and pedagogies that enable students to interact more effectively with other groups and individuals in public arenas, we could begin by considering where and to whom meaningful and productive public writing might be delivered. Luckily, when it comes to thinking about the location for public discourse—the public sphere—we need not reinvent the wheel; a number of social and cultural theorists have already written extensively and usefully about this notion from a variety of perspectives. By drawing principally upon the work of Jürgen Habermas—and perhaps more fruitfully upon critiques of his work as offered by Nancy Fraser, Oscar Negt, and Alexander Kluge—it is possible to develop a richer, more nuanced conceptualization of the public sphere than that which seems to underlie some traditional public-writing assignments. There are many parallels between the conversations of the public sphere in social and cultural theory and the more recent conversations in composition regarding public writing, and these similarities have allowed me to dispel several of my own initial misconceptions about the locations of public discourse. While it is impossible to fully address all of these parallels in this chapter, it may be useful to examine just a few of them to extend our current understanding of where and how public writing exists.

A PLACE IN TIME

A good place to begin this investigation is to examine the historical and contextual conditions that give rise to public discourse. One could assume that public writing is an activity that takes place in a relatively stationary sphere and that it requires little knowledge about the conditions that gave rise to the activity of public discourse or the conditions corresponding to each particular topic in the public sphere. Public writing may seem to be a comparatively ahistorical activity that calls for little prior knowledge of prior conversations or modes of conduct. However, effective public-writing assignments must account for the degree to which public discourse exists in a historically textured sphere that is the product of innumerable social and political forces. These forces have long histories and are in a constant state of flux. If we are to fully and cogently theorize public writing, we must begin by establishing it as a complex historical category.

Perhaps the best way to conceptualize this notion is to examine where public writing is thought to occur. The location of public discourse—labeled "the public sphere" by many theorists—has been seen primarily as a historical concept. Efforts to understand the history, foundations, and internal processes of public discourse have been central to the conversations about the public sphere in social and cultural theory. The debate on the public sphere has been influenced most deeply by Habermas's *The Structural Transformation of the Public Sphere*, a work that is, as Susan Wells writes, "both deeply problematic and astoundingly fruitful" ("Rogue Cops" 327). Essentially, the book builds its theoretical argument through an analysis of the historical growth of capitalism and democracy in Britain, France, and Germany in the seventeenth and eighteenth centuries. Thomas McCarthy argues that the book is "a historical-sociological account of the emergence, transformation, and disintegration of the . . . liberal public sphere that took shape in the specific historical circumstances of a developing market economy" ("Introduction" xi). The book envisions the public sphere as an *institutional location* where practical reason and debate arise out of material circumstances in order to promote more democratic ideals. That is, one of the most significant aspects of *Structural Transformation* is that it sees public discourse as occurring only as a *result* of a particular cultural climate. Habermas asserts that the public sphere "is a category that is typical of an epoch" and that "we treat public sphere in general as a historical category" (xvii). Similarly, Richard Sennett's *The Fall of Public Man* suggests the importance of a historical understanding of the concept of the public sphere. Sennett argues that his book attempts to "create a theory of expression in public by a process of interplay between history and theory" and that to have a clear understanding of the subject, it is necessary to examine "the social and political dimensions of the public problem as it has developed in modern society" (6). Both of these conceptions of the public sphere, and the many conversations that they have generated in social and cultural theory, see public discourse as arising from the distinct cultural conditions of capitalist and postcapitalist societies. They both suggest that public discourse occurs in the context of a particular cultural milieu.

If we agree that public discourse arises from a culture, and that social, political, and historical forces have constructed, shaped, and otherwise affected the locations, topics, and methods of public discourse, we are, in a sense, arguing that it is *ideologically interested.* (Of course, all discourse is ideologically interested. I mention the role of ideology here to emphasize it, not to suggest that public discourse is somehow different from other discursive situations in this respect.) In short, any understanding of public discourse as a product of a particular cultural climate must take into account the ways that ideology shapes and structures nearly every aspect of what, where, and how public discourse occurs as well as who gets to speak in public settings. While both Habermas and Sennett devote a great deal of attention to the historical emergence of the public sphere, they also (as their critics note) fail to recognize the degree to which ideology shapes public discourse. For example, in their analyses of the bourgeois public sphere of that time, both Habermas and Sennett overlook the degree to which dominant ideology shaped public debates, and, as a result, they both fail to account for the degree to which the discourse that occurred in this forum was controlled and manipulated by white property-owning males. Commonly, in public discourse, ideology naturalizes certain authority regimes—those of class, race, and gender, for example—and renders alternatives all but unthinkable. As James Berlin writes, ideology always brings with it "strong social and cultural reinforcement, so that what we take to exist, to have value, and to be possible seems necessary, normal, and inevitable—in the nature of things" (*Rhetorics* 78). Therefore, it is imperative that we recognize that public writing, and the spheres in which it occurs, is ideologically constructed. In short, recognizing that public discourse is historical, contextual, and ideologically influenced is an inherently rhetorical move, since it allows an author to better conceptualize his or her audience and the discourse that will suit it best.

Seeing public writing as a political move allows us to pay particular attention to both our audience and our subject. We recognize that the groups or individuals that we hope to persuade and possibly call to action are influenced by particular rhetorical modes and devices, and their reactions are often shaped by their prior experiences with public discourse. They may consider our public discourse more or less closely as a result of where we speak from and the style and type of discourse that we use. Furthermore, we can better conceptualize our subject if we see it as discursively constructed through a variety of previous public discussions. That is, our own conceptions of a particular topic are shaped by all of our previous encounters with it, and many of these encounters transpired in public spheres. Envisioning public writing in this way situates each public discursive moment as ideologically situated, itself an intervention in the political process. Public writing cannot deny its inescapable ideological predispositions. It cannot claim to be above ideology, a transcendent discourse that exists outside of history or culture. Like Berlin's social-epistemic rhetoric, public writing, when seen from a historical/cultural perspective, contains "within it a utopian moment, a conception of the good democratic society and the good life for all of its members" (*Rhetorics* 81). Public writing must be aware of its historical contingency and of its limitations and incompleteness.

I'm certainly not suggesting that we have our undergraduates read Habermas, Sennett, or any other historical investigation of the public sphere. Nor am I suggesting that they read Berlin to learn more about the relationships between ideology and discourse. What I am suggesting is that we should help them to recognize that culture, politics, and ideology shape public conversations. We should highlight the ways in which material forces shape what gets said, who gets heard, and how these forces have structured public discourse throughout history. This can be accomplished by choosing particular cultural issues that have been discussed in the public sphere, examining which voices have been heard and acknowledged, which voices have been marginalized, silenced, or excluded, and how discourse on particular issues has changed or developed as a result of the larger political and social climates in which they have been generated. Students are able to easily transfer these heuristics and skills to their own areas of interest, and, as a result, they are more capable of generating effective public writing. By looking at public writing in context, we allow students to see how to use the tools of language to their best interests and in the process discover how textual production—such as public writing—helps to shape and construct knowledge rather than simply reproduce it. Such an approach will necessitate that writers research the histories of the issues they choose to address to find out how the conversations surrounding them have been shaped, altered, and constructed. At the same time, they will need to consider what is *not* said, whose voices have been excluded from the conversation, and how ideology has normalized certain features of the public discussion they are entering.

A course or assignment focusing on public writing would need to consider how a particular issue—school vouchers, for example—has been shaped by the long history of educational debate in this country. Writers would need to consider how legislative programs such as school segregation, bussing, and standardized testing have been used in the past to justify the ideological perspectives of those in power. In addition, writers would need to consider what sorts of rhetoric might open up or foreclose further discussion from various groups in the public sphere. Regardless of the form or topic of the assignment or course, effective public writing necessitates a thorough investigation of the political, social, economic, cultural, and ideological forces that have influenced any public issue.

BRACKETING DIFFERENCE

It is easy to assume that a writer's identity can be put aside or "bracketed" in public discursive situations. The assumption goes that such writing, if done clearly and logically, frees the individual of his or her particular ethnic, gender, or class distinctions. Public writing, when examined as a category, is often assumed to be evaluated for its merits alone, disengaged and independent from the features and characteristics of its author. Furthermore, the audience for public writing is often assumed to be neutral, open-minded individuals who evaluate public discourse entirely on the merits of its argument. If writers would only express themselves with complete clarity and grammatical and mechanical correctness, some might argue, their positions would be accepted magnanimously, or at least evaluated honestly. The social inequalities that exist in the rest of society are often assumed to be set aside in the arenas of public discourse. In other words, it might be assumed that the differences and inequalities between the author of a piece of public writing and his or her audience can be overlooked. In addition, it is often supposed that all individuals—regardless of their race, class, gender, sexual inclination, or other distinguishing features—are as capable and authorized to produce public writing as anyone else. In short, the avenues of public discourse are often presumed to be open and accessible to all, free of any of the social inequalities that pervade other discursive situations.

Once again, it is useful to examine the discussions of the public sphere in social and cultural theory in order to most effectively theorize this aspect of public writing. Habermas's account of the bourgeois public sphere, which stresses the claim of open access to all, runs parallel with the assumptions outlined above. For Habermas, the idea of open access and participatory parity is one of the central aspects of public discourse. Habermas's interpretation of the bourgeois public sphere posits it to have been an arena where individuals would set aside "such characteristics as differences in birth and fortune and speak to one another as if they were social and economic peers" (Fraser, *Rethinking* 118). That is, Habermas assumed that a "social leveling" of all participants was an integral part of the liberal public sphere in the seventeenth and eighteenth centuries in Europe. He argues that "they preserved a kind of social intercourse that, far from presupposing the equality of status, disregarded status altogether. The tendency replaced the celebration of rank with a tact befitting equals" (*Structural* 36).

Nancy Fraser questions the assumption that it is possible for interlocutors in any public debate to actually bracket status differentials and to participate in discourse as if all of the members of a public sphere were social equals. She suggests that when analyzing the bourgeois public sphere, or any other public sphere for that matter, it has been impossible to effectively bracket social differences among interlocutors.

> But were they [the differences between interlocutors] really effectively bracketed? The revisionist historiography suggests that they were not. Rather, discursive interaction within the bourgeois public sphere was governed by protocols of style and decorum that were themselves correlates and markers of status inequality. These functioned informally to marginalize women and members of the plebeian classes and to prevent them from participating as peers. ("Rethinking" 119)

In this respect, Fraser is talking about informal impediments to participatory parity that can persist even after everyone is formally and legally licensed to participate. Certainly, there are no legal restrictions on public writing in the United States today, regardless of the circumstances. Such restrictions are not allowable by law. This fact has, unfortunately, created a situation that makes public discourse *appear* to be equally open to all, existing in arenas that *seem* to have overcome all social exclusions and marginalizations. However, public discourse is influenced by forces that cannot be easily disposed of through legislation. Fraser notes a number of these informal impediments to participatory parity in public discourse. She cites, for example, a familiar contemporary example drawn from feminist research. It has been documented that in mixed-sex deliberations, men tend to interrupt women more than women interrupt men, men also tend to speak more than women, and women's interventions are more often ignored or not responded to than men's. Deliberation and the appearance of participatory parity can serve as a mask for domination. These feminist insights into the ways that discourse is used to mask domination and imbalances of power can be applied to other kinds of unequal relations, like those based on class or ethnicity. They alert us to the ways in which "social inequalities can infect deliberation, even in the absence of any formal exclusions" (Fraser, "Rethinking" 119). In this respect, the bracketing of differences and social inequalities in public discourse cannot actually be enacted, and assuming that it can actually works to the advantage of dominant groups in a public sphere and to the disadvantage of subordinates. In most cases, it would be more appropriate to *unbracket* these inequalities by foregrounding and thematizing them. Doing this would help to eliminate some of the more pernicious uses of discourse in public deliberation. The assumption that public writing occurs in an arena that can overlook, bracket, or disregard social and cultural differences is counterfactual.

There is no reason to think that these conversational dynamics are somehow miraculously absent from the particular discursive situation of public writing. Since public discourse often brings together individuals from radically different perspectives and positions, and since these individuals often have no prior bonds or other incentives that would urge them to work toward participatory parity, it stands to reason that these status differentials are perhaps even more apparent and significant in public settings. For communicative situations such as public writing, gender-specific power differences cannot be disregarded. In fact, any course or assignment focusing on public writing must recognize the degree to which a number of other social forces—among them race, ethnicity, sexual orientation, age, occupation, class—influence the idealized statusfree public spheres envisioned by some writing instructors.

Compositionists should recognize that social differences shape public writing in significant ways. We also need to continue efforts to establish new theories of public writing that acknowledge differences in thinking and writing. At the same time, we need to assure that new theories identify the origins of many of these differences as ideologically constructed. For instance, new theories should acknowledge that the label "difference" can be used to reinforce and justify marginal or dominant status.

In composition courses focusing on public writing, it is important that instructors highlight for students the degree to which their social status and differences from others will affect how their writing is evaluated. Instructors will also need to examine with their students how differences themselves are often labels that are used to justify the dominance or subordination of certain classes or groups in public settings. Students will need to question whether it is possible, even in principle, for individuals to deliberate through public discourse as if they were social peers. If public discourse is situated in a larger societal context that is marked by structural relations of dominance and subordination—and students will often be the first to note these societal differences—it must follow that public writing will not be evaluated free of these systemic factors. In addition, it is also important to enable student writers to examine the ways that they themselves often evaluate the public discourse of others in biased and unproductive ways. Students need to understand that social inequalities are very real and significant factors affecting the reception and production of public writing. Such a recognition allows them to become more discerning users of the discourse they consume and produce. One task of an effective public-writing assignment is to render visible the ways that societal inequality infects formally inclusive existing public spheres and taints discursive interaction within them.

MULTIPLE SPHERES

Perhaps one reason why the letter to the editor is such a common public-writing assignment is that its forum—the local newspaper—appears to be the primary site available for students to reach a wide audience of diverse individuals who might be interested in what they have to say. It seems natural to think that student public discourse is only worthwhile if it reaches a large segment of the population that is able to act upon it in some way. In other words, students and teachers often assume that public writing must address the "general public," and the term *public* is often taken to encompass all members of a society, or at least a representative microcosm of them. However, it is incorrect to assume that newspapers are the only significant medium for reaching others through public writing, just as it is incorrect to assume that public writing must reach large segments of the population in order to be useful and constructive. Habermas, Negt, Kluge, and Fraser provide useful explanations as to why these assumptions are faulty and how we might more productively envision the full scope of public writing.

The belief that a large audience is mandatory for public writing, and that this audience must represent all or many individuals in a society, runs parallel to Habermas's conceptions of the public sphere. Habermas stresses the singularity of the bourgeois conception of the public sphere, its claim to be *the* public arena, in the singular, asserting that the bourgeois in seventeenth- and eighteenth-century Europe conceived of "the public sphere as something properly theirs" (*Structural* 24). On the whole, Habermas agrees with this bourgeois conception, as he casts "the emergence of additional publics as a late development signaling fragmentation and decline" (Fraser, "Rethinking" 122). That is, Habermas seems to suggest that any departure from this conception of a singular public sphere is a departure from the ideal. Like the conceptions of public writing I've just mentioned, Habermas's view is based upon an underlying assumption: that confining public discourse to a single, overarching public sphere is a desirable and positive move, whereas the proliferation of discourse in a multiplicity of public spaces represents a departure from, rather than an advance toward, democracy.

In contrast to Habermas, Oskar Negt and Alexander Kluge insist on the need to understand postbourgeois public formations in terms other than those of disintegration and decline. In *Public Sphere and Experience,* they assert that no singular form of the public did or ever could exist. They understand public discourse as existing in numerous sites that have "no homogenous substance whatsoever" (13). In their attempt to debunk the myth of a single, overarching public sphere, Negt and Kluge suggest that there are at least two other significant arenas of public discourse: the "public sphere of production," which is more directly rooted in spheres of capitalism, such as factory communities and labor unions, and the "proletarian public sphere," which is "substantively meshed with the history of the emancipation of the working class" (xliv). Moreover,

Negt and Kluge make the point that these other sites for public discourse cannot be viewed in isolation from one another; these public spheres must be seen as "mutually imbricated," overlapping, cohabitational, and often contradictory. In contrast to the conception that there must be one singular site of public discourse, and that it must embrace a diverse public, Negt and Kluge suggest that there are multiple arenas for public discourse, and these might best serve the needs of particular groups rather than a general public.

Nancy Fraser's analysis of this misconception is equally compelling. Counter to Habermas's confidence in an all-encompassing site for public discourse that is comprised of a cross-section of society, Fraser contends that in stratified societies, "arrangements that accommodate contestation among a plurality of competing publics better promote the ideal of participatory parity than does a single, comprehensive, overarching public" ("Rethinking" 122). As I explained earlier, she suggests that in societies whose basic structure generates unequal social groups in relations of dominance and subordination (as is the case in the United States), full parity of participation in public discourse is not feasible. Despite the fact that all members of a society may be *allowed* to participate in public discourse, it is impossible to insulate special discursive arenas from the effects of societal inequality. This being the case, she goes on to assert that the disadvantages marginalized groups face are only exacerbated where there is just one single arena for public discourse. If there were only one site for public discourse, members of subordinate groups would have no arenas for deliberation among themselves about their needs, objectives, and strategies. They would have no "venues in which to undertake communicative processes that were not, as it were, under the supervision of dominant groups" (123). In other words, if there were only a single public sphere, subaltern groups would have no discursive spaces in which to deliberate free of oppression.

Fraser suggests that it is advantageous for subordinated groups to constitute alternative sites of public discourse—what she calls *subaltern counterpublics.* She envisions these sites as "parallel discursive arenas where members of subordinated social groups invent and circulate counterdiscourses to formulate oppositional interpretations of their identities, interests, and needs" (123). Perhaps the most striking example of a subaltern counterpublic in contemporary history is the late-twentieth-century U.S. feminist subaltern counterpublic, with its diverse array of journals, bookstores, publishing companies, film and video distribution networks, lecture series, research centers, academic programs, conferences, conventions, festivals, and local meeting places (123). While subaltern counterpublics are not always inherently democratic or progressive, they do emerge in response to exclusions and omissions within dominant publics, and, as such, they help expand discursive space. In general, the proliferation of subaltern counterpublics means a widening of discursive contestation, and "that is a good thing in stratified societies" (124). Subaltern counterpublics can serve at least two functions. On the one hand, they function as spaces where oppressed others can withdraw, regroup, and heal; on the other hand, they function as "training grounds" and bases for the development of discourse or action that might agitate or disrupt wider publics.

Several scholars in composition have noted the usefulness of employing alternative or subaltern arenas for public writing. Susan Wells argues that compositionists "need to build, or take part in building, such a public sphere that . . . cannot, in our society, be unitary" ("Rogue Cops" 326) She goes on to suggest that given the intractable fragmentation of modern society, the representations of the public we offer students "beyond the classroom will be provisional; we will look for alternate publics and counter publics" (335). Wells offers a number of possible alternative publics that students might engage with through public-writing assignments that pair writing classes at different institutions, involve the collection of oral histories, and bring together computer-networked classes. Similarly, Irene Ward explores the potential for the Internet to become an alternative public sphere. While she rightly addresses the many problems with employing the Internet for public writing, she suggests at the same time that "some forms of the Internet . . . can potentially function in ways that print media functioned in the eighteenth century by delivering information, points of view, and extended argument to a growing sector of the public" (375).

Obviously, public writing need not be limited to a single discursive arena like the readership of a newspaper. Writing teachers should help students discover the various counterpublics where their public writing might have a receptive audience and, consequently, might result in significant outcomes. Public discourse is often difficult to generate and even more difficult to disseminate to large audiences—particularly when students have had little or no prior contact with these audiences.

Compositionists should work to create spaces for public writing if they don't exist or aren't readily entered by students. Public writing exists in a wide array of locations. Often, students feel most comfortable joining in conversation in Internet chat rooms, volunteer organizations, community outreach programs, or other smaller venues that target more specific issues and strive for and generate significant local results. Rather than feeling that they are just insignificant individuals who are unable to bring about sweeping changes—as is usually the case with letters to a newspaper with a wide circulation—students working with smaller, more specific groups often see tangible results from their public discourse. Enabling students to connect with counterpublics comprised of like-minded individuals is an important component of a successful public-writing assignment or course. In specific counterpublics, students often find that they can generate effective public discourse in a climate that is supportive and nurturing, which prepares them to enter larger public debates in the future. Also, these counterpublics allow them to see that they don't necessarily stand alone in their views and opinions; they learn from others with similar experiences and perspectives and often come away from such interactions with more complex and sophisticated views on public topics. Entering into discourse with specific counterpublics is often the most effective way for students to enter public space, and this move can encourage students to feel that public discourse is worth pursuing in the future.

OF COMMON CONCERN

An additional significant misconception of public writing must be debunked if we are to theorize and teach public writing more competently and productively: the misunderstanding that public writing must be confined to matters of "common concern" to all of the members in a society. Similar to the last misconception that I addressed, those who support this fallacy assume that the topic of public discourse must affect all (or at least many) members of society. By definition, such thinking limits public writing to public issues in general, to the exclusion of matters of specific or particular interest. This limitation reflects dualistic thinking that juxtaposes "public" with its apparent opposite, "private." It is easy to see how discursive topics might be placed into either of these two categories. If a topic does not seem to affect a large segment of the public, it is easily relegated to the realm of the private, and as such it is not seen as an appropriate topic for public writing. Students who choose to write about issues that do not appear to concern large segments of the population might be chastised for myopic thinking and encouraged to address topics that have wider implications and audiences. However, as I shall show, the myth that matters must be of "common concern" to be considered viable topics for public writing is based upon an ideologically interested notion of what counts as public matter.

Habermas envisions the bourgeois public sphere as a discursive arena in which private persons deliberate about public matters. He argues that discussion within this public sphere is grounded on the idea that areas that had previously been off-limits were to be problematized and questioned. Historically, public discourse first took the form of bourgeois discussions of the merits of art, music, and literature—subjects that had previously been confined to aristocrats and noblemen. Gradually, the commodification of cultural products made them more accessible to the public, taking them out of the control of the church and state. Habermas writes:

> [D]iscussion within such a public presupposed the problematization of areas that until then had not been questioned. The domain of "common concern" which was the object of public critical attention remained a preserve in which church and state authorities had the monopoly of interpretation not just from the pulpit but in philosophy, literature, and art, even at a time when, for specific social categories, the development of capitalism already demanded a behavior whose rational orientation required ever more information. (*Structural* 36)

Over time, public discussions of common concerns came to include not just art, literature, and philosophy, but economics and politics as well. In short, Habermas suggests that while the subjects of public discourse were quite diverse, they fulfilled an important criteria: they dealt with matters of common concern to all or nearly all members of a society.

Habermas limits his conception of the public sphere to sites where private persons deliberate about "public issues," and he suggests that the appearance of private issues and interests is always undesirable. However, this conception fails to recognize that the term *public* is ambiguous and open to interpretation. Fraser argues that there are several usages of the term beyond the sense of "of concern to everyone." She suggests that only participants can decide what is of common concern, and there is no guarantee that all of them will agree. Fraser suggests that the term *public* is "ambiguous between what objectively affects or has an impact on everyone as seen from an outsider's perspective, and what is recognized as a matter of common concern by participants" ("Rethinking" 128–29). Only participants can decide what is of common concern to them. However, there is no guarantee that they will all agree, and what will actually count as a matter of common concern will be decided through discursive contestation. Any consensus reached through such contestation will have been achieved "through deliberative processes tainted by the effects of dominance and subordination" (131). In other words, those who are in power get to decide what is a public issue and what is not.

Fraser asserts that the terms *public* and *private* are not simply straightforward designations of societal spheres; they are "cultural classifications and rhetorical labels" (131). As such, they function ideologically to delimit the boundaries of public discourse to the disadvantage of subordinate groups and individuals. For example, the issue of domestic violence was, until quite recently, considered to be a private matter between what was assumed to be a fairly small number of heterosexual couples. Feminists were in the minority in thinking that "domestic violence against women was a matter of common concern and thus a legitimate topic of public discourse" (Fraser, "Rethinking" 129). The feminist counterpublic, however, was instrumental in disseminating a view of domestic violence as a widespread systemic feature of male-dominated societies. Only through their sustained discursive contestation were they able to make it a matter of common concern.

A useful classroom heuristic is to ask students to talk about which issues are labeled "public" and which become "private." Such conversations often reveal the ideological mystification of these two categories. Matters that have heretofore been labeled private—such as sexual orientation, spousal and acquaintance abuse, and other matters of domestic or personal life—become important subjects for student writing. Students should feel free to address all of the issues that affect their lives—not just those that have been delegated "of common concern." In general, composition needs to take a more critical look at what we have determined are matters of public or private interest, and we must be willing to address issues that are often disturbing and unpleasant. We might begin by considering how the notions of public and private can be vehicles through which race, class, and gender disadvantages operate subtextually and informally, even after formal restrictions have been removed.

PUBLIC WRITING, DECISION MAKING, AND ACTION

There is one final assumption about public writing that I would like to address: that its only purpose is to sway public opinion and that it does not encompass actual decision making and action. If we employ newspapers as the primary venue for public-writing assignments, we imply that student discourse can rarely lead to substantial changes in public policy and can at best only convince others to "think differently." This presumption is especially pernicious because it forecloses real results from student writing and often turns public-writing assignments into pointless and futile exercises. While I'm not suggesting that public writing must *always* lead to decision making, I do believe that in certain circumstances it can. Public writing can form opinions *and* translate them into authoritative decisions, but only if we reconsider the presumption that public discourse is necessarily separated from legislative action.

Interestingly, Habermas suggests that a fundamental aspect of a functioning democratic public sphere is the sharp separation between civil society (the public) and the state (the government). He stops short of recognizing the power manifested in the eighteenth-century bourgeois public sphere, in particular, and suggests that there was no immediate implementation of the opinions produced through this sphere's deliberations. He notes that the bourgeois public "*readied* themselves to *compel* public authority" (*Structural* 27). This definition delineates the public sphere not as a site for the compulsion itself, but only for readying oneself to compel. Even that compulsion, had it been realized, was only a compulsion for the authorities to engage in further dialogue. Habermas suggests that members of the bourgeois public were not (and could not be) state officials, and their participation in the public sphere was not undertaken in any official capacity. As Fraser notes, Habermas's conception of public discourse does not "eventuate in binding, sovereign decisions authorizing the use of state power; on the contrary, it eventuates in public opinion" ("Rethinking" 133). Seen from this perspective, the public sphere is the polar opposite of the state; it is the informal body of discursive opinion that can serve as a "counterweight" to the state. Formal decisions on public issues cannot be made in the

Habermasian public sphere, because its scope is limited to conjecture, speculation, and debate about public matters. It is precisely this aspect of the public sphere that confers an aura of legitimacy, impartiality, and independence on the "public opinion" formed within it. Habermas's conception of the public sphere in effect implies that a sharp separation between civil society and the state is always desirable.

Fraser disagrees with this limited conception of the public sphere, arguing that the force of public opinion is strengthened, not weakened, when a body representing it is empowered to translate opinion into authoritative decisions. For example, self-governing institutions such as child-care centers, self-managed workplaces, or residential communities can be arenas of both opinion formation and decision making. She suggests that in these *strong publics*, whose discourse encompasses both deliberation and action, the "force of public opinion is strengthened when a body representing it is empowered to translate such 'opinion' into authoritative decisions" (*Rethinking* 134–35). The formation of these strong publics would be "tantamount to constituting sites of direct or quasi-direct democracy, wherein all those engaged in a collective undertaking would participate in deliberations to determine its design and operation" (135). While these internal public spheres would still be accountable to a larger public in many respects, their mere existence is a step toward a more egalitarian society, since they disseminate authority and power to a greater number of publics and individuals.

Students' public writing can have significant, tangible, immediate results if it is directed toward publics where both debate *and* decision making are central goals. It is both useful and important to help students locate strong publics where their discourse can lead to action. Asking students to write in spheres where discourse does not often lead to direct action, such as the local newspaper, is often pointless and futile. There are many arenas where student discourse can lead to palpable changes for them and others, and students may very well be members of these publics already. Students are often involved and engaged in student governments, campus organizations, resident-life committees, and workplace unions before they enroll in composition courses, and these and others are certainly sites where their discourse can have substantial effects. We should encourage students to write for publics where their discourse can have real significance, and we should help them to develop the rhetorical skills they will need to sway opinion and bring about change.

I have highlighted here just a few parallels between conversations about the public sphere in social and cultural theory and the more recent conversations of composition scholars about public writing. There is much more to be learned about public spheres and public discourse by looking outside of our own discipline. By drawing upon insights from cultural and social theory, we might develop more specific theoretical and pedagogical approaches to public writing. As a result, we should become more adept at facilitating critical public discourse in the writing courses that we teach.

REFERENCES

Alderman, Ellen, and Caroline Kennedy. 1995. *The Right to Privacy*. New York: Knopf.

Amin, Samir. 1995. *Capitalism in the Age of Globalization: Management of Contemporary Society*. London: Verso.

Annas, Pamela J. 1985. Style as Politics: A Feminist Approach to the Teaching of Writing. *College English* 47: 360–371.

Aristotle. 1984. *The Rhetoric and the Poetics of Aristotle. Rhetoric.* Trans. W. Rhys Roberts. *Poetics.* Trans. Ingram Bywater. New York: Modern Library.

Aston. T.H., gen. ed. 1984. *The History of the University of Oxford.* Vol. 1, ed. J. I. Catto. Oxford: Clarendon Press.

Baier, Annette. 1996. Trust and Antitrust. *Ethics 96* 2: 231–260.

Bakhtin, M. M. 1981. Discourse in the Novel. In *The Dialogic Imagination: Four Essays,* ed. Michael Holquist. Trans. Caryl Emerson and Michael Holquist. Austin: University of Texas Press. 259–422.

Bartholomae, David. 1985. Inventing the University. In *When a Writer Can't Write: Studies in Writer's Block and Other Composing-Process Problems,* ed. Mike Rose. NY: Guilford. 134–165.

Bartholomae, David. 1986. Wandering: Misreadings, Miswritings, Misunderstandings. In *Only Connect: Uniting Reading and Writing,* ed. Thomas Newkirk. Upper Montclair, N.J: Boynton/Cook Publishers. 89–118.

Bartholomae, David. 1997. Writing With Teachers: A Conversation with Peter Elbow. In Villanueva 1997. 479–488.

Bauman, Z. 1987. *Legislators and Interpreters: On Modernity, Post-modernity and Intellectuals.* Ithaca, NY: Cornell University Press.

Bawarshi, Anis S. 1997. Beyond Dichotomy: Toward a Theory of Divergence in Composition Studies. *JAC: A Journal of Composition Theory* 17: 69–82.

Baxter, Charles. 1999. Shame and Forgetting in the Information Age. In *The Business of Memory,* ed. Charles Baxter. St. Paul, MN: Graywolf. 141–157.

Baym, Nina. 2002. *American Women of Letters and the Nineteenth-Century Sciences.* New Brunswick: Rutgers University Press.

Belenky, Mary Field, Blythe McVicker Clinchy, Nancy Rule Goldberger, and Jill Mattuck Tarule. 1986. *Women's Ways of Knowing: The Development of Self, Voice, and Mind.* New York: Basic Books.

Bender, Thomas. 1984. The Erosion of Public Culture: Cities, Discourses, and Professional Disciplines. In *The Authority of Experts: Studies in History and Theory,* ed. T. L. Haskell. Bloomington: Indiana University Press. 84–106.

Berkenkotter, Carol, Thomas N. Huckin, and John Ackerman. 1988. Conventions, Conversations, and the Writer: Case Study of a Student in a Rhetoric Ph.D. Program. *Research in the Teaching of English* 22: 9–44.

Berlin, James. 1996. *Rhetorics, Poetics, and Cultures: Refiguring College English Studies.* Urbana: NCTE.

Berlin, James. 1992. Poststructuralism, Cultural Studies, and the Composition Classroom: Postmodern Theory into Practice. *Rhetoric Review* 1: 16–33.

Bernard-Donals, Michael. 2001. The Rhetoric of Disaster and the Imperative of Writing. *Rhetoric Society Quarterly* 31.1: 73–94.

Berry, Jason. 1992. *Lead Us Not Into Temptation: Catholic Priests and the Sexual Abuse of Children.* New York: Doubleday.

Billig, Michael. 1996. *Argument and Thinking.* New York: Cambridge University Press.

Bishop, Wendy. 1999. Places to Stand: The Reflective Writer-Teacher-Writer in Composition. *College Composition and Communication* 51: 9–25.

Bizzell, Patricia. 1982. Cognition, Convention, and Certainty: What We Need to Know About Writing. *Pre/Text* : 213–243.

Bizzell, Patricia. 1986: Foundationalism and Anti-Foundationalism in Composition Studies. *Pre/Text* 7: 37–57.

Bizzell, Patricia. 1992. *Academic Discourse and Critical Consciousness.* Pittsburgh: University of Pittsburgh Press.

Blakely, Edward J., and Mary Gail Snyder. 1997. *Fortress America: Gated Communities in the United States.* Washington, D.C: Brookings Institute.

Blanchot, Maurice. 1995. *The Writing of the Disaster.* Trans. Ann Smock. Lincoln: University of Nebraska Press.

Bleich, David. 1975. *Readings and Feelings.* Urbana: NCTE.

Bleich, David. 1978. *Subjective Criticism.* Baltimore: Johns Hopkins University Press.

Bloom, Lynn Z. 1972. *Doctor Spock: Biography of a Conservative Radical.* Indianapolis: Bobbs, Merrill.

Bloom, Lynn Z. 1999. The Essay Canon. *College English* 61: 401–430.

Bloom, Lynn Z. 2002. Once More to the Essay: The Essay Canon and Composition Textbooks. *Symplok* 8:1-2 20–35.

Boukreev, Anatoli, with G. Weston DeWalt. 1997. *The Climb: Tragic Ambitions on Everest.* New York: St. Martin's.

Bourdieu, Pierre. 1998. The Protest Movement of the Unemployed, a Social Miracle. *Acts of Resistance: Against the Tyranny of the Market.* New York: New Press.

Bourdieu, Pierre, Jean-Claude Passeron, and Monique de Saint Martin. 1994. *Academic Discourse: Linguistic Misunderstanding and Professorial Power.* Trans. Richard Teese. Palo Alto: Stanford University Press.

Brandt, Deborah. 2001. Protecting the Personal. In The Politics of the Personal: Storying Our Lives Against the Grain. The Symposium Collective. *College English* 64: 41–62.

Braverman, Harry. 1974. *Labor and Monopoly Capital: The Degradation of Work in the Twentieth Century.* New York: Monthly Review.

Braxton, Joanne. 1989. *Black Women Writing Autobiography: A Tradition within a Tradition.* Philadelphia: Temple University Press.

Breashears, David. 1999. *High Exposure: An Enduring Passion for Everest and Unforgiving Places.* New York: Simon and Schuster.

Bridwell-Bowles, Lillian. 1992. Discourse and Diversity: Experimental Writing within the Academy. *College Composition and Communication* 43: 349–368.

Brody, Miriam. 1993. *Manly Writing: Gender, Rhetoric, and the Rise of Composition.* Southern Illinois University Press.

Bucciarelli, Louis L. 1994. *Designing Engineers.* Cambridge, MA: The MIT Press.

Bunker, Matthew D., and Charles N. Davis. 2000. When Government 'Contracts Out': Privatization, Accountability, and Constitutional Doctrine. In *Access Denied: Freedom of Information in the Information Age,* eds. Charles N. Davis and Sigman L. Splichal. Ames, IA: Iowa State University Press.

Burke, Kenneth. 1968. *Counter-Statement.* 1931. Berkeley: University of California Press.

Burke, Kenneth. 1969. *A Grammar of Motives.* 1945. Berkeley: University of California Press.

Burke, Kenneth. 1969. *A Rhetoric of Motives.* 1950. Berkeley: University of California Press.

Burke, Kenneth. 1984. *Permanence and Change: An Anatomy of Purpose* (1935), Third edition. Berkeley: University of California Press.

Burke, Kenneth. 1951. Rhetoric—Old and New. *The Journal of General Education.* 202–209.

Burke, Kenneth. 1969. I, Eye, Aye—Emerson's Early Essay 'Nature': Thoughts on the Machinery of Transcendence. In *Emerson's Nature—Origin, Growth, Meaning,* ed. Merton M. Sealts and Alfred R. Ferguson. New York: Dodd, Mead. 150–163.

Burke, Kenneth. 1973. The Rhetorical Situation. In *Communication: Ethical and Moral Issues,* ed. Lee Thayer. London: Gordon and Breach Science Publishers. 263–275.

Burke, Kenneth. 1987. Letter to Bill Moyers. May 12. Copy in G. Clark's possession.

Burnett, Rebecca Emilynn. 1991. Conflict in the Collaborative Planning of Co-authors: How Substantive Conflict, Representation of Task, and Dominance Relate to High-Quality Documents. *Dissertations Abstracts International* 52: 1236A.

Butler, Judith. 1999. Politics and the Limits of Common Sense. The Second Biennial Feminism(s) and Rhetoric(s) Conference: Challenging Rhetorics: Cross-Disciplinary Sites of Feminist Discourse. Minneapolis, MN. Oct 8.

Caruth, Cathy. 1996. *Unclaimed Experience: Trauma, Narrative, and History.* Baltimore: Johns Hopkins.

Cazort, Mimi, Monique Kornell, and K.B. Roberts. 1996. *The Ingenious Machine of Nature: Four Centuries of Art and Anatomy.* Ottawa: National Gallery of Canada.

Charland, Maurice. 1987. Constitutive Rhetoric: The Case of the People Quebecois. *Quarterly Journal of Speech* 73.2 (May): 133–150.

Cheung, Charles. 2000. Presentations of Self on Personal Homepages. In Gauntlett. 43–51.

Cintron, Ralph. 1993. Wearing a Pith Helmet at a Sly Angle: Or, Can Writing Researchers Do Ethnography in a Postmodern Era? *Written Communication* 10: 371–412.

Clark, Gregory. n.d. Professional Ethics from an Academic Perspective. *Journal of Computer Documentation* 18.

Clark, Gregory. 1994. Rescuing the Discourse of Community. *College Composition and Communication* 45: 61-74.

Clark, Gregory, and Stephen Doheny-Farina. 1990. Public Discourse and Personal Expression: A Case Study in Theory-building. *Written Communication* 7: 456–481.

Clark, Gregory, and S. Michael Halloran. 1993. Transformation of Public Discourse in Nineteenth-century America. *Oratorical Culture in Nineteenth-century America: Transformation in the Theory and Practice of Rhetoric.* Carbondale, IL: Southern Illinois University Press. 1–26.

Collins, Randall. 1979. *The Credential Society: An Historical Sociology of Education and Stratification.* New York: Academic.

Connors, Robert J. 1997. *Composition-Rhetoric: Backgrounds, Theory, and Pedagogy.* Pittsburgh: University of Pittsburgh Press.

Cooper, Marilyn M. 1986. The Ecology of Writing. *College English* 48: 364–375.

Couture, Barbara. 1998. *Toward a Phenomenological Rhetoric: Writing, Profession, and Altruism.* Carbondale: Southern Illinois University Press.

Cramer, P. 2001. Arts Controversies and the Problem of the Public Sphere. Paper presented at the Argumentation and its Applications, Conference of the Ontario Society for the Study of Argumentation (OSSA), University of Windsor, Windsor, Ontario.

Crary, Jonathan. 1990. *Techniques of the Observer: On Vision and Modernity in the Nineteenth Century.* Cambridge: MIT Press.

Cressey, Donald R., and Moore, Charles A. 1983. Managerial Values and Corporate Codes of Ethics. *California Management Review* 25:53-77.

Crick, Bernard. 1980. *George Orwell: A Life.* Boston: Little, Brown.

Cross, Geoffrey A. 1994. *Collaboration and Conflict.* Cresskill, NJ: Hampton Press.

Cross, Geoffrey A. 2001. *Forming the Collective Mind.* Cresskill, NJ: Hampton Press.

Crouch, Stanley. 1995. *The All-American Skin Game, or, The Decoy of Race.* New York: Vintage.

Crouch, Stanley. 2001. Interview with G. Clark. May 15.

Daigneqult, Michael G. *Foreword, 2000 National Business Ethics Survey.* Ethics Resource Center. <www.ethics.org/2000survey.html>

Daly, Brenda. 1998. *Authoring a Life: A Woman's Survival in and through Literary Studies.* State University of New York Press.

Dannels, Deanna. 2000. Learning to be Professional: Technical Classroom Discourse, Practice, and Professional Identity Construction. *Journal of Business and Technical Communication* 14: 5–37.

Darnton, John. 2001. *Writers on Writing: Collected Essays from the New York Times.* New York: Henry Holt.

Davenport, Thomas, and Sirkka Jarvenpaa. 2001. Digital Marketing and the Exchange of Knowledge. In *Digital Marketing: Global Strategies from the World's Leading Experts,* ed. Jerry Wind and Vijay Mahajan. New York: John Wiley and Sons. 130–160.

Davis, D. Diane. 2001. Finitude's Clamor; Or, Notes Toward a Communitarian Literacy. *College Composition and Communication* 53: 119–145.

De Botton, Alain. 1998. What is Academia for? *Prospect* August/September. <www.prospect magazine.co.uk/highlights/academia for.html>

De Ridder-Symoens, Hilde, ed. 1992. *A History of the University in Europe.* Vol. 1. Cambridge University Press.

de St. Exupery, Antoine. 1942. *Flight to Arras.* New York: Reynal and Hitchcock.

Derrida, Jacques. 1997. *Politics of Friendship.* Trans. George Collins. London: Verso.

Didion, Joan. 1991. Why I Write. In *The Essay Connection,* ed. Lynn Z. Bloom. 3rd ed. Lexington, MA: Heath. 43–50.

Dixon, Kathleen. 1995. Gendering the 'Personal.' *College Composition and Communication* 46: 255–275.

Dixon, Laurinda. 1995. *Perilous Chastity: Women and Illness in Pre-Enlightenment Art and Medicine.* Ithaca: Cornell University Press.

Dobrin, Sidney I. 1997. *Constructing Knowledges: The Politics of Theory-Building and Pedagogy in Composition.* State University of New York Press.

Dobrin, Sidney I. 1999. Paralogic Hermeneutic Theories, Power, and the Possibility for Liberating Pedagogies. In *Post-process Theory: Beyond the Writing Process Paradigm,* ed. Thomas Kent. Southern Illinois University Press. 132–148.

Dobrin, Sidney I., and Christian R. Weisser. 2002. *Natural Discourse: Toward Ecocomposition.* Albany, NY: State University of New York Press.

Dobrin, Sidney I. Writing Takes Place. In Weisser and Dobrin 11-25.

Drorr, Otneil. 1999. The Scientific Image of Emotion. *Configurations* 7.3: 355–402.

DuBois, W.E.B. 1996. *The Souls of Black Folk.* 1903. New York: Penguin Books.

Eberly, Rosa. 1999. *Citizen Critics: Literary Public Spheres.* Urbana: University of Illinois Press.

Eggers, Dave. 2000. *A Heartbreaking Work of Staggering Genius.* New York: Simon and Schuster.

Elbow, Peter. 1973. *Writing Without Teachers.* New York: Oxford University Press.

Elbow, Peter. 1991. Some Thoughts on Expressive Discourse: A Review Essay. *JAC: A Journal of Composition Theory* 11: 83-93.

Elbow, Peter. 1994. Introduction: About Voice and Writing. In *Landmark Essays on Voice and Writing,* ed. Peter Elbow. Davis, CA: Hermagoras Press. xi–xlvii.

Elbow, Peter. 1995. Response. *College Composition and Communication* 46: 87–92.

Elbow, Peter. 1997. Being a Writer vs. Being an Academic. In Villanueva 1997. 489–500.

Elbow, Peter. 1997. Response. In Villanueva. 504–509.

Elbow, Peter. 2000. *College Composition and Communication* Online. News and Announcements. NCTE. <www.ncte.org/ccc/8/sub/50_2_98.html> Jun 3.

Ellison, Ralph. 2001. *Living With Music: Ralph Ellison's Jazz Writings,* ed. Robert G. O'Meally. New York: The Modern Library.

Evans, Bill. 1959. Liner notes. Portrait in Jazz: Bill Evans Trio.

Evans, Bill. 1963. Liner notes. Bill Evans: Conversations with Myself.

Evans, Bill. 1980. Interview. http: //www.njmetronet.com/billevans/molde.html

Everest. 1998. Dir. David Breashears, Stephen Judson, and Greg MacGillivray. Imax.

Expedition '96: Everest Quest. PBS Nova. http://www.pbs.org/wgbh/nova/everest/expeditions/96/

Falk, Gideon. 1982. An Empirical Study Measuring Conflict in Problem-Solving Groups which are Assigned Different Decision Rules. *Human Relations* 35: 1123-1148.

Farrell, Thomas B. 1993. *Norms of Rhetorical Culture.* New Haven: Yale University Press.

Farris, Christine. 1999. Feminist and Disciplinary Implications of the (re)turn to the Personal in Composition Studies. Feminisms and Rhetorics Conference. Minneapolis, MN.

Farris, Christine. 2001. Telephone conversation. Nov 14.

Fleck, Ludwig. 1979. *Genesis and Development of a Scientific Fact.* Chicago: University of Chicago Press.

Flynn, Elizabeth A. 1986. In Gender and Reading. *Gender and Reading: Essays on Readers, Texts, and Contexts,* ed. Elizabeth A. Flynn and Patrocinio P. Schweickart. Baltimore: Johns Hopkins University Press. 267–288.

Flynn, Elizabeth A. 1990. The Classroom as Interpretive Community: Teaching Reader-Response Theory and Composition Theory to Preprofessional Undergraduates. *Reorientations: Critical Theories and Pedagogies,* ed. Bruce Henricksen and Thais Morgan. Champaign: University of Illinois Press. 193–215.

Fox, Tom. 1999. *Defending Access: A Critique of Standards in Higher Education.* Portsmouth, NH: Heinemann.

Fraser, Nancy. 1989. *Unruly Practices: Power, Discourse, and Gender in Contemporary Social Theory.* Minneapolis: University of Minnesota Press.

Fraser, Nancy. 1996. Rethinking the Public Sphere: A Contribution to the Critique of Actually Existing Democracy. In *Habermas and the Public Sphere,* ed. Craig Calhoun. Cambridge: MIT Press. 109–142.

Fraser, Nancy. 1997. *Justice Interruptus: Critical Reflections on the Postsocialist Condition.* Routledge: New York and London.

Freedman, Aviva, Christine Adam, and Graham Smart. 1994. Wearing Suits to Class: Simulating Genres and Simulations as Genres. *Written Communication* 11: 193–226.

Freedman, Diane, Olivia Frey, and Frances Murphy Zauhar, eds. 1993. *The Intimate Critique: Autobiographical Literary Criticism.* Durham: Duke University Press.

Freidson, Elliot. 1986. *Professional Powers: A Study of the Institutionalization of Formal Knowledge.* Chicago: University of Chicago Press.

Frey, Olivia. 1990. Beyond Literary Darwinism: Women's Voices and Critical Discourse. *College English* 52: 507–526.

Galen. 1952. *On the Natural Faculties.* Trans. Arthur John Brock. Loeb Classical Library. Cambridge: Harvard University Press.

Garrison, Ruth. 1992. Feminism and the Public/Private Distinction. *Stanford Law Review* 45: 1–45.

Gass, William H. 1985. Emerson and the Essay. *Habitations of the Word: Essays.* New York: Simon. 9–49.

Gauntlett, David, ed. 2000. *Web Studies: Rewiring Media Studies for the Digital Age.* New York: Oxford University Press.

Geisler, Cheryl, Edwin H. Rogers, and Cynthia Haller. 1998. Disciplining Discourse: Discourse Practice in the Affiliated Professions of Software Engineering Design. *Written Communication* 15: 3-24.

Geisler, Cheryl. 1994. *Academic Literacy and the Nature of Expertise: Reading, Writing, and Knowing in Academic Philosophy.* Hillsdale, NJ: Erlbaum.

Geisler, Cheryl. 2004. *Analyzing Steams of Language: Twelve Steps to the Systematic Coding of Text, Talk and Other Verbal Data.* Pearson Longman.

Gibson, Walker. 1966. *Tough, Sweet, and Stuffy: An Essay on Modern American Prose Styles.* Bloomington: Indiana University Press.

Gilbert, James L., Francis H. Hare, Jr., and Stuart A. Ollanik. 1994. Negotiation and Settlement: The Price of Silence. *Trial* 30 (Jun): 17–21.

Gilmore, Leigh. 1994. *Autobiographics. A Feminist Theory of Women's Self-Representation.* Ithaca, NY: Cornell University Press.

Giroux, Henry. 2000. *Stealing Innocence: Youth, Corporate Power, and the Politics of Culture.* New York: St. Martin's.

Golding, Alan. 1995. *From Outlaw to Classic: Canons in American Poetry.* Madison: University of Wisconsin Press.

Goldman, Robert and Stephen Papson. 1996. *Sign Wars: The Cluttered Landscape of Advertising.* New York: Guilford.

Graff, Gerald. 2000. Scholars and Sound Bites: The Myth of Academic Difficulty. *PMLA* 115 (Oct): 1041–1051.

Green, Duncan. 1995. *Silent Revolution: The Rise of Market Economies in Latin America.* London: Cassell and LAB.

Gross, Paul R., and Norman Levitt. 1994. *Higher Superstition: The Academic Left and its Quarrels with Science.* Baltimore: John Hopkins University Press.

Gubrium, Jaber, and James Holstein. 1998. Narrative Practice and the Coherence of Personal Stories. *The Sociological Quarterly* 39 (Winter): 163–187.

Guetzkow, Harold, and Gyr, John. 1954. An Analysis of Conflict in Decision-Making Groups. *Human Relations* 7: 367–381.

Gurak, Laura J. 1997. *Privacy and Persuasion in Cyberspace: The Online Protests over Lotus MarketPlace and the Clipper Chip.* New Haven: Yale University Press.

Gusdorf, Georges. 1980. Conditions and Limits of Autobiography. 1956. In *Autobiography: Essays Theoretical and Critical,* ed. James Olney. Princeton: Princeton University Press. 28–48.

Haas, Christine. 1994. Learning to Read Biology: One Student's Rhetorical Development in College. *Written Communication* 11: 43–84.

Habermas, Jürgen. 1979. *Communication and the Evolution of Society*. Boston: Beacon.

Habermas, Jürgen. 1989. *The Structural Transformation of the Public Sphere: An Inquiry into a Category Bourgeois Society*. Cambridge: MIT Press.

Habermas, Jurgen. 1990. *Moral Consciousness and Communicative Action*. Trans. Christian Lenhardt and Shierry Weber Nicholsen. Cambridge: MIT Press.

Habermas, Jurgen. 1996. *Between Facts and Norms*. Trans. W. Rehg. Cambridge: MIT Press.

Haefner, Joel. 1992. Democracy, Pedagogy, and the Personal Essay. *College English* 54: 127–137.

Hans, Valerie P. 2000. *Business on Trial: The Civil Jury and Corporate Responsibility*. New Haven: Yale University Press.

Harris, Joseph. 1997. *A Teaching Subject: Composition Since 1966*. Upper Saddle River, NJ: Prentice Hall.

Harris, Joseph. 1989. The Idea of Community in the Study of Writing. *College Composition and Communication* 40 (Feb): 11–22.

Harris, Joseph. 1997. Person, Position, Style. In *Publishing in Rhetoric and Composition*, eds. Gary A. Olson and Todd W. Taylor. Albany: State University of New York Press. 47–56.

Harvey, Gordon. 1994. Presence in the Essay. *College English* 56: 642–654.

Hasian, Marouf, Jr. 2001. Vernacular Legal Discourse: Revisiting the Public Acceptance of the 'Right to Privacy' in the 1960s. *Political Communication* 18: 89–105.

Haskins, Charles Horner. 1957. *The Rise of Universities* [1923]. Ithaca: Cornell University Press.

Hawisher, Gail E., Paul LeBlanc, Charles Moran, Cynthia L. Selfe, eds. 1996. *Computers and the Teaching of Writing in American Higher Education, 1979–1994: A History*. Norwood, NJ: Ablex.

Heilbrun, Carolyn. 2002. *When Men Were the Only Models We Had*. Philadelphia: University of Pennsylvania Press.

Herrington, Anne. 2001. When Is My Business Your Business? In *The Politics of the Personal: Storying Our Lives Against the Grain*. The Symposium Collective. *College English* 64: 41-62.

Herrlinger, Robert. 1970. *History of Medical Illustration from Antiquity to 1600*. New York: Editions Medicina Rara.

Herzberg, Bruce. 1994. Community Service and Critical Teaching. *College Composition and Communication* 45: 307–319.

Hesford, Wendy. 1999. Reading Rape Stories: Material Rhetoric and the Trauma of Representation. *College English* 62: 192–221.

Hindman, Jane E. 2001. Introduction: Special Focus: Personal Writing. *College English* 64: 34–40.

Hine, Christine. 2000. *Virtual Ethnography*. London: Sage.

Hoagland, Edward. 1976. What I Think, What I Am. *New York Times Book Review*, Jun 27. Rpt. in Paul H. Connolly, ed. 1981. *On Essays*. New York: Harper and Row, 45–47.

Holdstein, Deborah H., and David Bleich, eds. 2001. *Personal Effects: The Social Character of Scholarly Writing*. Logan: Utah State University Press.

Horner, Winifred, ed. 1983. *Composition and Literature: Bridging the Gap*. Chicago: University of Chicago Press.

Horsburgh, H. J. N. 1960. The Ethics of Trust. *Philosophical Quarterly* 10: 354.

Howarth, William L. 1974. Some Principles of Autobiography. *Autobiography: Essays Theoretical and Critical*. 84–114.

Howell, Jeremy and Alan Ingham. 2001. From Social Problem to Personal Issue: The Language of Lifestyle. *Cultural Studies* 15: 326–351.

Into Thin Air: Death on Everest. 1997. Dir. Robert Markowitz. Columbia TriStar.

Mary Putnam Jacobi, M. D.: A Pathfinder in Medicine, with Selections from Her Writings and a Complete Bibliography. 1925. Ed. Women's Medical Association of New York City. New York: Putnam.

Jacobi, Mary Putnam. 1867. Our Paris Correspondent. *New York Herald Tribune.* Jan 2. Mary Putnam Jacobi papers. folder 29.

Jacobi, Mary Putnam. 1871. The Clubs of Paris. *Scribner's Monthly* 3 (Nov): 105–108.

Jacobi, Mary Putnam. 1875. Remarks upon the Action of Nitrate of Silver on Epithelial and Gland Cells. *Transactions of the New York State Medical Society*: 251.

Jacobi, Mary Putnam. 1877. *The Question of Rest for Women During Menstruation.* Boylston Prize Essay of Harvard University. 1876. New York: G.P. Putnam's Sons,

Jacobi, Mary Putnam. 1880. *On the Use of the Cold Pack Followed by Massage in the Treatment of Anaemia.* New York: G.P. Putnam's Sons.

Jacobi, Mary Putnam. 1885. Studies in Endometritis. *American Journal of Obstetrics* 18: 36, 113, 262, 519, 596; continued as Morbid Variations in the Greater or Parturient Cycle, Subinvolution and Chronic Metritis. (Studies in Endometritis), 802; Menstrual Subinvolution or Metritis of the Non-parturient Uterus (Studies in Endometritis), 915; and The Ovarian Complication of Endometritis (Studies in Endometritis), *American Journal of Obstetrics* 19 (1886): 352.

Jacobi, Mary Putnam. 1888. *Essays on Hysteria, Brain Tumor, and Some Other Causes of Nervous Disease.* New York: G. P. Putnam's Sons.

Jacobi, Mary Putnam. 1890. Remarks upon Empyema. *Medical News* 56: 120–121, 172–173.

Jacobi, Mary Putnam. 1891. Woman and Medicine. In *Woman's Work in America,* ed. Annie Nathan Meyer. New York: Holt. 139–205.

Jacobi, Mary Putnam. 1895. Case of Absent Uterus: With Considerations of the Significance of the Hermaphrodism. *American Journal of Obstetrics* 32.4 (Oct): 510–22.

Jacobi, Mary Putnam. 1902. Autobiographical manuscript. Typescript. Mary Putnam Jacobi papers. Schlesinger Library, Radcliffe College, Cambridge, MA. a-26, folder 2.

Jacobi, Mary Putnam. 1907. A Martyr for Science. *Stories and Sketches.* New York: G.P. Putnam's Sons. 212–261.

Jacobi, Mary Putnam. 1925. *Life and Letters of Mary Putnam Jacobi,* ed. Ruth Putnam. New York: G.P. Putnam's Sons.

Jacobi, Mary Putnam. 1925. *Mary Putnam Jacobi, M.D: A Pathfinder in Medicine,* ed. Women's Medical Association of New York City. New York: G.P. Putnam's Sons.

Jameson, Fredric. 1981. *The Political Unconscious: Narrative as a Socially Symbolic Act.* Ithaca, NY: Cornell University Press.

Jarratt, Susan. Introduction: As We Were Saying. In Jarrett and Worsham. 1–20.

Jarratt, Susan, and Lynn Worsham, eds. 1998. *Feminism and Composition Studies: In Other Words.* NY: MLA.

Jordanova, Ludmilla. 1989. *Sexual Visions: Images of Gender in Science and Medicine Between the Eighteenth and Twentieth Centuries.* New York: Harvester.

Karis, Bill. 1989. Conflict in Collaboration: A Burkean Perspective. *Rhetoric Review* 8: 113–126.

Katz, Steven B. 1992. The Ethic of Expediency: Classical Rhetoric, Technology, and the Holocaust. *College English* 54: 255–275.

Katz, Susan M. 1998. *The Dynamics of Writing Review: Opportunities for Growth and Change in the Workplace.* New York: Ablex.

Kaufer, David S., and Brian S. Butler. 1996. *Rhetoric and the Arts of Design.* Mahwah, NJ: Erlbaum.

Kaufer, David S., and Kathleen Carley. 1994. Some Concepts and Axioms about Communication: Proximate and at a Distance. *Written Communication* 11: 8–42.

Kent, Thomas. 1992. Externalism and the Production of Discourse. *JAC* 12: 57–74.

Kent, Thomas. 1993. *Paralogic Rhetoric: A Theory of Communicative Interaction.* Lewisburg, PA: Bucknell University Press.

Kent, Thomas. 1999. Introduction. In *Post-Process Theory: Beyond the Writing Process Paradigm,* ed. Thomas Kent. Carbondale: Southern Illinois University Press. 1–6.

King, Dennis J., and Janice Miner Holden. 1998. Disclosure of Trauma and Psychosomatic Health: An Interview with James W. Pennebaker. *Journal of Counseling and Development* 76.3: 358–363.

Kirsch, Gesa E. 1997. Opinion: Multi-Vocal Texts and Interpretive Responsibility. *College English* 59: 191–202.

Kirsch, Gesa E., and Joy S. Ritchie. 1995. Beyond the Personal: Theorizing a Politics of Location in Composition Research. *College Composition and Communication* 46: 7–29.

Kitzhaber, Albert Raymond. 1963. *Themes, Theories, and Therapy: Teaching of Writing in College. The Report of the Dartmouth Study of Student Writing.* NY: McGraw-Hill.

Krakauer, Jon. 1990. *Eiger Dreams: Ventures Among Men and Mountains.* New York: Anchor.

Krakauer, Jon. 1997. *Into Thin Air.* New York: Anchor.

Lakoff, Robin Tolmach. 1990. *Talking Power: The Politics of Language in our Lives.* New York: Basic Books.

Larson, M. S. 1977. *The Rise of Professionalism: A Sociological Analysis.* Berkeley: University of California Press.

Laub, Dori. 1992. Bearing Witness or the Vicissitudes of Listening. In *Testimony: Crises of Witnessing in Literature, Psychoanalysis, and History,* ed. Shoshana Felman. New York: Routledge. 75-92.

Law, John, and John Whittaker. 1988. On the Art of Representation: Notes on the Politics of Visualization. *Picturing Power: Visual Depiction and Social Relations. Sociological Review Monograph* 35, ed. Gordon Fyfe and John Law. London: Routledge. 160–183.

Leggo, Carl. 1991. Questions I Need To Ask before I Advise my Students to Write in their own Voices. *Rhetoric Review* 10: 143–152.

Lichtenstein, David. 1993. The Rhetoric of Improvisation: Spontaneous Discourse in Jazz and Psychoanalysis. *American Image* 50.2: 227–252.

Lindemann, Erika. 1995. Three Views of English 101. *College English*: 57: 287–302.

Lynch, Michael, and Samuel Edgerton, Jr. Aesthetics and Digital Image Processing. *Picturing Power: Visual Depiction and Social Relations.* 184–220.

Lyotard, Jean-Francois. 1984. *The Postmodern Condition: A Report on Knowledge.* Trans. Geoff Bennington and Brian Massumi. Minneapolis: University of Minnesota Press.

Maccoby, Michael. 1976. *The Gamesman: The New Corporate Leaders.* New York: Simon and Schuster.

MacKinnon, Catherine A. 1989. *Toward a Feminist Theory of the State.* Cambridge: Harvard University Press.

Mandel, Barrett J. 1980. Full of Life Now. In *Autobiography: Essays Theoretical and Critical,* ed. James Olney. Princeton: Princeton University Press. 49–72.

Marius, Richard. 1992. Composition Studies. In *Redrawing the Boundaries: The Transformation of English and American Literary Studies*, eds. Stephen Greenblatt and Giles Gunn. NY: MLA. 466–481.

Marsalis, Wynton. 2000. Interview with author. Mar 25.

Marsalis, Wynton. 2001. Interview with author. May 17.

Marsalis, Wynton, and Frank Stewart. 1994. *Sweet Swing Blues on the Road.* New York: Norton.

Marx, Karl. 1976. *Capital: A Critique of Political Economy.* Vol. I. Trans. Ben Fowkes. New York: Vintage.

Marx, Karl, and Friedrich Engels. 1970. *Manifesto of the Communist Party: Selected Works.* New York: International Publishers.

Matthews, M. Cash. 1987. Codes of Ethics: Organizational Behavior and Misbehavior. *Research in Corporate Social Performance.* Vol. 9. Greenwich, CT: JAI P: 107–130.

McCarthy, Thomas. 1978. *The Critical Theory of Jurgen Habermas.* Cambridge: MIT Press.

McCarthy, Thomas. 1989. Introduction. *The Structural Transformation of the Public Sphere: An Inquiry into a Category Bourgeois Society.* By Jürgen Habermas. Cambridge: MIT Press. xi–xiv.

McGee, Michael Calvin. 1999. In Search of 'the People: ' A Rhetorical Alternative. In *Contemporary Rhetorical Theory*, ed. J.L. Lucaites, C.M. Condit, S. Caudill. New York: Guilford Press. 341–356.

McQuade, Donald M. 1992. Composition and Literary Studies. In *Redrawing the Boundaries: The Transformation of English and American Literary Studies*, ed. Stephen Greenblatt and Giles Gunn. New York: MLA. 482–519.

McSweeney's News. 2002. <http: //www.mcsweeneys.net/news/feb00.html>. Oct 10.

Mehegan, John. 1997. Interview with Bill Evans. Liner notes for *The Complete Bill Evans on Verve.* 144–153.

Messbarger, Rebecca. 2001. Waxing Poetic: Anna Morandi Manzolini's Anatomical Sculptures. *Configurations* 9.1 (Winter): 65–97.

Meyrowitz, Joshua. 1985. *No Sense of Place: the Impact of Electronic Media on Social Behavior.* New York, Oxford.

Michael, John. 2000. *Anxious Intellects: Academic Professionals, Public Intellectuals, and Enlightenment Values.* Durham: Duke University Press.

Mill, John Stuart. 1863. *On Liberty.* Boston: Ticknor and Fields.

Miller, Carolyn R. 1993. Rhetoric and Community: The Problem of the One and the Many. In *Defining the New Rhetorics*, ed. Theresa Enos and Stuart C. Brown. Sage Series in Written Communication 7. Newbury Park: Sage. 79–94.

Miller, Richard E. 2001. Why Bother with Writing? In The Politics of the Personal: Storying Our Lives Against the Grain. *College English* 64: 41–62.

Mitchell, Silas Weir. 1978. *Fat and Blood and How to Make Them* [1877]. 2nd ed. Philadelphia: Lippincott.

Morgan, Janice. 1991. Subject to Subject/Voice to Voice: 20th-Century Autobiographical Fiction by Women Writers. In *Redefining Autobiography in Twentieth-Century Women's Fiction,* ed. Morgan, Janice and Collette Hall. NY: Garland Press. 1–15.

Murray, Albert. 1998. Improvisation and the Creative Process. In *The Jazz Cadence of American Culture*, ed. Robert G. O'Meally. New York: Columbia University Press. 111–113.

Myers, Greg. 1991. Stories and Styles in Two Molecular Biology Review Articles. In *Textual Dynamics of the Professions*, ed. C. Bazerman and J. Paradis. Madison: University of Wisconsin Press. 45–75.

Negt, Oskar, and Alexander Kluge. 1993. *Public Sphere and Experience.* Minneapolis: University of Minnesota Press.

Noble, David F. 1992. *A World Without Women: The Christian Clerical Culture of Western Science.* New York: Knopf.

Noddings, Nel. 1984. *Caring: A Feminine Approach to Ethics and Moral Education.* Berkeley: University of California Press.

Nussbaum, Martha. 1999. The Professor of Parody. *The New Republic.* Feb 22: 38.

Olney, James. 1972. *Metaphors of Self: The Meaning of Autobiography.* New Haven: Princeton University Press.

Olney, James, ed. 1980. *Autobiography: Essays Theoretical and Critical.* New Haven: Princeton University Press.

Olson, Gary A. 2002. Foreword: Public Discourse and the Future of Composition Pedagogy. *Moving Beyond Academic Discourse: Composition Studies and the Public Sphere.* By Christian R. Weisser. Carbondale: Southern Illinois University Press.

Ong, Walter J., S. J. 1981. *Fighting for Life: Contest, Sexuality, and Consciousness.* Ithaca: Cornell University Press.

Ong, Walter J., S. J. 1982. *Orality and Literacy.* New York: Penguin.

Orwell, George. 1954. Why I Write. 1947. *A Collection of Essays by George Orwell.* New York: Doubleday. 313–320.

Oye, Phil. 2001. Trade Center Survivor Recounts Harrowing Escape. *CNN.com.* <www.cnn.com.> Sep 21.

Paley, Vivian Gussin. 1990. *You Can't Say You Can't Play.* Cambridge: Harvard University Press.

Peitzman, Steven. 2000. *A New and Untried Course: Woman's Medical College and Medical College of Pennsylvania, 1850–1998.* New Brunswick: Rutgers University Press.

Penrose, Ann, and Cheryl Geisler. 1994. Reading and Writing Without Authority. *College Composition and Communication* 45: 71–86.

Petersen, Jennifer. 2001. Citizens and Spokesmen: Politics and Personal Expression on the Web. In *Our Virtual World: The Transformation of Work, Play and Life Via Technology*, ed. Laku Chidambaram and Ilze Zigurs. Hershey, PA: Idea Group. 152–165.

Petherbridge, Deanna, and Ludmilla Jordanova. 1997. *The Quick and the Dead: Artists and Anatomy.* London: National Touring Exhibitions.

Pettit, John D., Bobby Vaught, and Kathy Pulley. 1990. The Role of Communication in Organizations: Ethical Considerations. *The Journal of Business Communication* 27: 233–251.

Phillips, K. R. 1996. The Spaces of Public Dissension: Reconsidering the Public Sphere. *Communication Monographs* 63: 231–248.

Popper, Karl R. 1947. *The Spell of Plato.* London: Routledge, 1945. Vol. I of *The Open Society and Its Enemies.* 2 vols.

Popper, Karl. 1963. *The Open Society and its Enemies.* 4th ed. Princeton, NJ: Princeton University Press.

Potter, Nancy. 1995. On Becoming Trustworthy. Unpublished manuscript.

Poulakos, John. 1999. Toward a Sophistic Definition of Rhetoric.1983. In *Contemporary Rhetorical Theory: A Reader*, ed. John Louis Lucaites et.al. New York: Guilford Press. 25–32.

Prior, Paul. 1998. *Writing/Disciplinarity: A Sociohistoric Account of Literate Activity in the Academy.* Mahwah, NJ: Erlbaum.

Putnam, Linda L. 1986. Conflict in Group Decision-Making. In *Communication and Group Decision-Making,* ed. R.Y. Hirokawa and M. S. Poole. Beverly Hills: Sage. 175–196.

Ramsey, Maja, Justine Durrell, and Timothy W. Ahearn. 1998. Keeping Secrets with Confidentiality Agreements. *Trial* 34 (Aug): 38–43.

Rashdall, Hastings. 1997. *The Universities of Europe in the Middle Ages.* 3 Vols. 1895; 1936. Oxford University Press.

Rasula, Jed. 1996. *The American Poetry Wax Museum: Reality Effects, 1940–1990.* Urbana: National Council of Teachers of English.

Rentz, Kathryn C. and Mary Beth Debs. 1987. Language and Corporate Values: Teaching Ethics in Business Writing Courses. *The Journal of Business Communication* 24: 37–48.

Rheinberger, Hans-Jörg. 1998. Experimental Systems, Graphemic Spaces. In *Inscribing Science: Scientific Texts and the Materiality of Communication,* ed. Timothy Lenoir. Stanford: Stanford University Press. 285–303.

Rich, Adrienne. 1986. Notes Toward a Politics of Location. *Blood, Bread, and Poetry: Selected Prose 1979–85.* NY: Norton. 210–231.

Ritivoi, A. 2002. *Yesterday's Self: Nostalgia and the Construction of Personal Identity.* New York: Rowman and Littlefield Publishers.

Roberts, K.B., and J.D.W. Tomlinson. 1992. *The Fabric of the Body: History of Medical Illustration from Antiquity to 1600.* Oxford: Clarendon.

Root, Robert L., Jr. 1999. *E.B. White: The Emergence of an Essayist.* Iowa City: University of Iowa Press.

Rorty, Richard. 1991. Inquiry as Recontextualization: An Anti-Dualist Account of Interpretation. In *The Interpretive Turn: Philosophy, Science, Culture,* ed. David R. Hiley, James F. Bohman, and Richard Shusterman. Ithaca: Cornell University Press. 59–80.

Rose, Mike. 1989. *Lives on the Boundary: The Struggles and Achievements of America's Underprepared.* New York: Free Press.

Rothleder, Dianne. 1999. *The Work of Friendship: Rorty, His Critics, and the Project of Solidarity.* Albany: State University of New York Press.

Rousselot, Jean, ed. 1967. *Medicine in Art: a Cultural History.* New York: McGraw Hill.

Royster, Jacqueline Jones. 1994. When the First Voice You Hear Is Not Your Own. *College Composition and Communication.* 47.1: 29–40.

Royster, Jacqueline Jones. 2000. *Traces of a Stream: Literacy and Social Change Among African American Women.* Pittsburgh: University of Pittsburgh Press.

Ruegg, Walter. 1992. Epilogue: The Rise of Humanism. *A History of the University in Europe.* Vol. 1. Cambridge: Cambridge University Press. 442–468.

Ruskin, John. 1958. The Stones of Venice: The Nature of the Gothic. In *Prose of the Victorian Period,* ed. W.E. Buckler. New York: Houghton Mifflin. 361–392.

Sanders, Scott. 1997. Technical Communication and Ethics. In *Foundations for Teaching Technical Communication,* ed. Katherine Staples and Cesar Ornatowski. Greenwich, CT: Ablex. 99–117.

Sanders, Scott Russell. 1991. The Singular First Person.1989. *Secrets of the Universe: Scenes from the Journey Home.* Boston: Beacon Press. 187–204.

Sappol, Michael. 2002. *A Traffic of Dead Bodies: Anatomy and Embodied Social Identity in Nineteenth-Century America.* Princeton: Princeton University Press.

Sarwar, Beena. Brutality Cloaked as Tradition. *The New York Times.* www.nytimes.com/2002/08/06/opionion/06SAR.html?todaysheadlines

Scarry, Elaine. 1985. *The Body in Pain.* New York: Oxford.

Schacter, Aaron. 2001. Comfort Retailers. *Marketplace Morning Report.* Oct 9. Minneapolis: Minnesota Public Radio/Public Radio International.

Schaffer, Simon. The Leviathan of Parsonstown: Literary Technology and Scientific Representation. *Inscribing Science: Scientific Texts and the Materiality of Communication.* 183–222.

Scheman, Naomi. 1993. *Engenderings: Constructions of Knowledge, Authority, and Privilege.* New York: Routledge.

Scherman, Tony. 1996. The Music of Democracy: An Interview with Wynton Marsalis. *Utne Reader,* Mar–Apr: 29–35. Originally published in *American Heritage.*

Seigel, Jerrold E. 1968. *Rhetoric and Philosophy in Renaissance Humanism: The Union of Eloquence and Wisdom, Petrarch to Valla.* Princeton: Princeton University Press.

Sennett, Richard. 1974. *The Fall of Public Man.* New York: Norton.

Shaughnessy, Mina P. 1977. *Errors and Expectations: A Guide for the Teacher of Basic Writing.* New York: Oxford University Press.

Shay, Jonathan. 1996. Comment: Imagining the Citizen, Imagining the Enemy. *Literature and Medicine* 15.2: 221–223.

Shumway, David. 1989. Solidarity or Perspectivity? In *Gender and Theory: Dialogues on Feminist Criticism,* ed. Linda Kauffman. Oxford: Blackwell. 107–118.

Shumway, David. 1991. Comment. *College English* 53: 831–834.

Slevin, James M. 2000. *The Internet and Society.* Malden, MA: Blackwell.

Smith, Barbara Herrnstein. 1988. *Contingencies of Value: Alternative Perspectives for Critical Theory.* Cambridge, MA: Harvard University Press.

Smith, Dorothy E. 1987. *The Everyday World as Problematic: A Feminist Sociology.* Boston: Northeastern University Press.

Smith, Paul. 1997. *Millennial Dreams: Contemporary Culture and Capital in the North.* London: Verso.

Sokal, Alan, and Jean Bricmont. 1998. *Fashionable Nonsense: Postmodern Intellectuals' Abuse of Science.* New York: Picador Books.

Sokal, Alan D. 1996. Transgressing the Boundaries: Toward a Transformative Hermeneutics of Quantum Gravity. *Social Text* 46/47: 217–252.

Spellmeyer, Kurt. 2003. *Arts of Living: Remaking the Humanities for the Twenty-First Century.* Albany: State University of Albany Press.

Spigelman, Candace. 2001. Argument and Evidence in the Case of the Personal. *College English* 64: 63–87.

Stafford, Barbara. 1991. *Body Criticism: Imaging the Unseen in Enlightenment Art and Medicine.* Cambridge: MIT Press.

Stafford, Barbara. 1996. *Good Looking: Essays on the Virtue of Images.* Cambridge: MIT Press.

Stafford, Barbara. 1999. *Visual Analogy: Consciousness as the Art of Connecting.* Cambridge: MIT Press.

Steig, Michael. 1989. *Stories of Reading: Subjectivity and Literary Understanding.* Baltimore: Johns Hopkins University Press.

Stevens, Betsy. 1996. Using the Competing Values Framework to Assess Corporate Ethical Codes. *The Journal of Business Communication* 33: 71–84.

Stover, Andrea. 2001. Redefining Public/Private Boundaries in the Composition Classroom. In *Public Works: Student Writing as Public Text,* ed. Emily J. Isaacs and Phoebe Jackson. Portsmouth, NH: Heinemann Boynton/Cook. 1–9.

Swales, John, and Najjar, Hazem. 1987. The Writing of Research Article Introductions. *Written Communication* 4: 175–191.

Symposium Collective. 2001. The Politics of the Personal: Storying Our Lives Against the Grain. *College English* 64: 41–62.

Thoreau, Henry David. 1981. *Walden and Other Writings*, ed. William Howarth. New York: Modern Library.

Tompkins, Jane. 1987. Me and My Shadow. *New Literary History* 19. Rpt. *Gender and Theory: Dialogues on Feminist Criticism,* ed. Linda Kaufmon. Oxford: Blackwell. 121–139.

Tompkins, Jane. 1990. Pedagogy of the Distressed. *College English* 52: 653–660.

Torgovnick, Marianna. 1990. Experimental Critical Writing. *Profession* 90: 25–27.

Toulmin, Stephen. 1964. *The Uses of Argument.* Cambridge: Cambridge University Press.

Trimbur, John. 2000. Agency and the Death of the Author: A Partial Defense of Modernism. *JAC* 20: 283–298.

Trimbur, John. 1991. Literacy and the Discourse of Crisis. In *The Politics of Writing Instruction*, ed. Richard Bullock and John Trimbur. Portsmouth, NH: Boynton/Cook. 277–295.

Trimmer, Joseph, ed. 1997. *Narration as Knowledge: Tales of the Teaching Life.* Portsmouth, NH: Heinemann.

Trinkaus, Charles Edward, Jr., trans. and intro. Lorenzo Valla. 1948. *The Renaissance Philosophy of Mans*, eds. Ernest Cassirer, Paul Oskar Kristeller, and John Herman Randall, Jr. Chicago: University of Chicago Press. 147–154.

Trotsky, Leon. 1960. *Literature and Revolution.* Ann Arbor, MI: University of Michigan Press.

Villanueva, Victor, Jr. 1993. *Bootstraps: From an American Academic of Color.* Urbana: NCTE.

Villanueva, Victor, Jr., ed. 1997. *Cross-Talk in Comp Theory: A Reader.* Urbana: NCTE.

Villanueva, Victor, Jr. 2001. The Personal. Symposium Collective. The Politics of the Personal: Storying Our Lives against the Grain. *College English* 64: 50–52.

Wakeford, Nina. 2000. New Media, New Methodologies: Studying the Web. In Gauntlett. 31–41.

Ward, Irene. 1997. How Democratic Can We Get? The Internet, the Public Sphere, and Public Discourse. *JAC* 17: 365–380.

Warner, John Harley. 1998. *Against the Spirit of System: the French Impulse in Nineteenth Century American Medicine.* Princeton: Princeton University Press.

Warren, Charles, and Louis Brandeis. 1980. The Right of Privacy. *Harvard Law Review* 4: 194–221.

Weathers, Beck. 2000. *Left for Dead: My Journey Home from Everest.* With Stephen G. Michaud. New York: Villard.

Weine, Steven M. 1996. The Witnessing Imagination: Social Trauma, Creative Artists, and Witnessing Professionals. *Literature and Medicine* 15.2: 167–182.

Weisser, Christian R. 2002. *Moving Beyond Academic Discourse: Composition Studies and the Public Sphere.* Carbondale: Southern Illinois University Press.

Weisser, Christian R. and Sidney I. Dobrin, eds. 2001. *Ecomposition: Theoretical and Pedagogical Approaches.* Albany: State University of New York Press. 11–25.

Wells, Susan. 1986. Habermas, Communicative Competence, and the Teaching of Technical Discourse. In *Theory in the Classroom*, ed. Cary Nelson. Urbana: University of Illinois Press. 245–269.

Wells, Susan. 2001. *Out of the Dead House: Nineteenth Century Women Physicians and the Writing of Medicine.* Madison: Wisconsin University Press.

Wells, Susan. 1996. Rogue Cops and Health Care: What Do We Want from Public Writing? *College Composition and Communication* 47: 325–341.

Wess, Robert. 1996. *Kenneth Burke: Rhetoric, Subjectivity, Postmodernism.* New York: Cambridge University Press.

White, Bernard J., and B. Ruth Montgomery. 1980. Corporate Codes of Conduct. *California Management Review* 12: 80–87.

White, E. B. 1977. *Essays of E. B. White.* New York: Harper.

Wiggins, Osborne. 1995. Personal communication.

Williams, Martin. 1970. *The Jazz Tradition.* New York: Oxford University Press.

Williams, Patricia J. 1991. *The Alchemy of Race and Rights: Diary of a Law Professor.* Cambridge: Harvard University Press.

Williams, Raymond. 1977. *Marxism and Literature.* Oxford University Press.

Winsor, Dorothy. 1996. *Writing like an Engineer: A Rhetorical Education.* Mahwah, NJ: Erlbaum.

Woman's Medical College of Pennsylvania, Faculty Minutes, 1850–1864, MCP collection, Archives and Special Collections on Women and Medicine.

Worsham, Lynn. After Words: A Choice of Words Remains. Jarratt and Worsham 329–356.

Zappen, James P. 1987. Rhetoric and Technical Communication: An Argument for Historical and Political Pluralism. *Iowa State Journal of Business and Technical Writing* 1.2: 29–44.

Zappen, James P., Laura J. Gurak, and Stephen Doheny-Farina. 1997. Rhetoric, Community, and Cyberspace. *Rhetoric Review* 15: 400–419.

Zawacki, Terry Myers. 1992. Recomposing as a Woman: An Essay in Different Voices. *College Composition and Communication* 43: 32–38.

CONTRIBUTORS

BARBARA COUTURE is a professor of English and dean of liberal arts at Washington State University. Her scholarly interests include rhetoric and philosophy, technical communication, composition, and writing theory. Her publications on these topics include: *Toward a Phenomenological Rhetoric: Writing, Profession, and Altruism*; the edited anthology *Functional Approaches to Writing: Research Perspectives*; and *Cases for Technical and Professional Writing* (co-author, Jone Rymer Goldstein), as well as several chapters and articles in anthologies and journals.

THOMAS KENT teaches rhetoric and composition at Utah State University where he is professor of English and serves as dean of the School of Graduate Studies. He is the author of two books, *Interpretation and Genre: The Role of Generic Perception in Narrative Texts* and *Paralogic Rhetoric: A Theory of Communicative Interaction*, and he is the editor of *Post-Process Theory: Beyond the Writing-Process Paradigm.*

DAVID BLEICH teaches language, literature, writing, gender studies, science studies, and Jewish studies at the University of Rochester. His most recent book, edited and introduced with Deborah Holdstein, is *Personal Effects: The Social Character of Scholarly Writing.* He is also the author of *Know and Tell: A Writing Pedagogy of Disclosure, Genre, and Membership*; *The Double Perspective: Language, Literature, and Social Relations*; *Utopia: The Psychology of a Cultural Fantasy*; *Subjective Criticism*; and *Readings and Feelings.*

LYNN Z. BLOOM is Board of Trustees Distinguished Professor and Aetna Chair of Writing at the University of Connecticut. The most recent of her seventeen books are *The St. Martin's Custom Reader*, *The Essay Connection*, and *Composition Studies as a Creative Art.* She has published over eighty articles and essays in a variety of journals. Her forthcoming books include *The Essay Canon* and the coedited *Composition Studies in the 21st Century: Rereading the Past, Rewriting the Future.*

GREGORY CLARK is a professor of English at Brigham Young University, where he teaches courses in rhetoric, American literature, and American cultural studies. He has published books and essays in composition studies and American rhetorical history. He is currently editor of *Rhetoric Society Quarterly.*

GEOFFREY A. CROSS is a professor of English at the University of Louisville, where he teaches in the doctoral program in rhetoric and composition. His first full-length ethnography, *Collaboration and Conflict*, won the 1995 NCTE Best Book in Scientific and Technical Communication Award. In 1997, he won the Association for Business Communication Outstanding Researcher Award. His second ethnography, *Forming the Collective Mind*, is the first detailed rendering of large-scale group writing involving numerous subgroups.

SIDNEY I. DOBRIN is the director of writing programs and an associate professor of English at the University of Florida, where he teaches composition theory, technical and professional writing, ecocriticism, and environmental rhetoric. He also serves on the faculty of the College of Natural Resources and Environmental Studies. He has written or coauthored six books; his most recent book is *Ecocomposition: Theoretical and Pedagogical Approaches* (with Christian Weisser). His articles and essays cover a range of subjects about composition theory and writing and have appeared in a variety of journals and books.

CHERYL GEISLER is a joint professor of rhetoric and composition and information technology at Rensselaer Polytechnic Institute, where she conducts research on writing in workplace and professional contexts. She has published two books and numerous articles, most recently exploring the role that virtual objects play in supporting collaborative work.

MARGUERITE HELMERS is an associate professor in the Department of English at the University of Wisconsin–Oshkosh. She is the author of *Writing Students*, editor of *Intertexts: Reading Pedagogy in College Writing Classrooms*, and coeditor with Charles Hill of the forthcoming *Defining Visual Rhetorics*. She has contributed articles to *College English*, the *Journal of Advanced Composition*, and the electronic journals *Enculturation* and *Kairos*. She is also the coeditor of *WPA: Writing Program Administration*.

DOUGLAS HESSE directs the Center for the Advancement of Teaching at Illinois State University, where he is professor of English. Associate Chair of the Conference on College Composition and Communication, and past president of WPA, he publishes on writing program issues and creative nonfiction.

BRUCE HORNER is a professor of English at the University of Wisconsin–Milwaukee, where he teaches composition and composition theory and serves as director of composition. His books include *Representing the "Other": Basic Writers and the Teaching of Basic Writing*, coauthored with Min-Zhan Lu, and *Terms of Work for Composition: A Materialist Critique*, which was winner of the 2000 W. Ross Winterowd Award for the best book in composition theory.

DAVID KAUFER is a professor of English and rhetoric at Carnegie Mellon University, where he teaches courses in writing and textual analysis. He has authored or coauthored four books, the most recent titled *Rhetoric and the Arts of Design* and *Principles of Writing as Representational Composition*.

KRISTA RATCLIFFE is an associate professor of English at Marquette University, where she teaches rhetorical theory, writing, and women's literature. She is the author of *Anglo-American Feminist Challenges to the Rhetorical Traditions: Virginia Woolf, Mary Daly, and Adrienne Rich* and coauthor of *Who's Having This Baby? Perspectives on Birthing*. She is currently completing a manuscript titled *Rhetorical Listening*, which investigates the intersections of gender and ethnicity in cross-cultural communication.

JOHN TRIMBUR is a professor of writing and rhetoric at Worcester Polytechnic Institute, where he directs the technical, scientific, and professional communication program. He has published articles on writing theory and cultural studies of literacy. His most recent book is the edited collection *Popular Literacy: Cultural Practices and Poetics*.

CHRISTIAN R. WEISSER is an assistant professor of English at the University of Hawaii–Hilo. He is the author of *Moving beyond Academic Discourse: Composition Studies and the Public Sphere*. He coauthored, with Sidney I. Dobrin, *Natural Discourse: Toward Ecocomposition* and co-edited *Ecocomposition: Theoretical and Pedagogical Perspectives*. His work has also appeared in *College English*, the *Writing Instructor*, *Composition Forum*, and other journals.

NANCY WELCH is an associate professor in the Department of English at the University of Vermont, where she teaches courses in composition, rhetoric, and literacy politics.

Author of *Getting Restless: Rethinking Revision in Writing Instruction*, she has also published fiction and essays in *Prairie Schooner, Threepenny Review, College Composition and Communication, College English*, and other journals.

SUSAN WELLS is a professor of English at Temple University, where she teaches rhetoric and composition. She has published *The Dialectics of Representation*; *Sweet Reason: Intersubjectivity and the Rhetorics of Modernity*; and *Out of the Dead House: Nineteenth Century Women Physicians and the Writing of Medicine*. *Out of the Dead House* won the 2002 W. Ross Winterowd Award for the best book in composition theory.

INDEX

4455